THE ECONOMY OF SOCIALIST CUBA

THE ECONOMY OF SOCIALIST CUBA

A Two-Decade Appraisal

Carmelo Mesa-Lago

UNIVERSITY OF NEW MEXICO PRESS

Albuquerque

Library of Congress Cataloging in Publication Data

Mesa-Lago, Carmelo, 1934–

   The economy of socialist Cuba.

   Includes bibliographical references and index.
   1. Cuba—Economic conditions—1959–
I. Title.
HC152.5.M47   330.97291'064   80-54570
ISBN 0–8263–0578–4   AACR2
ISBN 0–8263–0585–7 (pbk.)

Manufactured in the United States of America.
Library of Congress Catalog Card Number 80–54570.
International Standard Book Number 0–8263–0578–4 (Cloth).
                              0–8263–0585–7 (Paper).
Second printing 1985

To Cuba
  which gave me a beginning
  and shaped my soul
To the United States
  which gave me a second chance
  and broadened my horizons

Contents

Tables

Graph

Foreword

During the twenty years of the Cuban Revolution, discussion of the Cuban economy under Castro has become a partisan debate. Sympathetic observers, comparing contemporary Cuba with its prerevolutionary orientation, have interpreted its socialist experiment, sometimes with unguarded optimism, as the pursuit of a romantic ideal. Others, mindful of the inherent limits of a planned economy and of government by an egalitarian ethic, have focused on Cuba's fundamental and, to them inevitable, failings. In either case, it seems to have been all too easy for the observer, following his ideological preconceptions, to treat hypothesis as if it were well-established fact.

The International Center for Economic Policy Studies determined, in its initial generation of public policy studies, to engage a well-informed and highly respected Cuban specialist to examine, with the objectivity that is associated with intimate knowledge of both history and data, these alternative views of Cuban economic performance. This book is the product of that effort. Its author, Professor Carmelo Mesa-Lago of the University of Pittsburgh, initially a partisan of the Cuban Revolution, came to the United States in 1962. He is currently Director of the Center for Latin American Studies at the University of Pittsburgh, having authored, in the interim, scores of publications on the subject of Cuba, including the well-received and much-cited monograph, *Cuba in the 1970s.*

As is readily apparent to the reader, *The Economy of Socialist Cuba* examines a large volume of data, some hitherto unavailable. Professor Mesa-Lago, drawing on his experience, employs this data very adroitly to demonstrate just how Cuba has succeeded, and how it has fallen short, pursuing shifting objectives of its twenty-year-old revolution.

The basic argument of *The Economy of Socialist Cuba* emerges from the data. Professor Mesa-Lago demonstrates, as the student of economic development would expect, that it is impossible to achieve a number of demanding socioeconomic goals simultaneously without confronting the tradeoffs that are the essence of economics. Mesa-Lago concentrates, in his discussion, on five such goals, discussing the relative emphasis accorded them and the attendant difficulties of attaining them in the various stages of the Cuban Revolution described in the initial chapter of the study. These goals—sustained economic growth, diversification of production, relative external economic independence, full employment, and a more equal distribution of income and social services—come into clear conflict in a number of ways.

It thus comes as no surprise that Cuba, in turning from a market to a socialist economy, has found it necessary time and again to reverse direction and attend to objectives it had underemphasized, objectives that would not have been violated, in the same measure, had markets been operating more freely; that dependence, in external economic relations, has simply been shifted from one set of trading partners to another; or that incentive problems have, in key economic sectors, led to the gradual reintroduction of some semblance of market allocation.

This is an important book to read to understand Cuba today. No reader, ideological preference aside, can be expected, in total, to agree with it. But its readers are bound to come away from it with a much more informed basis for discussing the economic success and the economic failings of the Cuban Revolution.

Harold M. Hochman
Professor of Economics
Baruch College and the Graduate Center
City University of New York

September 1980

1

Introduction

Twenty-two years after its victory, the Cuban Revolution continues to polarize opinion, being a source of uncritical admiration, passionate criticism, and intriguing curiosity. The exodus of more than 125,000 Cubans in the spring of 1980, one percent of the total population, made world news and heated the controversy on the performance of the Revolution. Although politics undeniably played a role in the exodus, economic factors—thoroughly analyzed in this book—were the underlying force in those events.

Within academia, the last decade has brought significant improvements in the amount and accuracy of data, in the depth and sophistication of analysis, and in topical specialization related to Cuban studies. A result of this research trend has been the emergence of consensus on some key issues, yet heated discussions persist among social scientists. Economists have their own value framework and biases and cannot claim to be objective in passing judgment.[1] Some scholars argue that the changes in the social component of development, particularly Cuban achievements in employment, distribution of income, goods, and wealth, and social services, demonstrate the success of the Revolution and its worthiness as a model for other Latin American and Third World countries. Other scholars, though, focus on the economic components of development to show that Cuba's lack of success in achieving sustained economic growth, in breaking away from monoculture, and in reducing economic dependency on a super power are evidence of the Revolution's economic failure; hence, for these researchers Cuba is a bad example for other developing countries.

Substantial progress has been made in the search for a global, balanced view that will delineate the relationship of social success and economic failure in the Cuban experience. But we still lack both a systematic analysis of this relationship and a comprehensive evaluation of Cuba's economic performance in the first two decades of the Revolution. This book adds substantial new research on the subject, while merging, filling gaps, and updating some of my previous works published in the last fifteen years. My goal has been to provide a concise but integrated view of the Cuban economy under socialism. To achieve this task, I analyze five major socioeconomic goals that are typical of most developing countries, including Cuba: (1) sustained economic growth; (2) diversification of production; (3) relative external economic independence; (4) full employment; and (5) more equal distribution of income and social services.[2]

The first three goals concentrate more on the economic component of development, while the last two focus on the social component. A major assumption of the book is that not all of these five goals can be pursued at the same time with similar intensity in the short run. The reason is that not all the goals are mutually reinforcing or compatible; in fact, some of them may be in conflict. For instance, if equality in distribution is intensely pursued, then economic disincentives and a dramatic shift of resources from investment to consumption can affect economic growth. Full employment, if mainly achieved through artificial job creation, generates a decline in labor productivity, inflationary tendencies, and a slowdown in real growth. An ill-conceived plan for rapid diversification of production in a monoculture type of economy may reduce both output and revenue from a major product such as sugar, which then undermines the financing of diversification and growth. The goal of external economic independence in a developing island that lacks vital resources and depends heavily on one product conflicts with its desperate need for foreign capital, technology, and trade.[3]

To compound these problems, conflicts emerge not only among goals but also between some of the policy instruments used by policy makers and the goals themselves. Thus a wide and rapid collectivization of most means of production, both domestic and foreign, can result in retaliation from foreign governments and investors, an exodus of managerial personnel, and grave problems of economic disorganization and inefficiency; all these effects, in turn, have a negative impact on growth. Excessive concentration of decision making in areas such as investment, allocation of resources, and so forth is difficult to apply to a labor-intensive, agricultural type of economy, without paying a heavy cost in efficiency. Reliance on moral stimuli, labor mobilization techniques, and unpaid voluntary labor usually lead to a decline in the labor effort and productivity. In the last decade or so, social scientists specializing on development have criticized economic growth as an exclusive goal of development and brought to the fore previously neglected social goals such as equality. I sympathize with this more balanced view of development but fear that the pendulum may swing to the other extreme. The Cubans painfully learned in the 1960s and acknowledged in the 1970s that when a goal such as more equal distribution is idealistically pushed beyond reasonable limits disregarding its economic costs with decline in productivity and growth, the survival of the whole system is in jeopardy. The continuation of the social accomplishments is then threatened.[4]

The above discussion suggests that policy makers must plan carefully and assign priorities to the various developmental goals before they initiate action. Otherwise the decision to sacrifice or assign a low priority to some goals is made later and only when facing economic adversity and the impossibility of achieving all goals simultaneously. Furthermore, the selection of policy instruments should take their viability into account in view of the economic reality of the nation, its level of development, infrastructure, and skills of the labor force, as well as impact on the selected goals.

Cuban policy makers in the first stages of the Revolution were unaware of the conflicting relationship of their ambitious goals and romantically tried to achieve all of them at the same time with similar intensity. But when economic reality imposed itself, goals such as growth had to be sacrificed to achieve such top-priority goals as equality. In subsequent stages of the Revolution, the Cubans learned the lesson and explicitly changed some of their goals; for example, industrialization (elimination of sugar monoculture) was postponed; dependency upon the Soviet Union was accepted although justified. In the current stage, begun in the early 1970s, goals such as growth have received first priority while emphasis on other goals—for example, equality—has been considerably reduced.

Some policy instruments have also been dropped or drastically modified when their impracticalness became obvious. For instance, the highly centralized Soviet style of physical planning briefly tried in an early stage of the Revolution was subsequently rejected and in its place were substituted loose sectorial miniplans. Later on, a modified version of the Soviet economic-reform type of planning was reintroduced, one which attempts to correct flaws of the previous approach by using selected market mechanisms and decentralized as well as cybernetic techniques. The romantic attempt in the second half of the 1960s to achieve development by rapidly raising consciousness and changing values through moral incentives, labor mobilization, and similar techniques has been reversed in the 1970s and is now criticized as an idealistic error.

The following topics are analyzed in the book: the various policies Cuba implemented in the first two decades of the Revolution in trying to achieve five major socioeconomic developmental goals; the results of such policies in terms of goal achievement; the changes in priority among goals in various stages; and the reasons behind such changes. Summarized in chapter 2 are the principal features of economic policy in five stages of the Revolution in 1959–79. Analyzed in chapters 3 to 7 are the performance of the economy in terms of growth, diversification, dependency, full employment, and equality in distribution. The overall economic performance of Cuba in the first two decades of the Revolution and the possibilities for the third decade are considered in chapter 8.

The resources available at the University of Pittsburgh have been very useful in the preparation of this book: the first-rate Cuban collection in the Hillman Library (see Appendix 3) and the generous help provided by the Latin American bibliographer, Eduardo Lozano; the exposure to thousands of items published on Cuba all over the world through my work as editor of *Cuban Studies/Estudios Cubanos,* now in its eleventh year of publication; and the efficient staff of the Center for Latin American Studies, particularly Carolyn Wilson, Administrative Assistant, who typed several versions of the manuscript, Erma MacPherson, Administrative Aide, who handled the correspondence and a myriad other things, and Felipe Morris, my research assistant in 1978–79, who helped in the computation of some tables and searching of sources. I am also in debt to Jorge Domínguez, Harold M. Hochman, Jorge Pérez-López, Sergio Roca, and two anonymous readers for their valuable comments and criticism; and to Nelson P. Valdés, Steven Reed, Edward Masferrer, and José Alonso, as well as numerous Cuban officials who provided valuable materials. The responsibility for what is said here, of course, is only mine.

Unlike my previous books and articles on Cuba published since 1962, this study greatly benefited from three trips to my native country, the first since 1961. After several unsuccessful attempts since 1973 to obtain a visa, in December 1978 I was invited by the Cuban government to visit the island for ten days as part of the committee that negotiated the freedom of 3,600 prisoners, as well as a freer exit from and entry to the island. This visit, although brief and limited to the city of Havana, provided a unique opportunity to have interviews with scholars, technicians, government officials, relatives and friends, and the man-in-the-street, collect recent statistical data and, above all, have a firsthand view of several aspects of the Cuban society. A second visit, for two weeks in July of 1979, was possible through the Institute of Cuban Studies, the financial support of the Ford Foundation, and the cooperation of several Cuban institutions and officials. This trip was even more fruitful since it included travel to four provinces, allowed me to check many tables, ask questions related to this book, obtain additional data, and interview more Cuban technicians and common people. I also benefited on this trip from the useful observations of my wife Elena, who was returning to the island after an absence of eighteen years. A third visit, for ten days in August 1980, as part of a seminar of the Institute of Cuban Studies, allowed me to discuss key issues with top Cuban economists and planners, clarify some of my remaining doubts, and gather recent statistics. It is my hope that the doors of Cuba will remain open for my wife and me as well as for our daughters Elizabeth, Ingrid, and Helena, all born in the United States, but anxious to see the land of their ancestors.

2

Revolutionary Economic Policies

This chapter is divided into two parts. The state of the Cuban economy on the eve of the Revolution is summarized in the first part by focusing on the key problems and goals selected for this study. Described in the second part are the economic policies followed in five stages of the Cuban Revolution in trying to solve the key socioeconomic problems of the prerevolutionary economy.

THE STATE OF THE CUBAN ECONOMY AT THE EVE OF THE REVOLUTION

The five crucial socioeconomic problems existing in Cuba in 1958 were the slow rate of economic growth, sugar monoculture or the excessive significance of this product in the generation of GNP and exports, the overwhelming dependence on the United States in regard to investment and trade, the high rates of unemployment and underemployment, and the significant inequalities in living standards, particularly between urban and rural areas.[1]

Slow Economic Growth. Some economists have claimed that the Cuban economy was stagnant either since the 1920s or throughout the republican periods beginning in 1902. Informed estimates are difficult to make because of the lack of data. National accounts began to be computed by the newly established National Bank of Cuba in the 1940s, and prior to that no reliable statistics existed in this field.

According to the National Bank, in 1950–58 the Cuban GNP estimated at current prices (not correcting for inflation) grew at an average rate of 4.6 percent annually. But taking population growth and inflation into account, the increase of real GNP per capita in 1950–58 was about 1 percent. Cuba's GNP devoted to investment in 1950–58 reached an average of 18 percent, and showed a steady tendency to climb, creating some hope that the rate of growth would rise in the 1960s. Hence, the Cuban economy was not stationary in the decade before the Revolution; indeed, it grew, but at a very slow rate, with some expectations for a higher rate in the future.

Sugar Monoculture. In the period 1949–58, an average of from 28 to 29 percent of GNP was generated by the sugar sector. However, a tendency toward the lessening of the importance of sugar was noticeable, not only during that period, but in comparison to the 1940s. Thus in the years 1957–58, sugar originated only 25 percent of GNP. On the other hand, nonsugar industrial output grew 47 percent between 1947 and 1958. As a typical export economy, Cuba depended heavily on foreign trade; thus, in 1949–58, some 36 percent of its GNP was generated by exports. Sugar and its by-products represented an average of 84 percent of the total exports, and the remaining ones were mainly tobacco and minerals. The price fluctuations of sugar on the international market, as well as the varying sugar quota policies and prices fixed by the United States, were exogenous factors that Cuba found impossible to control. As a result of the excessive importance of sugar, these fluctuations had a serious impact on GNP, provoking a situation of instability and uncertainty.

Economic Dependence. United States investment in Cuba by 1958 was possibly the second largest in Latin America, and in the period 1949–58, an average of two-thirds of Cuba's foreign trade was with the United States. This commercial dependence invariably resulted in a negative balance of trade for Cuba, building up a cumulative deficit of almost $350 million during that period. Some scholars argue that the proximity of Cuba to the United States, the world's most powerful economy, resulted in a total integration of the Cuban economy into the American economy; moreover, because Cuba was tied to the U.S. economy, the former could not achieve a satisfactory degree of independence or domestic integration. Others contend that heavy U.S. investment and transfer of technology to Cuba were largely responsible for the development achieved by the country in 1958, placing it among the top three or four nations in Latin America.

Unemployment and Underemployment. Between 1919 and 1957, the labor force employed in agriculture fell from 49 percent to 39 percent. The principal increases in employment were found in construction, commerce, and industry, in that order, but such increases were not high enough to absorb both the rapidly growing labor force and rural-to-urban migration. On the eve of the Revolution, 16 percent of the labor force was totally unemployed, and approximately 14 percent found itself in various forms of underemployment.

These figures represent annual averages, and they therefore do not reveal the fluctuations of unemployment during the year. From 20 to 25 percent of the labor force found work in the sugar sector, but due to the seasonal character of the sugar crop and its processing, this portion of the work force had stable work for only four months out of the year. During the so-called dead season (May to December), the proportion of employment in the sugar sector fell to 4 or 5 percent. It is difficult to determine what percentage of the temporarily unemployed sugar workers worked on their own land or on other crop harvests during the dead season, although it is known that about one-third of the sugar workers found employment for another three months in the harvesting of the coffee crop. Statistics on total unemployment in 1956–57 recorded an increase from 200,000 workers during the period of greatest activity in the sugar harvest (February to April) to 457,000 workers during the period of least activity (August to October). Although strict comparisons are not possible, a review of statistics from the years 1943, 1953, and 1956–57 suggest that unemployment was worsening.

Inequality in Distribution. An accurate study of income distribution in Cuba is impossible due to the absence of figures. Only a general index exists, indicating how the national income was distributed within two large categories: remuneration for labor (wages, fringe benefits, pensions), and remuneration for capital (rent, interest, dividends). Between 1949 and 1958, the average labor share was 65 percent, a figure surpassed in 1958 by only three developed Western countries: Great Britain, the United States, and Canada. Moreover, this percentage showed a noticeable tendency to increase. Employed labor had sufficient political and economic power to capture and increase its share of the national income, but those gains were obtained in large measure at the expense of the unemployed and the peasants.

In 1953, 44 percent of the Cuban population lived in rural areas, compared with 55 percent in 1919. During those years, legislation was enacted to better protect the peasants. Nevertheless, urbanization was accompanied by preferential state expenditures—especially to Havana and other large cities. In 1957–58, national averages in education, public health, and social security placed Cuba among the top three Latin American countries in delivery of social services: its literacy rate was the fourth highest; its percentage of the labor force covered by old-age, invalidity, and survivors social insurance was the second highest; its indices of number of inhabitants per doctor and hospital bed were the third lowest; its morbidity index was the second lowest; and its death rate and infant mortality rate were the lowest. But social-service facilities were mainly concentrated in the capital city and urban areas, whereas their availability and quality declined sharply in the rural areas. Results of a survey taken in 1956–57 revealed the disparity between urban and rural conditions. The caloric intake, diet, health, medical attention, housing, and income of peasants were very much below the national averages for 1953. The migratory movement from the countryside to the city was accentuated by the impoverished condition of the rural population, which made itself visible in Havana's shantytowns. A large number of these rural migrants found low paying work in the tertiary sector (for example domestic services and peddling) or they simply became beggars. The high and growing percentage of the work force engaged in tertiary activities was a clear symptom of underemployment in Cuba.

In summary, during the decade prior to the Revolution, the Cuban economy showed a small rate of real growth; however, the rate of investment was increasing. Even though development in the nonsugar sector occurred, sugar monoculture still dominated the economy. Cuba was heavily dependent on the United States for capital and trade, and the latter resulted in a deficit against Cuba. Both unemployment and underemployment were high and apparently worsening. The economic growth that occurred largely benefited capital and employed labor, as well as the urban sector, at the expense of the unemployed and the rural sector, all of which resulted in significant inequalities in living standards.

THE CHANGING ECONOMIC POLICIES OF THE REVOLUTION

The most important developmental goals announced by the triumphant Revolution were aimed at correcting the socioeconomic problems summarized above: to achieve high rates of economic growth; to eliminate sugar monoculture through rapid industrialization and agricultural diversification; to reduce economic dependence on the United States by varying trade and capital markets; to attain full employment; and to improve the standards of living of the peasants and the unskilled urban workers. But the economic policies used to achieve those goals were modified several times in the course of the first two decades of the Revolution. Furthermore, priorities among goals also changed. Hence a discussion of such policies must identify five stages of the Revolution: (1) 1959–60, liquidation of capitalism and erosion of the market; (2) 1961–63, attempt to introduce the Soviet pre-economic reform model of command economy; (3) 1964–66, debate over and test of alternative socialist economic models; (4) 1966–70, adoption and radicalization of the Mao-Guevarist model; and (5) 1971 on, shift to the current Soviet model of economic reform.

Discussion of economic policies in the five stages will distinguish among development strategy, organizational model, and goal fulfillment. By development strategy is meant the way in which the nation's material and human resources are allocated, to one or various sectors of the economy (for example, for industry or agriculture) to promote overall development in the long run. Organizational model refers to the form assumed by the economic structure (such as capitalism or socialism) and its corresponding set of instruments (including private versus collective ownership, market mechanisms versus central planning) to perform the basic economic functions. Goal fulfillment focuses on the actual performance in achieving the selected five goals rather than on ideal targets or rhetorical commitments. Each stage is discussed as follows: brief reference to the predominant ideology or set of beliefs; description of the organizational model used (with special reference to collectivization, planning, financing, management, labor, and incentives); and brief analysis of goal fulfillment and trade off among goals. A thorough analysis of the goals will be done in the subsequent five chapters.[2] The development strategy will be touched briefly in this chapter and will be fully analyzed in chapter 4.

The Liquidation of the Capitalist System and Erosion of the Market, 1959–60

The first stage of the Revolution lacked a clearly defined ideology. Some scholars have indicated that the "structuralist" philosophy of the Economic Commission for Latin America (which favors a mixed economy, decentralized-indicative planning, import substitution, industrialization, agrarian reform, and tax reform) exerted influence in the guerrilla period of the Revolution as well as in the early years in power. Others have attempted to prove that Marxism was the prevalent ideology of the revolutionaries. Whether there was an underlying ideology or not, the new leaders soon showed nationalist, statist, antimarket, antibureaucratic, and consumptionist attitudes. Fidel Castro and his close associates did not have any knowledge of economics (most of them were lawyers), and the few economists occupying government posts were soon dismissed and their jobs passed to enthusiastic but inexperienced revolutionaries. For example, Ernesto Guevara, a physician, first became the head of the Industrialization Department of the National Institute of Agrarian Reform (INRA), then president of the National Bank, and finally the Minister of Industry. Bureaucrats and technicians were viewed as opportunists who deliberately complicated economic and administrative matters in hope of making themselves indispensable. Partly due to their. ignorance in economic matters and partly because they were captivated by the Revolution's almost magical success against the supposedly technical army of Batista's dictatorship, the revolutionary leaders proposed the application of guerrilla techniques to the Cuban economy. It was widely believed that the nation's five major socioeconomic problems would be rapidly and simultaneously resolved by the power of the Revolution, the zeal and hard work of the leaders, the audacity of the improvisation, and the enthusiasm and support of the people. In summary, willingness, consciousness, morale, austerity, and loyalty were emphasized over material and human resources, technology, and knowledge and expertise.

Organizational Model. Collectivization of the means of production gradually increased and gained momentum in the second half of 1960. This occurred either because the leadership believed it was a necessary step to achieve their developmental goals or because they were forced to do it by domestic and international events or by a combination of both. In 1959 several means were used in the collectivization process: confiscation of property and assets embezzled by officials of the overthrown dictatorship; expropriation of latifundia (farms exceeding a ceiling of 400 hectares) through the first Agrarian Reform Law; expropriation of rental housing; state intervention in enterprises (factories, warehouses, transportation) abandoned by their owners or in which labor conflicts disrupted production; confiscation of assets of those who failed to pay due taxes; and confiscation of all property belonging to those convicted of counterrevolutionary crimes or who had become political exiles. In successive waves between June and October 1960, the collectivization process was rapidly extended. Involved were all foreign owned oil refineries, U.S. owned sugar mills, banks, telephone and electricity corporations, and all remaining U.S. properties as well as most domestically owned major industries, banks, and transportation business. By the end of 1960 all domestic wholesale and foreign trade and banking, and most transportation, industry, construction and retail trade, as well as more than one-third of agriculture was in state hands (see Table 1). This swift transfer of ownership liquidated the capitalist system and brought about the erosion of the automatic mechanisms of the market; as a result, production and distribution of goods and services partly ceased to be determined by the laws of supply and demand.

In the meantime several government agencies had been created to direct state domination over the economy. The first was INRA, which gradually grew to become a bureaucratic monster controlling one-third of agriculture and a good part of industry, and which developed the first experiments with central planning. The Central Planning Board (JUCEPLAN) was initially established to coordinate government policies and to guide the private sector through indicative planning; however, these functions were never exercised, and JUCEPLAN eventually became the agency for state central planning. Financing of the economy was increasingly done by the state, with private financing largely restricted to agriculture. The Ministry of Finance began to control the financing process through the state budget, while the National Bank expanded its command over credit and foreign exchange. The Ministry of Labor played an increasingly active role as labor arbiter and fixer of labor conditions as a step toward mastering trade unions. The collectivization process and the dissatisfaction of managers and technicians induced the exodus of this vital group. Their jobs were promptly filled with loyal but inexperienced revolutionaries, the cadres that eventually became responsible for the implementation of central planning as a substitute for the market forces.

Goal Fulfillment. Apparently economic growth continued at the same time the liquidation of the capitalist system occurred. This was accomplished mainly by full utilization of equipment, accumulated stocks and inventories, and foreign exchange reserves. Besides, confidence in the government was very high in 1959, and revenue from delinquent taxes flowed to the state. Much of that money was invested in a dynamic program of public works and housing construction. To reduce dependency on sugar, a program of agrarian diversification was launched in 1960, and large estates producing sugarcane began to be cleared off and replanted with rice, fruits or vegetables. However this cut in the size of cane was not yet important enough to affect sugar output, and the nationalization of sugar plantations and mills did not occur until the end of 1960. Hence the first two sugar harvests under the Revolution were fairly good and generated badly needed foreign exchange, while output of most agricultural products increased slightly. In 1960, a Soviet industrial fair was held in Havana, and Cuba began to sign contracts for the purchase of manufacturing equipment from the USSR, German Democratic Republic (GDR), and Czechoslovakia. The movement to cut economic dependence on the United States was accelerated in July 1960 when the U.S. quota to buy Cuban sugar was suspended. The USSR and China then made commitments to buy most of that sugar. Cuba started to import Soviet oil in early 1960 and by the end of the year was receiving most of its needed oil from the USSR. Trade with the United States began to decline in 1960 and shifted to socialist countries with whom Cuba signed commercial and economic aid agreements. In October 1960 all U.S. investment in Cuba had been nationalized; to retaliate, the United States imposed an economic embargo on Cuba, which would eventually terminate trade between the two nations.

In spite of the stated goal of full employment, the rate of unemployment increased in 1959–60. The government tried to cope with this problem by impeding job dismissals, by absorbing part of the unemployed in state agriculture, the growing armed forces, and social services, and by extending education thus keeping young people from entering into the labor market. The collectivization of most means of production, real estate, and banking practically eliminated nonwage income (that is dividends, rent, and interest) except in agriculture. On the other hand, raises were enacted for overall monetary wages, the minimum wage in agriculture, and minimum pensions. The net results of these two actions was a decrease in extreme income differentials. Moreover, the disposable income of the poorest sector was augmented as a result of the reduction of housing rent and electricity rates, subsidized public housing, and the expansion of free education and medical care. Most of the expansion in social services took place in rural areas, which helped begin to close the gap of living standards with urban areas. The consumptionist policy, however, sharply reduced the proportion of GNP devoted to investment. Also consumption increased faster than production and imports, rapidly depleting existing stocks.

In this stage of the Revolution the leaders tried to achieve all the five goals at the same time but with divergent results. Although a clear policy to promote growth did not exist, moderate growth was achieved by taking advantage of underutilized equipment, stocks, and reserves and by being aided by fair sugar crops and an active government expenditures policy. Little of significance was done to reduce sugar monoculture, and unemployment grew worse in spite of some government measures to stop it. On the other hand, economic dependence on the United States was substantially reduced, and distribution in favor of rural areas and low-income urban groups was improved.

The Attempt to Introduce the Soviet Pre-Economic-Reform Model, 1961–63

The year 1961 brought the break of diplomatic relations with the United States, the defeat of the Bay of Pigs invasion which consolidated the Revolution, and the declaration that the Revolution was socialist and that its leader was a Marxist. Facing the collapse of the market mechanisms and having established a survival pipeline with the Soviet Union, the revolutionary leadership attempted to apply to Cuba the model of economic organization prevalent in the USSR and the strategy of development of heavy industrialization successively tried by the Soviets in the 1930s. Although this development was influenced by western Marxist scholars and planners such as Leo Huberman, Paul Sweezy, and Paul Baran, most technical advice came from the USSR and Czechoslovakia.

Organizational Model. The process of state collectivization continued in this stage but at a slower rate than in the previous one (see Table 1): in 1961 all private educational institutions were nationalized; in 1962, private agricultural cooperatives established since 1959 in nationalized latifundia were transformed into state farms; in 1963 the second Agrarian Reform Law expropriated land of farms having more than 67 hectares, hence eliminating the middle-sized farmer; finally, the state exerted control of private agriculture through INRA introducing compulsory procurement quotas (acopio, that is, the sale of part of the crop to the state at prices set below the market price).

The Cubans tried rapidly to convert an economy in chaos into a command economy through highly centralized physical planning for which the island lacked the needed infrastructure. The novel economic organization began to be introduced in early 1961 with the creation of a new administrative structure. JUCEPLAN was charged with formulating annual and medium-range macro development plans to be submitted for consideration of the political leadership. A network of central ministries and agencies was created or modified to take charge of the various economic sectors, mostly as state monopolies dealing with foreign trade, industry and mining, domestic trade, finance, labor, and banking. State enterprises producing the same type of goods were merged into

TABLE 1. Collectivization of Ownership of Means of Production and Services in Cuba, 1961–77[a] (in percentages)

Sector	1961	1963	1968	1977
Agriculture	37	70	70	79[b]
Industry	85	95	100	100
Construction	80	98	100	100
Transportation	92	95	98	98
Retail trade	52	75	100	100
Wholesale and foreign trade	100	100	100	100
Banking	100	100	100	100
Education	100	100	100	100

[a]Figures in the table refer to property not to production. In 1976, the output of the private sector represented about 4 percent of national output (excluding trade) with the following shares by economic sector: 25 percent in agriculture, less than 7 percent in transportation, and less than 1 percent in communication. (The percent in the latter statistics refers not to national output but to the private share of output in each economic sector.)

[b]Private farmers owned about 33 percent of the cattle and produced 80 percent of tobacco, 50 percent of coffee, 50 percent of vegetables and fruits, and 16 percent of sugar.

Sources: Carmelo Mesa-Lago, ed. Revolutionary Change in Cuba (Pittsburgh: University of Pittsburgh Press, 1971), p. 283; Direct from Cuba, no. 169, 15 May 1977; and Banco Nacional de Cuba, Present Planning and Management System of the National Economy of the Republic of Cuba (La Habana: Banco Nacional 1978), p. 3.

trusts (*consolidados*) controlled by the proper central ministry. Financing of the economy was done in all state enterprises through budgetary allocations; annual state budgets were prepared but applied using primitive accounting techniques. Most prices began to be centrally fixed and, in 1962, physical allocation of consumer goods through rationing began. The 1962 annual plan was prepared with the aid of Czech planners. Their efforts, though, were hamstrung by lack of both accurate statistics and trained cadres and because the Czech model was inappropriate. It was too centralized, shaped by a developed, industrialized economy, and was rigidly applied with no effort to adapt it to Cuba's insular, monoculture, developing economy. Figures were grossly estimated or invented, there was no real input and feedback from lower echelons, and hence production goals were too optimistic with no basis in reality. When the final version of the plan was ready, its gross miscalculations made it practically useless. Apparently other plans were elaborated from 1963 and 1964 but never really enforced. A medium-range plan for 1962–65 was also drawn up with the aid of Polish and Soviet planners, but the lack of sophisticated knowledge of the economy and of clear economic directives from the leadership made that plan a theoretical study divorced from reality and impeded its practical usage. Other reasons contributed to the failure of planning in this stage. The collectivization was too wide and rapid, hence millions of economic microrelations were destroyed at once, breaking the automatic mechanisms of the market when the state was not ready to take over these functions. The new central ministries and agencies lacked coordination among themselves, were hastily organized and staffed with inexperienced personnel, and operated in a freewheeling manner with no control procedures. Economic decisions were taken by the political leadership without consultation with JUCEPLAN, which resulted in serious inconsistencies. No investment plan existed, investment decisions were not coordinated but made in an arbitrary manner lacking mechanisms to assure their efficiency; the result was poor capital productivity. Land collectivization and the acopio system dislocated the flow of supplies from the countryside to the towns. Due to lack of information or managerial control, agricultural products badly needed in the cities were lost in the ground or, after being harvested, spoiled because of unavailability of transportation. Because of price rigidity, many state stores did not reduce prices and lost perishable goods. Moreover, irrational prices discouraged private farmers from producing the badly needed crops.

Goal Fulfillment. In view of the above explained problems, it was a miracle that economic growth continued in 1961. The main reason behind this success was an exceptionally good sugar harvest, conducted in the first four months of the year, when the full impact of collectivization and administrative reform had not taken place. But in the next two years, the situation rapidly deteriorated resulting in one of the worst recessions of the Revolution. In the sugar sector, reduction of the cultivated area of sugar cane (down 25 percent over 1958), scarcity of professional sugarcane cutters (who had shifted to easier jobs), and disorganization created by administrative changes and the new state farm structure had a heavy toll on sugar output, which in 1963 reached the lowest level under the Revolution. At the same time several key agricultural products (for example, tobacco, coffee, beans, and tubers) suffered output declines, hence in 1963 agricultural output was 23 percent below 1959. Cuban officials had predicted that by 1965 Cuba would lead Latin America in per capita output of steel, cement, tractors, electricity, and refined petroleum. By 1963 Cuba was neither producing steel nor tractors, and its overall output of cement, electricity, and most important manufactures (such as cigars and beer) was below the 1961 level. Furthermore, the output of minerals (except for nickel) in 1963 was below the 1957 level. Contributing to this economic failure were lack of spare parts—most Cuban factories were still U.S. made—the exodus of U.S. and Cuban industrial managers and technicians, and the poor planning for the installment and integration of the newly bought factories.

Decreasing revenues from the sugar sector created a bottleneck in the ambitious program of industrialization. The decline of production of the principal exports (sugar, minerals, and tobacco) induced a cumulative trade deficit of more than half a billion pesos in 1962–63. The USSR provided credits to back up the deficits, but this aid rapidly increased Cuba's foreign debt. In 1962 almost 83 percent of Cuban trade was with socialist countries—almost one-half with the USSR, which held 80 percent of the island's trade deficit. Cuba achieved full economic independence from the United States only to become dependent on the USSR. It is true that the latter did not have direct investment in Cuba, but still the island could not survive without the vital Soviet pipeline of oil, credit, weapons, and a myriad of other imports.

By 1963 open unemployment in Cuba had probably been cut to one-half the prerevolutionary rate, but this was achieved by transforming most of the open unemployment into underemployment. Such a shift meant solving in the short run the social problem but spreading the economic costs to all the population and negatively affecting growth. In state farms, workers enjoyed guaranteed jobs and minimum wages the year around, but their productivity was one-half that of the private farmers. Industrial mergers and shutdowns should have generated unemployment but instead of being dismissed, unnecessary workers remained on the enterprise payroll waiting for retraining. The tertiary sector became hypertrophied with the expansion of the bureaucracy, social services, the armed forces, and internal security. An artificial manpower deficit appeared in 1962 in the main crops, particularly sugar. To cope with it, the government resorted to mobilization of "voluntary" unpaid labor trying to transfer the urban labor surplus to the countryside. In many cases, however, the cost of mobilizing the inexperienced volunteers was higher than the value of the product created by them. The hope was to employ productively the urban sector in the new industries, but in spite of overstaffing, not much of the force was absorbed because the industrial sector was small.

The increase in demand for consumer goods and the stagnation or decline in their supply resulted in a widening gap. In a market economy, such an unbalance would have corrected itself automatically through inflationary price increases; the Cuban government, however, chose the egalitarian path and, trying to protect the poorest sector of the population, froze prices and imposed rationing. The black market soon appeared, and the resulting high prices served to discriminate against the lowest income brackets, who could not afford the high prices that realistically reflected the underlying forces of supply and demand. Income distribution probably became more equal with the elimination of the middle-sized private farmer and the introduction of acopio, which operated like a tax on private farmers most of which had an income above the national average. On the other hand, the deterioration of the economy impeded the expansion of social services (particularly housing), which received lower proportions of both state investment and the budget than in the early years of the Revolution. The quality of educational and medical services suffered because of the emigration of about one-half of the physicians and the majority of university professors.

In this stage, the decline in sugar revenue provoked a serious economic crisis in 1962–63. Priority was given to diversification but without significant increases in nonsugar output and with the negative result of expanding trade deficits and declining growth rates. Economic independence from the United States was consolidated at the cost of worsening dependence on the USSR. Open unemployment was significantly cut and the emphasis in equality in distribution continued, but these achievements had an adverse effect on productivity and growth.

The Debate Over and Test of Alternative Socialist Economic Models, 1964–66

The failure of the Stalinist model of economic organization and development strategy in Cuba prompted that country's leadership to question whether another model was more appropriate for an insular, plantation economy. As a result, it was decided to postpone heavy industrialization and return to sugar as the engine for development. Accompanying this change in development strategy was a lively ideological debate between two alternative models of economic organization: Mao-Guevarism and Libermanism.

Ernesto Che Guevara and a group of devoted followers, indirectly influenced by War Communism (tried in the USSR in 1918–20) and more directly by the Maoist Great Leap Forward (applied in China in 1958–60), endorsed an idealistic line of thought contrary to the conventional Soviet doctrine of the 1960s. Guevara believed that "subjective conditions" (ideas, consciousness, willingness; all belonging to the superstructure in Marxist terms) could decisively influence "objective conditions," that is, the material base, the forces of production, the structure which in the conventional interpretation of Marxism determines the superstructure. Guevara and others argued that the successful development of consciousness ahead of the material-base development could enable a country to skip the transitional, socialist stage between capitalism and communism or to build socialism and communism simultaneously. Two sets of actions were proposed to achieve that end: in the material realm the basic objective was the total elimination of the market or the law of supply and demand. This was to be achieved through the following measures: full collectivization of all means of production; a highly centralized mathematical-physical planning apparatus; the organization of state enterprises as simple branches of a central enterprise (agency, ministry); central financing of all state enterprises through the state budget (the so-called budgetary financing based on nonrepayable, interest-free grants with transfer of all enterprise profits to the state, cancellation of any resulting deficits, and allocation of state investment disregarding enterprise profitability); elimination of mercantile relations among state enterprises (selling and buying using money were substituted by simple accounting transactions); gradual eradication of money (limited only as a unit for accounting purposes but not as a means for assessing profitability); steady downplaying of economic or material incentives (for example, wage differentials, production bonuses, overtime payments, awards in kind); and state physical allocation and pricing of consumer goods to substitute for the law of supply and demand. In the ideal realm, economic incentives to assure productivity, quality, investment efficiency, and reduction in costs should be largely replaced by raising the consciousness of managers and workers. Therefore Guevara's model, to be successful, had to create a New Man who, contrary to the economic man, would be unselfish, frugal, egalitarian, motivated not by greed but by patriotism and solidarity, and who would give his maximum labor effort to the collectivity and receive from it the basics to satisfy his needs. This ideal human being would be the product of mass consciousness-raising through education, mobilization, unpaid voluntary labor, moral incentives (for example, banners, medals won in fraternal competition), and the gradual expansion of state-provided free social services. If conducted simultaneously the two sets of actions (in the material and ideal realms) would be reinforcing rather than conflicting and result in economic and consciousness development.

Confronting Guevara was a moderate, pragmatist group led by the economist Carlos Rafael Rodríguez (then Director of INRA) and composed mostly of members of the prerevolutionary pro-Soviet communist party. This group was indirectly influenced by "market socialism"—the application of selected market mechanisms within the framework of a socialist economy. That model had influenced economic reform in Eastern Europe and eventually the Russian economist E. G. Liberman's program of economic reform, which had been experimented with in the USSR by Khrushchev in the early 1960s and moderately implemented by Brezhnev-Kosygin since 1965 to revive the sluggish Soviet economy. Rodríguez's group, sticking to the Soviet interpretation of Marxism, argued that subjective conditions cannot ignore objective conditions, that a socialist country cannot go farther than its structure allows it to go, that the material base has to be developed first and will, in turn, raise consciousness, and that it is impossible to skip the transitional—socialistic—stage between capitalism and full communism. Soviet ideologists actually subdivide the transitional stage into three steps: "building the foundations of socialism," "full socialism," and "building the foundations of communism." Such ideologists place the USSR in the third step as the most advanced country in the socialist camp, but, in practice, all of these countries are in the transitional stage and none have reached the full communist stage. In the necessary transitional stage, there will be traits of the capitalist past and some features of the communist future. It would not be possible in this stage to eliminate the law of supply and demand and hence some market mechanisms should be used (for example, money, profit, interest, and differential rent). Foreign supporters of this group, including René Dumont and Charles Bettelheim, were against excessive collectivization, particularly in agriculture, small retail trade, and personal services, and in favor of small individual farms and middle-sized private cooperatives rather than gigantic state farms. The Cuban group endorsed central planning but coupled it with cybernetic and input-output techniques, economic accounting, and market mechanisms. Local enterprises would have much more autonomy than in the Guevarist approach in hiring and dismissing labor, making investment decisions, and so forth, and they could buy and sell among themselves using money as a means of exchange. This group was against budgetary financing and instead advocated "self-financing": state enterprises would be responsible for their profits and losses; receive repayable loans with due interest from the banking system, which would exert supervision through monetary calculation; enterprises would retain part of their profit for reinvestment and distribution and would face closing if incapable of eliminating persistent deficits. Finally, to foster labor productivity, the group advocated material rather than moral incentives in the transitional stage and the need of work quotas connected with wages. The work quotas would fix the output to be produced by a worker in a given time period and fulfillment of it would result in a full wage, but nonfulfillment meant a proportional wage cut. This group believed that to ignore the law of supply and demand and cut down material incentives would have a negative effect on production and the development of the material base.

Organizational Model. The two models operated at the same time in different sectors of the Cuban economy, although the Libermanist model was adulterated with such features of the Mao-Guevarist model as covering enterprise deficits with budgetary grants. The Libermanist model was tried in one-third of Cuban enterprises, mostly agriculture and domestic and foreign trade; the Mao-Guevarist model operated in two-thirds of the state sector, primarily in industry. Guevara's centralistic model could work in the concentrated small industrial sector in which labor is skilled and its output relatively easy to check. But in agriculture, there are natural factors impossible to predict and control, and production is dispersed and in the hands of hundreds of thousands of unskilled workers and peasants whose output is difficult to monitor. The Cuban economy is essentially agrarian and depends heavily on foreign trade. Market mechanisms seemed more appropriate to agriculture and foreign trade, and in the latter sector Cuban officials faced the real outside world of internationally set market prices, tough competition based on costs, and the need for foreign exchange. Each of the two groups also controlled the key financing institution akin to its respective model; the Guevarists had the Ministry of Finance, which was in charge of the budget and capital grants; Rodríguez's group had the National Bank, the traditional dispenser of loans to be repaid with interest.

This stage of the Revolution seemed to be mainly concerned with the shift in development strategy, and few significant decisions were made on national economic organization. Collectivization did not advance. While both sides in the debate advocated a central plan, no annual plans were enforced nor was there discussion or preparation for a 1966–70 medium-range plan. Instead, sectorial plans began to proliferate, the first and most important one in the sugar industry. Capital accumulation increased moderately. Budgetary finance ruled in two-thirds of the economy and self-finance (often adulterated) prevailed in the rest. Perhaps the only nationally important step was the introduction of the Soviet system of work quotas and wage scales, which was quite advanced by the end of 1965.

Goal Fulfillment. Economic growth resumed in 1964–65 mainly as a result of fair sugar harvests and higher sugar prices in the international market, but also probably helped by better incentives in agriculture, increases in labor productivity through work quotas and economic incentives, and pay-off of capital accumulation with slightly improved efficiency in investment allocation and use. The goal of diversification suffered a severe blow with the return to sugar. The leadership attempted to justify and embellish that development strategy with the following rationale: the return to sugar was temporary and eventually would generate the necessary impetus for industrialization; sugar output would increase gradually in the 1960s to reach record crops that would allow a significant improvement in living standards in the 1970s; Cuba was suited to produce sugar cheaper than the USSR and other developed socialist countries, which in turn could produce machinery cheaper than Cuba; exchange of sugar for machinery and manufactures would result in mutual benefit because the USSR and other socialist countries would not take advantage of their privileged position in their trade with Cuba. In this spirit Cuba and the USSR signed a five-year economic and trade agreement (1965–70) in which the latter committed to increase imports of Cuban sugar by 150 percent and at a higher price than the Soviets had paid before. Just prior to that trade pact, though, market conditions favored trade with nonsocialist countries. The increase in sugar prices in the international market augmented the value of Cuban exports, particularly in 1964, but imports escalated reaching new records and trade deficits continued. Interestingly in this stage Cuba had a valued product (sugar) to trade with market economies, and as a result trade with socialist countries declined, reaching a low ebb in 1964 when the sugar price was high. This economic development seemed to call into question the assumption that trade with socialist countries was more advantageous than trade with market countries. In mid-1964 the Organization of American States imposed a collective embargo on Cuba applied by all members except Mexico, hence most Cuban trade with market economies in this stage was with Europe and Japan.

Open unemployment was further reduced in this stage using the same approach as in the previous stage. But postponement of the industrialization plan ended the expectation that the urban labor surplus would become productively employed in the industrial sector. On the other hand, the return to agriculture boosted the demand for manpower in the countryside. The government attempted to detect the labor surplus through the application of work quotas, to cut down the surplus with a campaign to reduce the bureaucracy by relocating redundant workers, and to transfer the urban surplus to the countryside by compulsory military service, mobilization of voluntary labor, restrictions of labor mobility, and selective incentives in the countryside rather than in the cities. Concerning distribution, the national establishment of wage scales set the basis for equal wage for equal work within the state sector. But the resilient forces of the market impeded the total elimination of old wages when they were higher than the new wages and were needed to keep technicians in vital sectors of the economy. Those who performed well or gave an extra effort were rewarded with production bonuses and overtime payments. The rising income of private farmers also contributed to some income inequalities.

In this stage, to save the economy from the 1962–63 crises, growth was emphasized with fair results, particularly in 1964 with the aid of higher sugar prices. This was achieved, however, at the cost of sacrificing industrialization and returning to sugar, a shift in strategy justified on theoretical and long-term grounds. Dependence on the USSR continued and yet trade partner concentration diminished somewhat aided by higher sugar prices. Full employment and distribution continued to be emphasized but slightly subordinated to productivity and growth.

The Adoption and Radicalization of the Mao-Guevarist Model, 1966–70

The discussion and confrontation between two competing economic ideologies and organization models could not last too long. For three years, Fidel Castro abstained from open participation in the controversy, but by the end of 1965 the leaders of the two groups were no longer in command. Guevara resigned as minister of industry and left Cuba to lead the revolution in South America, where he eventually met death; Rodríguez resigned as director of INRA but cleverly stayed in Cuba as a minister without portfolio. In the summer of 1966, Fidel Castro announced the new directions in economic organization—the Mao-Guevarist approach embellished with Fidelista features.

Organizational Model. Collectivization was reactivated in agriculture by taking family plots away from state farmers, state buying of private farms, expansion of the acopio, and banning sales from the farmers to individuals. In the spring of 1968 collectivization climaxed with the launching of the "Revolutionary Offensive." The remainder of the nonagricultural private sector passed to state control—56,000 small businesses such as street food outlets, consumer service shops, restaurants and bars, repair outfits, handicraft shops, even street vendors (see Table 1). The most important economic decisions were not grounded in a "scientific and objective" central planning apparatus capable of achieving some kind of optimality in resource allocation or development, rather those decisions were made by the political leadership. By the end of 1966, the annual plan lost its directive nature and was reduced to a tool for internal calculation (actually the plan was probably dropped altogether in the second half of the 1960s) and JUCEPLAN was limited to research and the logistic functions of assuring the needed inputs to meet the output targets fixed by the political leadership and of solving eventual discrepancies. In place of medium-range and annual macroplans, medium-range miniplans were developed for specific sectors (for example sugar, cattle raising, fishing, and electricity). The official reason for such an approach to planning was that Cuba lacked both statistics and cadres for highly abstract exercises and was better off concentrating its scarce resources on the vital sectors of the economy. Furthermore, special and extra plans were also introduced in a case-by-case manner by the leadership to tackle urgent economic problems. The administration of those plans was usually entrusted to loyal revolutionaries and the allocation of resources to the plans done by "superior order," outside of JUCEPLAN. This resulted in the reduction of resource allocation made to central projects already in operation but ranked lower in priority than the special or extra plans. Incompatibilities between central and special plans were resolved in an arbitrary manner by the political leadership as conflicts arose.

A significant reorganization of the government apparatus took place in 1966. The Ministry of Finance was abolished and all its functions consolidated into the National Bank. This act, instead of signaling the demise of the budgetary financing system, facilitated its expansion to all the economy because the National Bank was changed from a lender to an overseer of the financing of the economy. The number of state enterprises was reduced to 300, some of them embracing whole industrial branches—for example, the sugar industry was made up of well over 100 mills and related operations. Following Guevara's model, the use of monetary calculation and market mechanisms in agriculture and trade were discontinued. But the state budget, which was supposed to play a key role in the Mao-Guevarist model, also lost importance and apparently disappeared for a decade (1967–77). Accounting techniques were downplayed; student enrollment in universities and technical schools in the fields of economics and management in 1969 was one-twelfth that of 1965 (see Table 2).

Capital accumulation was emphasized over consumption, which resulted in increasing investment ratios and stagnating or declining consumption per capita. But capital productivity sharply declined because neither the interest rate nor the Soviet "coefficient of relative effectiveness"—a formula to evaluate efficiency among alternative investment projects based on the time required

TABLE 2. Student Enrollment in Economics and Management, 1959–76

Years[a]	Technical Schools	Universities
1959–60	14,280	5,931
1960–61	14,634	5,901
1961–62	15,613	2,846
1962–63	21,697	3,575
1963–64	27,363	4,443
1964–65	29,314	4,818
1965–66	13,172	2,796
1966–67	13,576	2,169
1967–68	2,869	1,518
1968–69	1,630	1,230
1969–70	2,538	1,338
1970–71	3,953	1,395
1971–72	6,770	2,147
1972–73	10,165	2,793
1973–74	11,925	4,757
1974–75	15,490	6,832
1975–76	18,214	9,286

[a]School year begins in September and ends in June.

Sources: *Sources: Anuario 1973*, pp.237, 243; *Anuario 1974*, pp. 240, 246; *Anuario 1975*, pp. 210–11, 216; *Anuario 1976*, pp. 199, 204. For full citations of Cuban statistical compendia see Appendix 3.

to pay them off—were used. Labor productivity also fell due to the negligence of work quotas, its disconnection with wage scales, the suppression of production bonuses, and the gigantic labor mobilization that disregarded costs. Interest charges on loans to private farmers and all personal taxes were eliminated. Monetary currency was not reduced but substantially increased; hence, with fewer consumer goods available, money began to lose value as a means of exchange and incentive for the labor force. Material incentives were dramatically curtailed or eliminated. The ultimate goal was proclaimed: eradication of wage differentials (thus an engineer and a sugarcane cutter would eventually earn the same wage) and gradual application of the communist principle of distribution according to needs instead of the socialist principle of distribution according to work. In theory, the so-called New Man was supposed to substitute for both automatic market mechanisms and central planning commands. Contrary to expectations, the old "economic man" was not transformed and economic chaos ensued.

The absence of a central plan and of coordination among special plans provoked shortages in inputs, bottlenecks, shutdowns, and proliferation of incompleted projects. Advances in certain sectors were offset by declines in others. Imported equipment lay unutilized for years (sometimes rusting on the docks, including vital oil tanks) because the building to house it had not been finished. Factories were nearly completed but could not start because of a missing component or part. The construction of small dams was not matched by the development of irrigation, hence most of the accumulated water could not be used. The lack of centralized information compounded with poor management had damaging effects: perishable goods spoiled on the docks or in warehouses; certain crops like pumpkins were lost due to excessively wet terrain, while others such as coffee dried up because of lack of water; still others like *malanga* (a tuber) were partly lost due to lack of manpower; and valuable seedlings for pine trees were stored and forgotten. The lack of maintenance and the rejection of depreciation costs resulted in the deterioration of installation and equipment, with eventual slowdown or shutdown, for example electricity blackouts and water supply shortages. Finally relaxed maintenance controls and standards plus either the lack of labor or its deficiencies in knowledge and expertise resulted in breakdowns of costly equipment. Half of the locomotives in existence were wrecked by careless workers creating a crisis in railroad transportation; 50,000 imported tractors were reduced to about 7,000 in terms of years of service due to misuse and lack of care.

Goal Fulfillment. As previous examples illustrate, the absence of mechanisms to use efficiently the significant increase in capital investment and labor mobilization resulted in significant waste of material and human resources. Hence the economy deteriorated, declining in terms of per capita growth rates. Grandiose plans in the sugar sector set increasing output targets in 1965–70 to reach 10 million tons of sugar at the end of the period and twice that target for the 1970s. But the sugar plan was fulfilled only in its first year; total accumulated output during the six years was 25 percent below the goal. The 1970 sugar harvest set a historical output record, but it still was 15 percent short of the target. Furthermore this was a Pyrrhic victory achieved by depleting resources from other sectors of the economy, which in turn suffered output declines offsetting the increase in sugar output. The fiasco of the sugar plan brought failure to both the developing strategy and model of organization nurtured in the second half of the 1960s. Huge sugar crops in the 1970s were expected to generate the necessary resources to reanudate the industrialization effort, repay the enormous debt to the USSR, and substantially increase the standards of living of the population. Actually industrial production with few exceptions peaked in 1965–67 and thereafter declined. Trade with the USSR set a record of 56 percent in 1967, and trade deficits also increased setting a record of more than half a billion pesos in 1969. The USSR held 80 percent of such deficit, and the main cause was that Cuba failed to deliver the committed sugar exports to the USSR. From 1966 to 1969, the cumulative deficit in sugar deliveries was about 10 million tons. In spite of the increasing dependency upon the Soviet Union in this stage, Cuba confronted the latter in several crucial areas, including an opposite model of economic organization and the claim that the island was ahead of the USSR in approaching full communism. The Soviets attempted to retaliate against the irritant and costly Cuban economic experiment by reducing the supply of oil to the island in 1968. The Cubans initially responded with open criticism of this move and put several members of the prerevolutionary communist party on trial; soon, however, they had to accept economic reality and endorsed the Soviet invasion of Czechoslovakia in the summer of 1968.

Full employment was practically achieved in 1970, but studies conducted in 1968 in state enterprises showed that in many of them from one-fourth to one-half of the workday was wasted. Unemployment had been disguised but not significantly reduced. To harvest the gigantic sugar crop in 1970, the government stepped up labor mobilization; however, the inefficiency and high economic cost of the volunteers actually contributed to the failure of the crop. Labor absenteeism increased sharply in this stage— reaching 20 percent of the labor force after the 1970 harvest was over—because of lack of incentives, disenchantment over the failure of the sugar crop, and ability to stay home and still be able to buy the scarce goods available with money already earned. Egalitarianism was advanced by the reduction in wage differentials, the elimination of production bonuses and overtime payments, the selective expansion of free social services (to burials, public phone calls, sports), and the decline in value of money. But the black market boomed in 1969–70 in spite of government restrictions.

Although growth was a priority goal in this stage—as the policy in favor of investment at the cost of consumption testified— in practice inefficiency and mismanagement provoked grave economic decline and dislocation. Diversification continued to be sacrificed and greater emphasis put on sugar, with the hope of generating the resources for both economic independence and industrialization in the long run, but the failure of the sugar plan destroyed those expectations. Economic dependency persisted, while full employment and egalitarianism were pushed forward at a significant economic cost for the nation.

The Shift to the Soviet Economic Reform Model, 1971 On

The failure of both the development strategy and model of economic organization tried in 1966–70, along with the subsequent economic dislocation, labor absenteeism, and spiraling foreign debt (combined with other political and international factors), forced the Cuban leadership to a significant shift in the 1970s. They entered into a new mature and pragmatic stage usually referred to as the "Institutionalization of the Revolution." In several speeches delivered in the 1970s, Castro criticized the previous stage as idealistic, utopian, and unreal. He explained the mistakes committed in the following manner: Although the Cubans lacked good economists, scientists, and theoreticians to make a significant contribution to the construction of socialism, they tried to invent a new approach. In doing so they showed contempt for the experiences of other more advanced socialist countries, experience which could have helped them considerably. The Cuban approach (Mao-Guevarism) was highly idealistic, minimized actual serious difficulties, and pretended that willingness could overcome the lack of objective conditions. The leadership was guilty of idealism in assuming that the attitude of a conscious minority was typical of the overall society, and this misconception proved detrimental to the economy. Now it is realized that it is easier to change the economic structure than man's consciousness, that the latter has a long way to go, and that material-base development should precede efforts to raise the consciousness of society. It is also currently accepted that the transitional stage between capitalism and communism cannot be skipped: it was folly to believe that the Cuban society could leave capitalism and enter into, in one bound, a society in which everyone would behave in an ethical and moral manner. It is hence accepted that currently Cuba is only building the foundations of socialism while the USSR has gone beyond full socialism and is building the foundations of communism. In the future, Cuba should advance slowly, carefully, and realistically; if it tries to go farther than possible, it will soon be forced to retreat. Measures of a communist character that were previously put into effect should be reconsidered: when it might have seemed as though we were drawing nearer to communistic forms of production and distribution, we were actually pulling away from the methods proper to the stage of building the foundations of socialism.[3]

Organizational Model. In the new stage, Cubans have gradually introduced the model of economic reform currently in force in the USSR. Collectivization has slowly advanced in agriculture through gradual transformation of private farms into cooperatives (like Soviet *kolhkoz*) and to a lesser extent into state farms (see Table 1). On the other hand, private farmers have been authorized to sell their surplus to individuals in free peasant markets, at prices set by supply and demand. State prices for acopio have been increased also. In addition there is a trend to decollectivize such individual services as repairs and minor construction; these services have to be provided under state license and usually are performed outside the regular work schedule and without paid employees.

Central planning has been reinstated as the main tool in the economy, and lower-level plans like mini, sectorial, and special are subordinated to the former. The 1970s saw annual macro plans since 1973; a global economic model for 1973–75; the first five-year plan (1976–80); and the preparation of the second five-year plan (1981–85) and a twenty-year development and forecast plan (1980–2000). Since 1977, statistical gathering, standardization, and publication is centralized in the State Committee of Statistics. Planning is being aided also by the development of computation with equipment imported from the USSR and Western and Eastern Europe as well as old U.S. equipment. During the Mao-Guevarist stage, profit, interest, taxes, depreciation, and cost analysis were despised as tools of "bourgeois economies" contrary to communist morale; that attitude is now criticized as a mistake resulting from ignorance of economic matters, and such market tools are now accepted as key economic instruments of Cuba's socialist economy. There has been a revival of economic, accounting, and managerial studies that suffered a serious setback in the second half of the 1960s: from Table 2 it is seen that enrollment in these fields increased sevenfold in 1970–76; and to push enrollment forward, a National School of Economic Management and three provincial schools were established in 1976. The loss of valuable technicians who fled in the 1960s is now blamed on the excessive radicalism of the leadership, and the substitution of political cadres for technocrats is acknowledged as a costly economic error. Technicians who do not embrace socialism but have "national conscience" have been guaranteed in their jobs, while incompetent managers with revolutionary credentials have been admonished to improve their skills or else face dismissal. In early 1979 more than half of the directors of state enterprises were either graduates of or were studying in managerial schools. A new Soviet-style System of Economic Management and Planning (SDPE) was gradually introduced in the second half of the 1970s, should be completed in 1980, and is expected to be in full operation in the mid-1980s. The SDPE takes into account the law of supply and demand and the need of monetary and mercantile relations in the transitional stage. To improve efficiency in the allocation and utilization of capital and human and material resources, the new economic system uses market instruments such as credit, interest, rational prices, budgets, monetary controls, and taxes. State enterprises have been decentralized—from 300 in 1968 to less than 3,000 in 1979—and enjoy more independence to hire and dismiss labor, request loans, and make investment decisions. Along with this they are held responsible to balance revenue with expenses and generate a profit. The efficiency of Cuban enterprises is measured by a set of indicators with profit as the main one and including others such as output, quality, cost, and productivity. The price fixed for enterprises and wholesalers includes production costs (labor, capital amortization and interest, and depreciation) and a profit, out of which the enterprise has to pay a sort of corporation tax and a social security tax and develop an economic incentive fund for workers. Retail prices are expected to include, in addition, a sales tax which will be aimed at balancing supply and demand as well as generating revenue for the state. In the initial model, part of the enterprise revenue went to a development fund for self expansion, but this has been temporarily discarded and expansion is to be decided centrally. The state budget was reintroduced in 1978, after being discarded for almost a decade, and economic calculation began also in that year. The budgetary system of finance has been largely substituted by self-finance: the state provides to its enterprises and farms, and to private cooperatives and farms, repayable loans with interest ranging from 4 to 12 percent.

The Soviet system of work quotas and wage scales, briefly tried in 1964–65, has been gradually reintroduced to control and foster labor productivity. Material incentives have also been reintroduced, including wage differentials which take skills and special effort into account, bonuses for fulfilling and over-fulfilling work quotas, payments for overtime, priorities in the allocation of housing and durable consumer goods, and vacations according to certain skills and productivity. The size of the economic incentive fund, introduced in 1979 in 7 percent of the enterprises, is determined by enterprise profitability. It is partly used to provide economic rewards for its workers—both collectively (for example, enterprise restaurants and day-care centers) and to individuals (for example, cash bonuses). In order for these new incentives to be effective, "socialist inflation," which is monetary surplus, has been reduced by curtailing demand through higher prices and increasing supply of consumer goods.

Goal Fulfillment. Economic growth, so neglected in 1966–70, took first priority in the 1970s. The measures introduced to strengthen capital and labor productivity, as well as the more rational approach in planning and financing, combined with booming sugar prices in the international market resulted in impressive rates of growth in 1971–75. But the decline in sugar prices, compounded by difficulties in implementing the new model of economic organization and by agricultural plagues and other problems, provoked a slowdown in economic growth in 1976–80. The economic strategy of the 1970s continued to be fundamentally based on sugar but with a more balanced and rational approach. The government sought to produce as much sugar as possible with the material and human resources allocated to the sugar sector without depleting resources from other economic sectors and by relying on technology—including mechanization of cane-cutting and modernization of mills—rather than on labor mobilization. Sugar harvests declined in 1971–75, but this loss was more than compensated by the booming sugar prices; the latter resulted in increased value of exports which, paradoxically, worsened the dependency on sugar with a record high in 1975. Harvests in 1976–79 increased in volume although not in value. Industrial output rapidly recuperated in the first-half of the 1970s, although it leveled off in the second-half of the decade. Performance of nonsugar agriculture, with some exceptions, was not as good as in industry but certainly better than during the Mao-Guevarist experiment. Helped by the favorable conditions in the sugar market, Cuba gradually reversed her balance of trade from a deficit of half a billion pesos in 1971 to a small surplus in 1974—the first in fifteen years. Yet decaying sugar prices built up the deficit again in 1975–78. With high sugar prices in the international market, Cuban trade moved away from socialist to market economies in 1974–75, but declining international sugar prices and Soviet subsidies to Cuban sugar reversed the trend again since 1976. Cuba entered COMECON in 1972 and signed trade agreements with the USSR for 1973–75 and 1976–80, actions which reinforced her dependency with the socialist camp. In 1972 the enormous debt with the USSR was postponed (and interest cancelled) until 1986 thus giving Cuba a most needed break. But new Soviet credits both to cover trade deficits and for development kept building up the debt in the 1970s reaching probably more than six billion pesos in 1975, for the highest per capita debt in Latin America.

With the shift in economic model in the 1970s, both employment and distribution were negatively affected. It was officially accepted that the previous policy of subsidized employment and labor mobilization had resulted in low labor productivity and a burden for the economy. The new model of economic organization stresses efficiency and gives more power to enterprise managers for dismissals, while the application of work quotas releases surplus labor from state enterprises, hence unemployment pockets have appeared. Voluntary labor is now only used when its net productivity can be proved beforehand. Previous emphasis on egalitarianism came also under official criticism as an idealistic mistake. The reintroduction of material incentives, the increasing use of prices, the halt or curtailment of some free social services, and the restoration of the value of money as a buying tool resulted in a retrenchment in egalitarianism and some stratification.

Facing economic chaos and danger to the survival of the Revolution at the end of the 1960s, the Cuban leadership dramatically rearranged goal priorities in the 1970s. Economic growth became the most important goal to which the others were subordinated. Diversification continued to be sacrificed and external economic dependence increased. The most significant change, though, was that adoption of policies which stressed efficiency and growth resulted in the downgrading of full employment and egalitarianism.

3

Sustained Economic Growth

This chapter opens with a discussion of global and sectorial indicators of Cuban economic growth followed by an analysis of the causes behind the divergent economic performance in the first and second decade of the Revolution. Special attention is then given to the impact of population, investment, inflation, and military costs in economic growth.

GLOBAL INDICATORS OF ECONOMIC GROWTH

Cuba's national accounts do not follow the Western concept of the gross national product (GNP), instead they correspond to the Soviet concepts of global social product (GSP) and gross material product (GMP). Both GSP and GMP include the production of "material goods" in agriculture, fishing, mining, industry, and construction. In addition, GSP includes the value of such "material services" as transportation, trade, and communication that are directly connected with the production of material goods. Conversely GMP excludes the value of material services. Both GSP and GMP exclude the value of "nonmaterial services" such as education, health care, and so forth. Other methodological differences with Western economic indicators result from the process of aggregation, changes in definitions, and whether figures are given in constant or current prices (correcting inflation or not). These procedures make it difficult to evaluate Cuba's macroeconomic indicators (see Appendix 1).

Official data is given in Table 3 on the value in pesos (for exchange rates see Appendix 1) of both GSP and GMP as well as total and per capita growth rates. The latter are shown both annually and in averages corresponding to three of the five stages described in the previous chapter. Technically speaking (See Table 3), the whole series cannot be connected because it is cut in three

TABLE 3. Economic Growth in Cuba, 1962–80

Years	GSP	GMP	Annual Rates[a]		Stage Averages[a]	
	(In Million Pesos)		Total	Per Capita	Total	Per Capita
1962	6,082.1	3,698.2	—	—		
1963	6,013.2	3,736.7	1.0%	−1.6%		
1964	6,454.5	4,076.4	9.0	6.4 ⎤	5.2%	2.7%
1965	6,770.9	4,137.5	1.5	−1.0 ⎦		
1966	6,709.3	3,985.5	−3.7	−5.7 ⎤		
1967	7,211.6	4,081.0	2.4	0.5		
1968	7,330.9	4,352.6	6.7	5.0	0.4%	−1.3%
1969	7,236.1	4,180.6	−4.0	−5.6		
1970	8,355.6	4,203.9	0.6	−0.9 ⎦		
1971	8,936.4	4,818.2	14.6	12.8 ⎤		
1972	10,349.2	6,026.9	25.1	23.0		
1973	11,910.3	6,710.4	11.3	9.4	16.3%	14.5%
1974	13,423.5	7,414.1	10.5	8.9		
1975	15,799.3	8,886.3	19.8	18.3 ⎦		
1976	15,860.5	8,881.8[c]	−0.1	−1.5 ⎤		
1977	16,510.8[b]	9,246.0[c]	4.1	2.9		
1978	18,062.8[b]	10,115.2[c]	9.4	8.4	4.1%	3.1%
1979	18,830.5[b]	10,545.1[c]	4.3	3.6		
1980[d]	19,395.4	10,861.4[c]	3.0	2.3 ⎦		

[a]GMP; in 1962–66 at constant prices, in 1967–80 in current prices.
[b]Official estimate.
[c]Author estimate based on the average ratio of GMP/GSP in the previous ten years.
[d]Goal.
Sources: GSP 1962–66 *Boletín 1966*, p. 20; 1967–69 *Anuario 1972*, p. 31; 1970 *Anuario 1973*, p. 35; 1971–74 *Anuario 1975*, p. 39; 1975–76 *Anuario 1976*, p. 45; 1977 *La economía cubana 1977*, p. 1; 1978 *La economía cubana 1978*, p. 5; *Granma Weekly Review*, 6 January 1980, pp. 2–3; GMP 1962–66 *Boletín 1966*, p. 20; 1967–75 Banco Nacional de Cuba, 1977, p. 11. Population from Table 6 infra. A new GSP series for 1975–78, with a different methodology, appears in *Anuario 1978*, p. 50.

points by shifts in methodologies and because inflation affected data, particularly since 1967. There are no data for the years 1959–61, although we know they were years of steady growth; annual estimates for these three years range between 4 and 6 percent (2 to 4 percent per capita). Data for 1962 are available but do not show the relation with the previous year. Estimates by foreign planning advisors to Cuba on the decline in 1962 fluctuate between 10 and 20 percent; my own conservative estimate is of −8 percent.[1] Hence the 1962–63 attempt to apply the Soviet pre-economic-reform model cost at least 7 percent in total growth, or 12 percent per capita. Economic recuperation during the stage of debate of alternative economic models generated average annual rates of 5.2 percent and 2.7 percent per capita. The Mao-Guevarist experiment (1966–70) resulted in economic stagnation (0.4 percent annually) and actual decline in per capita terms (−1.3 percent annually). The economic recuperation in the current stage is impressive, particularly in 1971–75 when record average annual rates of 16.3 percent and 14.5 percent per capita were reached. And yet in the second half of the decade there was a slowdown to 4.1 percent and 3.1 percent per capita, the former equal to two-thirds of the modest target of an average 6 percent growth set by the 1976–80 plan. GMP per capita declined in 1962 (to 505 pesos) and again in 1963 (to 497 pesos); after a brief recuperation in 1964–65 when it reached a high (528 pesos), it declined once more in 1966–70, reaching a trough of 488 pesos in the latter year. In 1971–77 GMP per capita rapidly rose to reach 988 pesos, which represented in the latter year about twofold the levels of 1964 and 1970.[2]

The dismal economic performance of the 1960s, and particularly of the second-half of that decade, was caused by several factors: the rapid and wide collectivization of the means of production, which largely destroyed the automatic mechanisms of the market without an adequate substitute; the numerous changes (an average of one every three years) in the model of economic organization and development strategy, which made it impossible for any policy to consolidate; the idealistic errors and inefficiency of the Mao-Guevarist stage, which cost anywhere from 20 to 80 percent in lost growth, depending on which historical periods are used as norms for the comparison; the exodus of experienced managerial, technical, and professional personnel and its substitution by loyal but incompetent revolutionaries; the decline of economic and managerial studies; and the predominance of politics and subjective conditions over expertise and objective conditions— all of which negatively affected the efficiency of human resources; the low sugar output in various years combined with low sugar prices in the international market; the consumptionist policy of the early years of the Revolution, which induced a significant decline in investment, and the poor efficiency in the allocation and use of capital when investment increased; the cost of the economic embargo imposed by the United States and the OAS upon Cuba and of shifting the entire set of international economic relations away from the United States towards the USSR and the socialist camp; and the heavy burden of military expenditures for internal defense and subversion abroad.

The vigorous economic recuperation of the first half of the 1970s was induced by the following factors: the more efficient model of economic organization and a better balanced and rational development strategy, which were tried for almost a decade; the pay-off of previous investment in human and capital resources and the current emphasis in training of managerial personnel, both of which were reinforced by the current policy that stresses expertise over politics in economics and enterprise administration; the record prices of sugar in the international market in 1971–75; the 1972 postponement of the payment of the Cuban debt to the USSR for fifteen years and the new Soviet credits provided; and the lifting of the OAS embargo and the relaxation of U.S. economic sanctions against Cuba, combined with a substantial flow of credit from market economies.[3]

The slowdown of 1976–80 was caused by these conditions: the decline in sugar prices in the international market (although attenuated by Soviet subsidies in buying of Cuban sugar and nickel and in selling oil to the island; see chapter 5); agricultural plagues that adversely affected sugarcane, tobacco, and coffee plantations, combined with an epidemic of porcine cholera and problems in the fishing and nickel industries; a sharp reduction of the flow of credit from market economies since 1979; some complications in the implementation of the new System of Economic Management and Planning; and the heavy burden of Cuban involvement in Africa.

AGRICULTURAL AND INDUSTRIAL OUTPUT

Cuban figures on physical output are more reliable to assess economic growth than global indicators since they are not distorted by methodological diversity or inflation. Industrial figures since 1962 are more accurate than agricultural ones because the former practically cover all production, which is controlled by the state. In agriculture, however, since 1963 output figures (with a few exceptions, including sugar) refer to production of state farms plus acopio (private farms sales to the state), excluding private farmers' own consumption and a small amount of barter and sales.

Summarized in Table 4 are production trends in thirty-two major agricultural, fishing, mining, and manufacturing products. These were selected for their importance to both domestic consumption and exports, and they represent traditional and modern agriculture and industry. Output is compared at the end of the first stage of the Revolution (1960) before the economy was collectivized; towards the end of the third stage(1965) on the eve of the implementation of Mao-Guevarism; at the end of the fourth stage (1970); in the middle of the current stage (1975 and 1976) indicating the height of the economic recuperation and its subsequent slowdown. Goals of the current five-year plan set for 1980 are also shown when available.

Production of practically all products was slightly lower in 1958 than in 1960, important exceptions being nickel, tobacco, and cigars. In the few modern, capital intensive sectors—including steel, electricity, nickel, fishing, and eggs—production steadily

TABLE 4. Physical output of Selected Products in Cuba, 1960–76
and 1980 Goals (in thousand metric tons unless specified)

Products	1960	1965	1970	1975	1976	1980
Sugar	5943	6156	8538	6314	6155	8–8700
Tobacco	45	43	32	41	51	60
Citrus fruits	73	160[d]	124[f]	182	199	350–550
Coffee	42	24	20	18	19	—
Eggs (MU)	430	920	1509	1851	1829	2000
Rice	323	50	291	338	335	600
Yuca	255	62	22	85	84	—
Malanga (a tuber)	257	47	12	32	45	—
Potatoes	97	84	77	117	145	—
Tomatoes	116	120	62	184	194	—
Beans	37	11	5	5	3	—
Pork	38	48	15	43	52	80
Milk	767	575	380	591	682	1000
Fish	31	40	106	143	193	350
Nickel	13	28	37	37	37	100
Salt	59	106	89	157	150	—
Electricity (Mkwh)	2981	3387	4888	6583	7198	9000
Steel	63	36	140	298	250	440
Cement	813	801	742	2083	2501	5000
Fertilizers	438[c]	860[e]	577	749	803	—
Textiles (Mm²)	116[c]	96	78	144	139	260–280
Tires (TU)	314	451	202	368	266	—
Shoes (M)	14	16	16	23	21	35
Soap	34[c]	37	33	41	43	—
Refrigerators (TU)	0	12	6	50	44	100
Gas ranges (TU)	9[c]	46[d]	6	54	50	—
Radios (TU)	0	82	19	113	94	300
Beer (TH)	1394[b]	993	659	2111	2169	—
Liquor (TH)	154[c]	170	170	295	277	—
Sodas (TH)	2372[c]	2406	871	1570	1502	—
Canned fruits and vegetables	64[c]	80	39	98	104	—
Cigars (MU)	591[a]	657	277[f]	383	359	—

[a]1959 [b]1961 [c]1963 [d]1966 [e]1969 [f]1971

M=millions T=thousands U=units H=hectolitres m²=square meters
Kwh=kilowats/hour

Sources: C. Mesa-Lago, *Cuba in the 1970s: Pragmatism and Institutionalization* (Albuquerque: University of New Mexico Press, 1978), p. 59; expanded and updated with *Anuario 1975; Compendio 1976; Anuario 1976;* Banco Nacional de Cuba, *1977;* and *Guía Estadística 1977.*

increased throughout the 1960s and 1970s. But output of most products in traditional agriculture and industry either increased in the first half of the 1960s then declined in the second half and recuperated in the 1970s, or declined throughout most of the 1960s and recuperated by 1975. Sixty percent of the products had a higher output in 1965 than in 1960, but 65 percent of the products had declined in their output in 1970 over 1965. By 1975, however, 88 percent of the products had surpassed their output levels of 1970, and 70 percent were also above the 1960 level. Thirty percent of these products, all of which were agricultural, and include tobacco, coffee, malanga, and beans, had not recuperated their prerevolutionary output level in 1975. In 1976 about half of the products suffered a decline in output, although scattered information suggests that there was some recuperation in 1977–78.

Cuba's output performance as described above is corroborated in a study by Jorge Domínguez. Using official data, he systematically followed the annual output performance of 353 products in agriculture, cattle raising, forestry, fishing, and industry throughout 1963–73, registering the highest and lowest output of each product. His computations show that in the year 1970 one-fifth of the products were at the lowest ebb and, in 1963, 18 percent of the products were in a trough. In 1973, however, one-fourth of the products reached a peak and in 1964 10 percent of the products peaked. Domínguez also checked the total number of products rising or falling in their output in two-year periods, and even more dramatic results were recorded: the worst period was right after the Revolutionary Offensive in 1968–70 in which almost two-thirds of the products suffered a decline in output; the best period was 1970–72 when more than two-thirds of the products increased their output.[4]

Indices of agricultural and industrial output are contrasted in Table 5, and performance in the latter has been substantially better than in the former. The two indices, however, have different sources as well as base years and are not strictly comparable. The United Nations' Food and Agricultural Organization agricultural index is based on 1959, which was a good production year. It shows that total output reached its lowest point in 1963, and even in 1976 output was only slightly above the 1959 level. In per capita terms the picture is gloomier: output in 1976 was two-thirds that of 1959. According to FAO, Cuba's agricultural performance in 1961–76 was the worst—tied with that of Chile—in Latin America.[5] The index of industrial output is based on Cuban data and poses several problems: it starts in a low year (1962) and does not show output in the good years of 1959–61; it is distorted by inflation in 1967–76; and it cannot be truly connected due to several changes in methodology. It should be noted that industrial output increased at an annual growth rate of 5.7 percent in 1962–77, while GMP supposedly grew at an annual rate of 6.3 percent, something unusual in developing countries in which industrial output grows faster than overall output. Industrial growth in 1961 over 1959 has been estimated at 20 percent, but while 1962 and 1963 were among the worst

TABLE 5. Indices of Agricultural and Industrial Output in Cuba, 1959–77

Years	Agricultural Output (1959=100)		Industrial Output[a] (1967=100)	
	Total	Per capita	Total	Per capita
1959	100.0	100.0	—	—
1960	101.8	100.0	—	—
1961	109.0	105.0	—	—
1962	89.3	84.2	86.2	96.8
1963	76.8	71.3	84.7	92.7
1964	83.9	74.3	88.3	94.1
1965	100.0	88.1	91.4	95.0
1966	83.9	71.3	89.7	91.4
1967	102.7	87.1	100.0	100.0
1968	94.6	78.2	98.2	96.6
1969	88.4	72.3	99.8	96.5
1970	126.8	101.1	125.6	119.8
1971	99.5	77.8	131.1	122.9
1972	85.4	65.8	139.9	128.5
1973	96.9	73.0	156.6	141.1
1974	106.5	77.8	169.3	150.1
1975	111.0	80.2	188.6	164.8
1976	105.7	73.8	194.8	167.9
1977	—	—	197.1	167.9

[a]1962–66 in constant (1965) prices; 1967–76 in current prices.

Sources: Agriculture from FAO *Monthly Bulletin of Agricultural Economics and Statistics,* 19 (July-August 1970), pp. 14–17, and *Production Yearbook 1976* (Rome: 1977), pp. 75, 79 (the two series were statiscally connected by the author with 1959 as the base year). Industry computed by the author using population figures from Table 6 and production figures from *Boletín 1966,* pp. 20–22; *Anuario 1972,* p. 31; *Anuario 1974,* p. 35; *Anuario 1975,* p. 39; and *Compendio 1976,* p. 14.

years in the Revolution we do not know the magnitude of the decline. It has been said, though, that the prerevolutionary level of industrial output was not recuperated until 1967,[6] and the latter date has been taken as the base year in this study. We can assume that the levels of output in 1959 and 1967 were roughly comparable. If my assumptions are correct, total industrial output doubled in the first two decades of the Revolution, for an average annual rate of 5 percent. In per capita terms, the increase was about 70 percent or 3.5 percent annually. In reality, however, stagnation of industrial output occurred in the 1960s followed by impressive growth in the first half of the 1970s, which was partly pushed by booming sugar prices and inflation but also was a result of real industrial expansion.

The different performance between agriculture and industry can be explained in some measure by considering the effects of hurricanes, droughts, and plagues on crops. Such natural disasters

cannot be controlled by policy makers. But perhaps the fundamental reason for the disparity in performance is that agriculture
has traditionally been the Achilles heel of command economies.
This difficulty is aggravated in Cuba, basically an agrarian
country which, in spite of significant improvements in the last
twenty years in irrigation, mechanization, increased use of
fertilizers and pesticides, still has to deal with a relatively
backward, dispersed, labor-intensive agriculture. Excessive collectivization, poor incentives for both state and private farmers, and
difficulties in controlling labor productivity certainly have complicated rather than helped the problems. Only the most concentrated, modern, mechanized, and capital intensive agricultural
enterprises—such as eggs—have been successful. The same factors
explain the outcome of modern industrial sector in which capital
investment, improved organization, better incentives, and control
of labor output have resulted in a better performance in the
1970s.

Few of the goals set by the current five-year plan for 1980 will
probably be fulfilled, and most of those that are not will be in the
modern sector, including electricity, steel, and eggs (see Table 4).
The cement goal will not be achieved until the mid-1980s even if
two plants under construction, which will increase output by two
million tons, are inaugurated, as expected, in 1980. A new textile
plant scheduled to start production in 1979 or 1980 will increase
production by 60,000 metric tons but hardly could help to reach
the goal. Production of nickel was expected to boom in 1980 with
the addition of two new plants, but their construction has
apparently been delayed. Output goal set for rice, citrus fruits,
fish, refrigerators, and radios call for a twofold increase in
1975–80, a target difficult to achieve in view of the stagnation,
slowdown, or decline in output suffered by most of these products
in 1976–77.

POPULATION CHANGES AND GROWTH

A summary of demographic trends in Cuba in 1958–77 is
presented in Table 6. Birth rates steadily increased in 1959–63,
probably due to rising standards of living and expectations among
low-income groups, mass mobilizations, sexual freedom among
females, and increasing numbers of marriages in which the
average age of females was lower than in the past. But high birth
rates were more than offset by increases in general and infant
mortality rates and migration, resulting in lower population
growth rates in 1960–62. Birth rates leveled off in 1964 and
steadily declined thereafter probably as a result of several factors:
expansion of education, increasing number of females entering
the labor force, severe restrictions in consumption (rationing
began in 1962), scarcity of housing, and introduction of a three-

TABLE 6. Vital Statistics of Cuba, 1958-78

Year	(Thousands)[a]	Rates per 1,000			Migration[d]	Percent of Population Growth
		Birth[b]	Mortality[b]	Infant Mortality[c]		
1958	6,824	26.1	6.3	33.4	− 4,449	1.8
1959	6,977	27.7	6.4	34.7	−12,345	2.2
1960	7,077	30.1	6.1	35.9	−62,379	1.4
1961	7,191	32.5	6.4	37.6	−67,468	1.6
1962	7,318	34.3	7.1	41.5	−66,264	1.6
1963	7,512	35.1	6.7	37.1	−12,201	2.6
1964	7,713	35.0	6.3	37.4	−12,791	2.6
1965	7,907	34.3	6.4	37.8	−18,003	2.5
1966	8,064	33.1	6.4	37.2	−53,409	2.0
1967	8,215	31.7	6.3	36.4	−51,972	1.9
1968	8,353	30.4	6.5	38.2	−56,755	1.7
1969	8,489	29.2	6.6	46.7	−49,776	1.6
1970	8,613	27.7	6.3	38.7	−56,404	1.5
1971	8,768	29.5	6.2	37.4	−49,631	1.8
1972	8,951	28.0	5.5	27.4	−16,856	2.1
1973	9,118	25.0	5.7	28.9	−7,073	1.9
1974	9,266	21.9	5.6	29.0	−3,893	1.6
1975	9,405	20.7	5.4	27.3	−2,891	1.5
1976	9,537	19.8	5.5	22.9	−2,891	1.4
1977	9,649	17.5	5.8	24.8	−968	1.2
1978	9,738	15.3	5.7	22.3	−3,462	0.9

[a]At the end of the year.
[b]Per 1,000 inhabitants.
[c]Per 1,000 infants born alive.
[d]Balance of migratory movement.
Sources: *Anuario 1974*, p. 26; *Anuario 1975*, p. 30; *Anuario 1976*, pp. 28, 35; *Anuario 1977*, p. 38; and *Anuario 1978*, pp. 28, 38.

year compulsory military service starting at age sixteen. Mortality rates increased in the early 1960s and then leveled off due to the exodus of about half of the physicians, the scarcity of medicines, and the spread of contagious diseases (see Chapter 7)[7]. In the 1970s, however, mortality rates declined as a result of the significant expansion of the number of physicians, the increase in the medicine supply, and the control of contagious diseases through vaccination. The decline in birth rates (combined with heavy emigration) has helped to cut by half Cuba's population growth rate—from 2.6 percent in 1963 to 0.9 percent in 1978— with a positive impact in per capita economic growth.

Until recently, the Cuban government had an ambiguous attitude toward family planning and birth control. While they criticized such policies as "imperialist formulas for the underdeveloped world," they occasionally published information on birth control, made contraceptives available to those who wanted them, and allowed free abortions within the first month of pregnancy.[8] In 1974 the official position was that population was not a limiting factor in development, hence government officials remained critical of economists from "capitalist countries" who blamed the demographic explosion for underdevelopment and promoted birth control to help in developmental efforts. According to Cuban demographers, their nation introduced structural changes that promoted development, without the need for birth control, and eventually the process of modernization curbed birth rates.[9] But in 1975, Castro referred to the burden imposed on Cuba's development by demographic factors and urged the party to design a scientifically-based population policy.[10] The baby boom of the 1960s changed the composition of the population. More youth meant a corresponding decline in the productive-age bracket and increases in both the dependency ratio—in 1970 there were two inactive persons for each active person in the labor force— and in the burden of state-provided services such as education. However, as those born during the baby boom enter the labor force and as birth rates decline, the population will become older, the productive-age bracket will expand again, and the dependency ratio will be somewhat reduced. The decline in birth rates means fewer youngsters to teach and so will reduce the cost of education, but the cost of social security will rise since the proportion of those 65 and older will increase. Cuban awareness of the demographic factor is reflected by the number of articles published in the past few years on this subject, some of them with new approaches. Thus one article acknowledged that a high rate of population growth is an obstacle for development because it increases consumption, reduces savings and investment, slows down growth, and puts an excessive burden on both the productive population and the state for the provision of services. The article quoted a Soviet demographer, who supported a reduction in population growth to increase social welfare, and it concluded by accepting a population policy, combined with structural change and socioeconomic policies, as a package to fight underdevelopment.[12] Cubans are now producing the pill (also being imported from Czechoslovakia), which is sold in pharmacies without prescription and has become the most popular contraceptive followed by the ring. Vasectomies are unknown in Cuba. The number of abortions has dramatically increased: in 1978 at the Hospital of Havana 20 abortions were done daily versus 12 births.[13]

Migration of some 800,000 Cubans (about 8 percent of the current population) has had both negative and positive effects on the economy. The loss of managers, technicians, professionals, and skilled workers—especially in the big migration wave of 1960–62—was a serious blow to production and productivity.[14]

But after the missile crisis of October 1962, most commercial airlines ceased to fly to Cuba, which resulted in a dramatic reduction in the exodus in 1963–65 to one-fifth of the number who fled in 1960–62. In the meantime the Cuban government introduced tighter controls for the exit of technicians or skilled personnel and barred the exit of those between 15 and 26 years of age. In 1966–72 the exit was reopened with an airlift established between Cuba and the United States. Another big migrational wave began, but this time with significantly less loss of managerial, professional, and technical personnel.

After a period of restricted exit in 1973–79, in the spring of 1980 there was a massive exodus of about 125,000 people in less than five months, mostly leaving by sea from the port of Mariel— west of Havana. Precise data on the composition of this group were not available at the time this book went to the printers.

The decision to allow opponents and discontents to leave the island contributed to elimination of political dissent and to achievement of stability and consensus. Furthermore, the migrants left behind significant assets, which were immediately seized. For example, houses were seized to ease somewhat the grave housing deficit. Because those leaving in 1959–72 overrepresented older persons in Cuba and, in 1965–72, they also overrepresented children, their departure helped to reduce the heavy burden on education and social security.[15] The exodus was a key factor in the decline of population growth rates, and this in turn had a positive impact, at least statistically, in per capita economic growth rates. Since 1979 Cuban exiles returning for short visits have become an important source of foreign exchange. Finally the exodus of 1980 has probably contributed toward reduction of unemployment.

INVESTMENT, CONSUMPTION, AND GROWTH

The average ratio of gross investment over GNP in the decade prior to the Revolution steadily climbed, reaching an annual average estimated between 17.5 and 19.8 percent in 1955–58. Although no official figures are available, a planner-advisor to Cuba has stated that investment declined to an annual average of 14 percent in 1959–60. No estimates exist at all for 1961, but possibly investment was stagnant in that year.[16] Investment in 1962—the year in which rationing began—rose to 16.4 percent and continued to climb reaching 25.3 percent in 1967 (see Table 7). The last three columns in the table show that real GMP per capita was stagnant in 1962–67, but at the same time investment (also measured in constant prices) was increasing at impressive rates (particularly at the beginning of the Mao-Guevarist stage), and consumption (measured in current prices) rose slightly until 1965 and then declined in the frugal years of 1966–67. In the

TABLE 7. Growth of GMP, Investment, and Consumption Per Capita in Cuba, 1962−67[a]

Years	Investment Ratio[b]	Index Numbers (1962=100)		
		GMP	Investment	Consumption[c]
1962	16.4	100.0	100.0	100.0
1963	19.2	98.4	114.2	103.8
1964	19.5	104.5	122.8	105.9
1965	20.3	103.6	124.6	107.4
1966	23.3	97.8	135.6	100.9
1967	25.3	98.2	146.8	95.9

[a]Consumption at current prices; GMP and investment in 1962−66 in constant prices, in 1967 in current prices.

[b]Gross investment as a percentage of GMP.

[c]Personal consumption; excludes social consumption, for example, services provided by the state.

Source: Author calculations based on Tables 3 and 6 infra; *Boletín 1971*, p. 44; and *Anuario 1972*, p. 30.

latter year, investment was almost 47 percent above 1962, while GMP and particularly consumption were below the 1962 level and certainly below the 1961 level. If consumption had been measured at constant prices, it probably would have been stagnant or declining throughout the period 1962−67. With GMP and consumption stagnant, investment increased at the cost of expanding the trade deficit and the foreign debt (more on this in chapter 5).

What happened to investment since 1967 is a matter of speculation. The official target for investment in 1968 was 31 percent of GMP. This target was justified by Fidel Castro as necessary to assure a minimum GMP per capita growth rate of 5 percent in the rest of the decade, which took into account the average population growth rate of 2.3 percent of the previous years.[17] Data published in Cuba's statistical yearbook of 1972, however, suggest that the investment ratio actually declined in 1968 and was stagnant in 1969. Fragmented data available on capital accumulation (investment plus stocks) hint a further decline in 1970 to less than 16 percent.[18] These figures go against the previous consensus of foreign specialists (including myself) that investment kept growing in the second half of the 1960s.[19]

If investment did decline in 1969−70, then it is proof that the Mao-Guevarist policy failed to achieve its grandiose capital accumulation goals in spite of the heavy demands it put on the population in terms of labor mobilization and frugality in consumption. On the other hand if the investment ratio did increase in 1969−70, it failed to boost economic growth because it could not overcome the grave waste and inefficiency in the allocation and use of capital provoked by the model of economic organization prevalent in those years. Castro has said on the subject: "Frequently the desire to accomplish a great deal in a short time led us to gather together a large amount of resources. And the result was that we did not make the most effective use of them—we squandered them."[20]

The only data ever published on the distribution of state investment by the socioeconomic sector are also more than a decade old and are reproduced in Table 8. It shows that the percentage of investment going to social services—housing, education, and health—steadily declined from a combined 23.6 percent in 1962 to 15.2 percent in 1966. At the same time the percentage of investment in the "material" sector steadily climbed, with the exception of construction and commerce. Personal consumption per capita in 1969 was at the same level of 1965, and total consumption per capita, which includes personal and "social consumption" (that is, the value of social services provided by the state), in 1970 was only 3 percent above 1965.[21]

Statistics on investment and consumption are even more scarce for the 1970s. No data exist on investment, but it is known that the ratio for capital accumulation over GMP (in current prices) increased from 22.4 percent for 1974 to an impressive 32.6 percent for 1975. The latter was a booming year in terms of prices in the international market and capital inflows to Cuba both from

TABLE 8. Percentage Distribution of State Investment by Sector in Cuba, 1962–66 (based on current prices)

Sectors	1962	1963	1964	1965	1966
Agriculture	29.4	24.3	30.5	40.5	40.4
Industry	23.1	31.6	29.1	18.1	16.7
Construction	4.3	5.8	4.6	3.8	2.2
Transportation and communication	9.5	9.6	9.1	11.7	14.3
Commerce	4.4	3.3	3.5	4.6	3.2
Housing and community services	13.5	11.5	11.4	9.4	9.6
Education, culture, research	8.1	7.0	5.3	5.0	4.4
Health	2.0	1.6	1.9	1.6	1.2
Others[a]	5.7	5.3	4.6	5.3	8.0
Total	100.0	100.0	100.0	100.0	100.0

[a]Includes administration and finance, defense and internal security, and other minor activities in the material and nonmaterial sectors.

Sources: Boletín 1966, p. 102. This is the only time that this information has been published in twenty years of the Revolution. In the draft of the next five year plan (1981–85) 75 percent of total investment is devoted to the productive sphere—a proportion similar to that of 1963. "Cuba," BOLSA Review, 13:2 (February 1979): 78.

socialist and market economies. There are figures on total rather than personal consumption and they indicate substantial increases over 1970 (as well as 1965): about 41 percent in 1974 and 52 percent in 1975.[22] Paradoxically, the dreamed target of one-third of GMP going to investment probably was not reached in the 1960s in spite of the sacrifices of the population imposed by Mao-Guevarism. That target may have been accomplished in the mid-1970s and accompanied by an improvement in consumption. These improvements were partly made possible by external factors but also as a result of the use of market mechanisms—considered anathema in the previous stage—to increase capital productivity.[23]

Information on what happened in the second half of the 1970s is not available, but an educated guess suggests stagnation or decline in both investment and consumption.[24] JUCEPLAN prepared three variants of the 1976–80 plan (optimal, average, and minimal) to take into account the decline in sugar prices. Since prices fell more than expected, planners had to take the minimal variant; as a result, twenty-two major investment projects had to be dropped.[25] In 1979, Fidel Castro acknowledged that in 1975 all experts, domestic and foreign, thought that sugar prices would never fall below 16 or 17 cents per pound. Since sugar prices dropped to 7 cents, Cuba suffered a severe capital shortage and had to borrow heavily from nonsocialist banks in 1977–78. That source of capital declined sharply in 1979 and came to a halt in 1980. As a result, the 1981–85 plan contemplates a reduction in investment and a freeze in social consumption.[26] The attempt to increase efficiency in the use of capital has been jeopardized by difficulties in the implementation of the new System of Economic Management and Planning. In 1978–79 a national survey conducted by JUCEPLAN among Cuba's enterprises to check the application of twenty different aspects in the new System found that numerous enterprises did not apply or violated the new rules in such areas as accounting, costs, capital amortization, and inventories. Moreover, about half of the enterprise managers had not been trained in management schools, while those who had such schooling were significantly underutilized.[27]

The current model of economic organization, although significantly more rational than the Mao-Guevarist one, has not been able so far to duplicate the efficiency of the market system as acknowledged by none less than Castro:

> We cannot deny the fact that, when it comes to running a factory, the capitalist is usually efficient. What should we expect from a socialist manager? We should expect him to be, as a rule, more efficient than the capitalist. And not because he is the owner—because he does not own any factories—but because he is in charge of a factory that belongs to the workers, to the people. . . . One thing we are is inefficient,

inefficient! Inefficiency lies with us, the managers, the leaders. . . . [28]

INFLATION AND ITS EFFECTS

Since 1961 spiraling inflation in Cuba has been generated by a widening gap between the demand for and the supply of consumer goods. Demand swelled because the population income (or disposable income) rose through full employment, guaranteed annual wages in agriculture, increases in minimum wages and pensions, expansion of free social services, and reduction in the cost of other services. On the other hand, the supply of consumer goods was negatively affected by stagnation or the small increase in domestic output, reduction of imports, and exportation of goods previously assigned to internal consumption.

In a market economy this disequilibrium would have resulted in a steady increase in prices. But the Cuban leadership, for social and political reasons, froze prices and introduced rationing of consumer goods in 1962 and expanded it throughout the 1960s. Most families, however, received an income that exceeded their personal consumption—that is, the cost of the monthly-ration basket of goods and of the few nonrationed goods and fee-charging social services available in the market. The difference between the population income and the total value of personal consumption is the monetary surplus—that is, excess money in circulation with which nothing can be bought in the market.[29]

An attempt to roughly estimate Cuba's population income and monetary surplus in the 1970s is made in Table 9. The monetary surplus steadily increased in the 1960s and in 1970 reached a peak of 86 percent over the population income; in other words, the total income of the population exceeded by almost twofold the value of available supply. Hence the population could have lived one year without working, and indeed 20 percent of the labor force did precisely that. Prices in the black market also boomed in 1970 in spite of government restrictions.

Castro described the situation as one of "tremendous inflation" resulting from "throwing more money in circulation than the value of goods and services available." He explained some of the effects of this phenomenon as follows: "All this superabundance of money in circulation was having adverse economic effects; there was a need for workers in many critical sectors—sometimes even in hospitals—and nobody wanted to do the work . . . the textile mills had come to a halt, factories had no workers because 60 percent of them quit." The money in circulation—said Castro— had to be reduced to achieve a "balance between the people's total income and the available goods and services in the market, to

TABLE 9. Inflation in Cuba, 1970–78 (in million pesos)

Year	Population Income	Monetary Surplus	Extraction or Addition	Ratio M. Surplus over P. Income
1970	4032	3478	+747	86.2
1971	4117	3328	−150	80.8
1972	4347	2648	−680	60.9
1973	4750	2248	−400	47.3
1974	5040	2088	−160	41.4
1975	5544	2022	− 66	36.5
1976	5800	2172	+150	37.4
1977	6055	2377	+205	39.2
1978	6555	2494	+117	38.0

Sources: Author's reconstruction based on scattered figures and information provided by *Anuario 1972*, p. 36; Fidel Castro, "Speech at the Closing Congress of the 13th Congress of the CTC," *Granma Weekly Review*, 25 November 1973, pp. 9–10; Banco Nacional de Cuba, *Desarrollo y perspectivas de la economía cubana* (La Habana, 1975), p. 105; *Compendio 1976*, p. 60; Rafael Díaz Balaguer, "Apuntes metodológicos para el cálculo del nivel de vida," *Economía y Desarrollo*, 39 (January-February 1977): 173–85; Roberto Veiga, "Informe Central en la Apertura del XIV Congreso de la CTC," *Granma*, 30 November 1978, p. 3; and Table 45, infra.

impede the rise of black market prices and labor absenteeism, and to make material incentives effective."[30]

In order to reduce the money in circulation, the decision was made to decrease consumer demand and increase supply of goods. To cut demand several steps were taken: some promises made in the late 1960s were abandoned or postponed, including canceling the abolition of house rent and the raising of minimum wages; inflationary measures in force like the granting of 100 percent salary to sick or retired vanguard workers were chopped; social services such as public phone calls and day-care centers, previously provided free, were assigned a charge; and prices were raised for certain goods and services, including cigarettes, beer, rum, electricity, water, worker-canteen meals, long-distance transportation, restaurants, and night clubs. To increase the supply, the government expanded domestic output of some consumer durables—for example, refrigerators, gas ranges, radios, and pressure cookers—or their imports—for example, cars, TV sets, air conditioners, and fans—and raised their prices significantly. Also an official parallel market was created in which consumer goods could be bought from three to eight times the rationing price. As a result of these measures, in the second half of 1971 personal consumption increased faster than the population income and hence the monetary surplus over the population income decreased from 86.2 percent in 1970 to 36.5 percent in 1975 (see Table 9). Castro summarized this situation as follows:

A deflationary process, reducing the money in circulation has been in effect since 1971 . . . this has been accomplished by making more goods available and by raising prices of certain nonessential goods. . . . The effects of the gradual reduction in the amount of money in circulation are already evident. . . . Money has started to have some value![31]

World inflation, accelerated after 1973 by the energy crisis, had its impact in Cuba as has been described by a high Cuban official:

The abrupt decline in the capitalist-market prices of sugar combined with the enormous increase in prices of products that we buy in that market has reduced our buying power. . . . In 1976, we began to feel the economic contraction and the process of reducing the money in circulation was stopped . . . and reversed until recently by a process of monetary expansion, hence the population began to buy less with their income. . . . In 1973–78 the population income increased by 38 percent but its consumption only by 25 percent.[32]

According to the National Bank of Cuba, current accounts and Cuban bank notes increased threefold in 1977, from an average of 717 million pesos in 1974–76 to 2,252 million pesos.[33] The monetary surplus seen on Table 9 expanded again in 1976–78 with a subsequent increase in its ratio over the population income. This forced the halt of a series of measures passed in 1973 that would have added 314 million pesos to the circulation. Suspended were extra payment for work done in extremely dangerous or hard conditions, payment of accumulated unused vacations, and raise in wages in the agricultural sector.

Although the above discussion clearly shows the importance of inflationary pressures in Cuba and its effects, it is quite difficult to quantify inflation.[34] It is impossible from the scattered information available to calculate a consumer price index for Cuba much less a deflator because prices of capital and intermediate goods are fixed by the state and there are no data on them. The last column of Table 9, however, provides a rough measure of inflation. In Cuba all investment is done by the state; individual income that is not spent cannot be invested except by the small private sector in agriculture. Savings apparently are quite low because interest is not paid on deposits, although there are plans to pay interest in the near future. The state facilitates credit to buy consumer durables in installments, but practically no possibility exists for buying homes or traveling abroad. Under these circumstances one could argue that the ratio of monetary surplus over population income approximates the rate of inflation. If prices were set by supply and demand in Cuba, in 1978 the prices of consumer goods would have increased by 38 percent. And yet this is not the case since about 30 percent of all consumer goods were rationed in that year and sold at state-fixed (subsidized) prices below the market price. Also the most important social services—education, health, social security, and housing—are either provided free or at a very low cost. The Cubans argue that all prices of rationed consumer goods have been frozen since 1962 or 1965. Indeed most food prices remain unchanged although a few have increased substantially—such as the cost of eggs rose 60 percent between 1964 and 1974.[35] In the official parallel market, which takes supply and demand into account, an increasing number of goods are sold from three to eight times the rationing price. In the illegal black market, goods are sold from five to fifteen times the rationing price.[36] Prices of meals in cafeterias and restaurants have also increased substantially, and the prices of the few durable consumer goods available are from four to six times what they would cost abroad (see Table 42 in chapter 7).

THE MILITARY BURDEN ON THE ECONOMY

Through most of the 1960s the Cuban Revolution faced formidable external and internal security threats. The climax of U.S. intervention occurred in 1961–62 with the Bay of Pigs invasion and the missile crisis. As part of the agreement between the United States and the Soviet Union defusing the crisis of October 1962, the former promised not to invade the island. Although minor attacks by Cuban exiles and acts of sabotage and espionage continued, the external threat gradually diminished through the rest of the 1960s. Internally the Revolution faced peasants' insurrections in 1963–65 but these were eventually defeated. Until 1967 Cuba was also sending armed expeditions or promoting revolution and subversion in other Latin American countries, but Che Guevara's death in Bolivia largely put an end to those activities. Tensions between the U.S. and Cuba subsided in the 1970s, particularly in the early years of the administrations of presidents Ford and Carter; several agreements were signed by both countries (on hijacking, fishing, and maritime boundaries) and "offices of interests" were established in 1976. Cuba's armed forces were at a peak of 350,000 in the early 1960s and military expenditures in 1961 were probably as high as 500 million pesos. The real cost of defense and internal security is probably underestimated in Table 10, but it shows important trends.[37] In 1962 when the missile crisis occurred, the military budget took 6.7 percent of Cuba's GMP and 13.3 percent of the state budget. In the next three years the military budget declined but it still

TABLE 10. The Burden of Military Expenditures in Cuba: 1962–65 and 1978–79
(in current pesos)

Year	Military Budget[a] (million pesos)	Pesos Per Capita	Military Expenditures as Percent of	
			GMP	Total Budget
1962	247	33.8	6.7	13.3
1963	214	29.4	5.7	10.2
1964	221	28.7	5.4	9.2
1965	213	26.9	5.2	8.4
1978	784	80.5	7.8	8.6
1979	841[b]	85.7	—	8.9

[a]Budgetary expenditures for national defense and internal order.
[b]Planned.
Sources: Budget from *Gaceta Oficial*, 9 January 1962; *La Tarde*, 8 January 1963; *El Mundo*, 10 January 1964, p. 1; *Revolución*, 2 January 1965, p. 2; *Granma*, 23 December 1977; and *Granma Weekly Review*, 21 January 1979, p. 3. GMP and population from Tables 3 and 6 infra.

represented 5.2 percent of GMP and 8.4 percent of the budget in 1965.

In 1971, Castro referred to the negative impact on the economy of the heavy military burden during the first revolutionary decade:

> For ten years our main problem was survival . . . a great number of other tasks were relegated to a second or even third place. It was not a question of development, nor could it be, since in order to develop, we first had to survive. And this effort took the bulk of our strength, our best cadres. . . . This is the reason why it is only recently that we could really tackle a number of tasks aimed at the development of the country.[38]

It should be noted that a large part of Cuba's defense burden was shared by the Soviet Union, which supplied 1.5 billion pesos worth of armaments, apparently free of charge, in 1965–71 alone. In the early years of the 1970s, the size of the professional armed forces was reduced and reached a trough of about 150,000 in 1974. Instead of taking full advantage of this situation to shift increasingly resources from defense to development, in the second half of the 1970s Cuba did the opposite: her intervention in Africa (mainly in Angola since 1975 and Ethiopia since 1977) resulted in a big jump in military expenditures. In 1975 the number of reservists doubled and probably kept growing during the rest of the decade, and the armed forces swelled to more than 200,000 by

1978. Unfortunately we do not have accurate figures for 1975–77, but as seen in Table 10, military expenditures in 1978 probably took 7.8 percent of GMP—the highest proportion in the history of the Revolution. In 1979, military expenditures had increased fourfold over the 1963 level, in per capita terms were equivalent to the monthly minimum wage, and were rising as a percentage of the state budget to almost 9 percent. In 1978 Cuba had approximately 38,650 military technicians and combat troops in Angola, Ethiopia, and a dozen countries of Africa and the Middle East; this represented 75 percent of the total communist countries' military personnel—including the USSR, Eastern Europe, and China—stationed in the Third World. Cuba also had approximately 12,525 nonmilitary technicians, such as economic advisors for foreign trade and international banking, civil servants, experts on agriculture, fishing, and public health, physicians, dentists, nurses, teachers, construction workers, and mechanics, stationed in Angola and other Third World countries. This contingent was equivalent to 12 percent of total communist nonmilitary personnel abroad.[39]

The Soviet Union supplied Cuba with heavy weapons for the operations in Africa and also has provided increasingly sophisticated weapons, aircraft, and other matériel for the island's armed forces. It is not clear whether Cuba has had to pay for Soviet armaments for her own defense in the 1970s. At least these weapons have been supplied at lower prices than in the international market.[40]

Information on the magnitude of the economic cost of the operations in Africa is kept strictly secret by the Cuban government for obvious political and military reasons, but scattered data provide some hints on such costs.[41] Troops, weapons, and equipment were transported mainly by sea using part of the fishing fleet and the merchant marine. When the Angola operation began in 1975, fish output declined by 14 percent, and it declined again by 6 percent in 1977 when the Ethiopian operation started. The fluctuations are significant because fish output increased eightfold in 1959–74, falling only in 1975 and 1977.[42] In 1975 two more ships were added to the Cuban merchant marine and its total tonnage increased by 13 percent. In addition, the number of rented ships doubled from 42 to 87, and their tonnage increased by one-and-one-half times; however, the cargo transported increased only by 3 percent. In 1976 the number of rented ships declined to sixty-one while the cargo transported was about equal.[43] This suggests that most of the rented ships added in 1975 were used for the Angola operation. Cuba has sent abroad almost 2 percent of her employed labor force, and such a drainage of skilled personnel must have aggravated the shortage of qualified personnel and created serious bottlenecks in production. In late 1975 some state managers resisted the military draft to keep skilled personnel, arguing that it was indispensable to maintain production, and only after Castro's intervention did the managers yield.[44] The President of the Central Planning Board (JUCEPLAN) has acknowledged that Cuba's involvement in Angola and Ethiopia "undoubtedly has affected the application of the System of Economic Management and Planning" because "numerous and valuable cadres were sent to the front hence depriving the nation's domestic tasks of their experience."[45] The increasing burden of military expenditures and the depletion of personnel probably had an influence in the declines in output experienced in 1976–77 and the general economic slowdown of those years.[46] Cuba's involvement in Africa also cooled off the trend toward reestablishment of economic relations with the United States, provoked the cut of economic aid provided by Canada, the Netherlands, and Sweden, and affected economic relations with France and the Federal Republic of Germany. Fidel Castro would do well to heed the advice he offered to the United Nations in 1979: "Arms expenditures are irrational. They should cease, and the funds thus released should be used to finance development."[47]

4

Diversification of Production

Economic diversification is normally associated with development. This is because the more varied the output mix is, the more self-sufficient the country is in meeting its domestic needs, and the less dependent it is on imports and vulnerable to price fluctuations in the international market. The degree of economic diversification of a country can be measured by its level of industrialization, variety of agricultural crops, and share of other economic sectors in the generation of GNP. Analyzed in this chapter are first the changes that have taken place in the composition of Cuba's GSP under the first two decades of the Revolution. The continued predominance of the sugar sector is then discussed, following which are considered the contribution of other important sectors such as nonsugar agriculture, livestock, fishing, nickel, manufacturing, energy, and tourism.

THE OVERALL COMPOSITION OF GSP

In western countries, the best indicator to check economic divesification is the composition of GNP through time but, as we know, this is not the case in socialist countries. Because of the exclusion of the value of nonmaterial services and other distortions introduced by the price structure, double counting, and inflation, the value of industrial output in Cuba's GSP is greatly overestimated. The value of commerce and transportation services are probably somewhat overestimated, the value of agricultural output is seriously underestimated, and no data exist on the value of nonmaterial services.[1] Trends in the composition of GSP in 1962−78 are given in Table 11.

The shares of agriculture and industry declined through the period, while communication was about stagnant, construction and transportation rose slightly, and commerce increased significantly after a sharp decline during the Mao-Guevarist stage. In 1962, industry generated 48 percent of GSP but only 36 percent

TABLE 11. Percentage Distribution of Global Social Product by Economic Sector, 1962–78 (all based on current prices)

	1962	1963	1964	1965	1966	1967	1968	1969	1970	1971	1972	1973	1974	1975	1976	1977	1978
Agriculture[a]	17.8	15.5	15.1	16.5	15.6	15.4	18.5	17.8	14.7	12.9	11.7	10.6	9.9	12.1	12.6	12.6	12.0
Industry[b]	48.2	45.1	41.7	42.5	43.0	44.2	42.7	43.9	47.9	46.5	42.8	41.9	40.2	37.4	37.8	36.9	36.1
Construction	7.2	6.2	6.4	7.7	7.6	8.3	7.2	6.2	5.2	6.4	7.7	9.0	8.8	9.0	9.4	9.9	9.5
Transport[c]	5.6	5.3	5.2	5.1	5.5	5.3	8.3	8.4	9.4	8.8	7.9	6.6	6.3	7.2	7.4	7.5	7.2
Communication	0.9	0.8	0.7	0.8	0.8	0.8	0.8	0.8	0.8	0.8	0.7	0.6	0.5	0.6	0.6	0.7	0.7
Commerce[d]	20.3	27.1	30.9	27.4	27.5	26.0	22.5	22.9	22.0	24.6	29.2	31.3	34.3	33.7	32.2	32.4	34.5
Total GSP	100.0	100.0	100.0	100.0	100.0	100.0	100.0	100.0	100.0	100.0	100.0	100.0	100.0	100.0	100.0	100.0	100.0

[a]Includes sugar and nonsugar agriculture, cattle, forestry, and fishing; also services in 1962–69 that are excluded in 1970–76.

[b]Includes sugar and food (the most important components), tobacco and beverages, electricity and other industries.

[c]Includes air, sea, railroad, and motor-vehicle transportation.

[d]Includes domestic and foreign trade, restaurants, hotels, night clubs, tourism, and a small amount of other productive activities in 1962–66.

Sources: 1962–66 Compendio 1968, p. 8; 1967–69 Anuario 1972, p. 32; 1970–72 Anuario 1973, p. 36; 1973–74 Anuario 1975, p. 40; and 1976–78 Anuario 1978, p. 52.

in 1978; on the other hand, commerce generated 20 percent of GSP in 1962 but 34 percent in 1978.[2] The shrinkage of the industrial share of GSP in Cuba goes against the trend of most Latin American countries in this period, while the reduction in the agricultural share and increase in the commerce-service share are similar to the Latin American experience. What is most surprising in the case of Cuba, a socialist country, is that commerce instead of industry appears as the most dynamic sector of the economy.

The disaggregation of the major economic sectors into specific lines of production[3] shows that, in 1962–76, sugar remained the most important line of production—combining its agricultural and industrial shares. Within the agricultural sector, sugar increased from 30 to 37 percent, while livestock and nonsugar agriculture respectively declined from 34 to 31 percent and from 35 to 29 percent, and forestry increased by about one percentage point (see Appendix 2A). The composition of the industrial sector did not change as dramatically as that of the agricultural sector. The three leading industrial lines in 1976 were linked with agriculture: food continued to be the most important product and increased from 21 to 23 percent; sugar declined from 15 to 10 percent falling to third place, while chemistry (mainly products for agricultural use) increased from 9 to 12 percent becoming the second most important product; finally, beverages-tobacco, leather, mining, oil, and electricity declined about one percentage point each, while metallurgy-metallic products and construction materials increased by five and one percent respectively (see Appendix 2B). Within the transport sector, railroad declined somewhat, while sea and land transportation increased sharply and air slightly. No disaggregated data are available on the composition of the commerce sector except for the years 1970–72. These show that the most important lines were restaurants, domestic trade, and foreign trade in that order, with the shares of the first two rising and the share of the third declining.[4]

In summary, little diversification of the Cuban economy occurred during the first two decades of the Revolution. The overall GSP shares of industry and to a lesser extent agriculture declined while that of commerce increased. The most important single product continued to be sugar: within agriculture, the sugar share increased while the share of other production lines declined; within industry, the share of food remained the largest, but the share of sugar declined, its place taken by chemistry.

SUGAR: UPS AND DOWNS BUT STILL THE KING

An overall picture of the performance of the sugar sector in the first two decades of the Revolution is found in Table 12.[5] The highest sugar output of the prerevolutionary period was achieved

TABLE 12. Sugar Production and Yields in Cuba, 1952 and 1958−79

Years	Grinding Days	Industrial Yield[a]	Sugar Output[b]	
			Raw	Refined
1952	120	12.26	7,298.0	713.0
1958	84	12.82	5,862.6	624.5
1959	89	12.57	6,038.6	592.7
1960	88	12.51	5,942.9	616.3
1961	104	12.66	6,875.5	694.4
1962	76	13.31	4,882.1	741.1
1963	68	12.36	3,882.5	843.0
1964	82	12.03	4,474.5	947.7
1965	105	12.15	6,156.2	1,022.1
1966	76	12.32	4,537.4	735.9
1967	101	12.26	6,236.1	1,127.9
1968	87	12.19	5,164.5	1,012.2
1969	86	11.02	4,459.4	892.9
1970	143	10.71	8,537.6	1,002.7
1971	101	11.49	5,924.8	548.3
1972	91	9.93	4,324.8	671.4
1973	92	11.07	5,252.7	712.0
1974	95	11.95	5,924.9	746.2
1975	99	12.44	6,314.4	677.9
1976	127	11.84	6,155.7	700.0
1977	139	11.55	6,484.9	742.5
1978	153	10.96	7,350.5	860.6
1979	—	10.94	7,991.8	898.7

[a]Proportion of sugar obtained in the mills in relation to the weight of the cut cane. Thus in 1952, 12.26 tons of sugar were produced out of 100 tons of sugar cane at 96 degrees of polarization.

[b]Thousand metric tons.

Sources: *Compendio 1976*, p. 18; *Anuario 1976*, pp. 85−86; *La economía cubana 1977*, p. 7; *Anuario 1978*, pp. 90−91; and *Cuba en cifras 1979*, pp. 26−30.

in 1952 with 7.3 million tons. Production declined in the next three years due to a world production surplus and low prices, but the Korean War and the Suez Canal crisis pushed prices up and thus production increased in 1956−58. The first three harvests of the Revolution were good, particularly that of 1961, which was the second largest in history. But the leaders' antisugar bias and desire to promote agricultural diversification led to the reduction of sugarcane land by 25 percent between 1958 and 1963 to make space for other cultives. This action combined with problems induced by the collectivization of sugar plantations and mills, a decline in investment in the sugar sector, a deficit of professional canecutters, and shorter harvests provoked a sharp decline in sugar output in 1962 and 1963. The sugar harvest in the latter year was the lowest of the Revolution, one-half the 1961 harvest. The failure of the industrialization plan, the increasing deficit in the balance of payments, and the desperate need for foreign exchange reversed the development strategy in 1964. As a result, sugar was restored to its traditional predominance.

The core of the so-called new development strategy was embodied in the Prospective Sugar Plan (1965–70), which projected an investment of more than one billion pesos. Improvements included the following: a 50 percent expansion of the sugarcane land to be planted with higher-yield sugarcane varieties; the substantial increase of irrigation and fertilization of sugar fields in order to step-up their yield; the almost total mechanization of the sugar harvest (planting, cutting, cleaning, lifting/loading, and transporting the sugarcane) to solve the manpower shortage; and the boost of the grinding capacity through the modernization of existing sugar mills and the construction of three new sugar mills.[6] State investment was to shift from industry to agriculture and within the latter to sugar. Indeed state investment in agriculture—which had declined from 29 to 24 percent in 1962–63—gradually increased to reach more than 40 percent in 1965–66 (see Table 8). Based on this heavy concentration of resources on the sugar sector, the plan set increasing sugar production targets: 6 million tons in 1965; 6.5 in 1966; 7.5 in 1967; 8 in 1968; 9 in 1969; and 10 in 1970. Under the sugar plan of 1971–80, output would rise to 11–12 million tons of sugar plus 14–15 million tons of molasses, the latter to be used as cattle fodder and for the development of sugar by-products. The increase in sugar output, in turn, would solve the balance of payment problems, allow Cuba to repay the Soviet debt, provide foreign exchange to augment capital imports and resume the industrialization effort, and enhance the standard of living of the population. In short, Cuba attempted to apply the theory of unbalanced economic development or intentional disequilibrium, centering all the nation's resources and efforts on the sugar sector. One sympathetic foreign observer termed this reliance on sugar "the turnpike of development," and the hope was that the expansion of this sector would pull up other agricultural and industrial lines of production and generate, in the long run, a vigorous and more balanced development.

One can see from Table 12 that the Prospective Sugar Plan did not succeed. Only in the first year—1965—was the output target met, but the starting target was not a great feat in itself—700,000 tons below the 1961 output. The percentage of the annual target left unfulfilled in 1966–70 varied, reaching as high as one-half of the target in 1969. The actual accumulated output of 1965–70 was 25 percent below the planned accumulated output. The 1970 harvest broke the 1952 sugar output record by more than one million tons, but it still fell 15 percent below the target. This output, though, was the result of various manipulations: borrowing sugarcane scheduled for the 1969 crop (the annual average output of 1969–70 was only 6.5 million tons); expanding the crop period to 334 days and the grinding period to 143 days (as compared to respective averages of 225 and 91 days in 1965–69), which resulted in a sharp decline in sugar yields and wreckage of the machinery; and deploying substantial material and human resources from the nonsugar sector, which provoked a serious decline in practically all other productive sectors.

The reasons behind the fiasco of the 1965–70 plan and, particularly of the 10 million tons harvest, were varied and complex.[7] The government put part of the blame on the weather. There was a drought in 1966–68, but it was not an impediment to having a good crop in 1967. Moreover, the weather in 1969–70 was optimal. The lack of managerial and technical personnel played a significant role in the failure. After the 1961 sugar harvest was over, most of the administrators of the recently nationalized sugar mills were replaced by totally inexperienced people, many of them young, militant teachers who had participated in the literacy campaign. The old sugar technicians were alienated and most of them retired or left the country. During the 1965–67 "Campaign Against Bureaucracy," most of the remaining experts, who worked on control and supervision, were fired because their jobs were considered "unproductive." Another cause of the failure was that prices fixed arbitrarily by the state did not take into account real costs. Finally, the state failed to check productivity. The lack of technicians, controls of productivity, and rational prices left the sugar industry in economic limbo. Nobody really knew what was going on. Cuba's most renowned sugar historian, Manual Moreno Fraginals, has said that during the 1970 harvest one of the best sugar mills (Central Baraguá) did not keep any indicator of production and productivity, and gross output was estimated by an unskilled worker by rule of tumb.[8]

The goals of the Prospective Sugar Plan were set by the political leadership without a previous technical study of feasibility and opportunity costs. In fact, the plan was drafted only after Castro announced the 1970 output target. With this background, it is not surprising that practically none of the goals were fulfilled. Of the projected investment of one billion pesos, only 40 percent came through. The sugarcane land was indeed expanded by 50 percent, but this colossal feat was accomplished in the eighteen months prior to the harvest, hastily done with significant seed losses, and the new high-yield varieties of cane planted did not reach optimal yields in time for the harvest. Only one-third of the planned target for irrigation was completed and nonfulfillment of the fertilization target was even worse. Moreover, the crucial goal of full mechanization of the harvest was not accomplished. Shortfalls were evident at every level: plowing by less than 40 percent, canecutting by one percent, lifting and loading the cane into carts by 83 percent, and cleaning the cane of leaves and dirt by 25 percent. Thus an army of 350,000 canecutters was mobilized for the 1970 harvest. While this number of canecutters was about equal to the 1952 harvest, a significant difference existed: in 1970 only one-fourth of the canecutters were professionals (79,752) and the rest were inexperienced volunteers who cost dearly to the harvest in terms of sugarcane badly cut, wasted in the field, or left uncleaned. In the industrial front the situation was not better: none of the three planned sugar mills were built and the modernization of the old mills was seriously delayed, so when the complex new equipment arrived it was either too late or the operators did not know how to handle it. Thus the actual installed capacity in operation was about one-half of the planned capacity and, due to the deterioration of the mills in the 1960s, below the 1952–58 installed capacity. Transportation became a nightmare when the government tried quickly to move surplus cut cane from plantations to mills that had underutilized capacity. If one is to summarize the 1970 sugar debacle with a single figure it should be the industrial yield—that is, the percentage of sugar produced in relation to the cane cut. The industrial yield averaged 12.4 percent in 1959–68, but declined to 11 percent in 1969 and 10.7 percent in 1970—the lowest on record since the 1930s (see Table 12). The low yield resulted from several factors. The low sugar content of the cane, either because it was not ripened, had been cut too high leaving in the ground the segment with highest sugar content, or because it was left too long in the field after being cut. Low yield was also related to the high amount of leaves and dirt left on the cane and the inefficiency of the equipment. The sugar that was produced was done so at a very high cost. This fact coupled with the overall decline in production in the nonsugar sector made it evident that the development strategy of 1965–70 was a forlorn hope.

In the 1970s, although sugar continued to be the engine of the Cuban economy, a more rational policy was implemented. Sugar technicians gradually returned to the sugar industry, output targets were set at feasible levels to be accomplished only with the resources allocated to the sugar sector, and mobilization of voluntary labor was sharply cut and emphasis placed on finding technological alternatives to the manpower deficit. The Australian alternative of burning the cane tried in 1971–72 failed, but the mechanization alternative seemed to have succeeded. The old technicians were attracted back to leading positions through offers of economic incentives, job security, and public recognition. Foreign technicians were also hired and intermediate technical sugar schools established to train cadres both in the agricultural and manufacturing process. A notable effort was made to improve statistical gathering and accuracy, including the installation of computers in the mills with a terminal in Havana. Controls on productivity were also reintroduced.[9] The number of harvest days declined from 334 in 1970 to an average of 200 in 1971–75, while the number of grinding days declined from 143 to 95.[10] It was decided to calculate costs of voluntary labor beforehand to assure a "net" contribution to the harvest and that unions selected the most productive canecutters. As a result, 60,000 fewer volunteers were mobilized in the 1971 harvest, another 35,000 less in the 1972 harvest, 25,000 less in the 1973 harvest, and 28,000 less in the 1974 harvest. The number of canecutters was cut by 60 percent in 1978 over 1970—a reduction from 350,000 to 143,000 canecutters. The goal for 1980 was to reduce it further to 50,000 canecutters, but they actually increased to 190,000.

Partly to cope with the manpower deficit, the Cubans tested the Australian system of burning and cutting the cane in the 1971 harvest. Supposedly burned cane did not have to be cleaned of leaves and dirt, weighed less, and was easier to pile. But for the system to work effectively, the terrain had to be leveled off, a special variety of cane planted, the burning process carefully planned, and the burned cane rapidly ground to avoid sugar loss. Additional difficulties were that neither the mechanical lifting nor the manual cutting tool (the machete) were designed for the burned cane. Adjustments made late in 1971 resulted in a modified Australian system, which was acknowledged to be only one-third as productive as the pure system but twice as productive as the traditional method used in Cuba. The modified system was thoroughly applied in the 1972 harvest with disastrous effects: the agricultural and industrial yields plunged respectively to 37.2 and 9.9 percent, the lowest in recent history (see Table 12). After this experiment, the Cubans concentrated on mechanization.

The scarce data available on the mechanization of the sugar harvest are presented in Table 13. Plowing and lifting the cut cane are the two most advanced processes of mechanization. Cleaning the cane of leaves and dirt was done mostly in conditioning centers in the late 1960s and early 1970s. The new harvesters largely do the cleaning now, hence that operation probably has improved at rates comparable to cane cutting. The latter has been the most difficult step to mechanize, and a number of pieces of equipment have been tried. In 1963–66, Soviet-made harvesters were imported, but they were too heavy and broke easily. The Cubans in 1967–70 turned out their own harvesters ("Henderson" and "Libertadora"), but they could not be mass produced. British-Australian Massey-Ferguson harvesters were imported in 1971–72 with good results. In 1972, Soviet and Cuban engineers designed a new harvester, the KTP-1, based on the Massey-Ferguson model, which was tested successfully in 1973 and modified to produce an improved version—the KTP-2. An assembly plant of these harvesters was inaugurated in Cuba in 1977. Key components come from the USSR and some parts are built in Cuba. Production was reported to be 250 KTP-1 and 50 KTP-2 in 1978 and would increase to a total of 600 harvesters

TABLE 13. Mechanization of the Sugar Harvest in Cuba, 1965−80

Years	Percentage Mechanized			
	Plowing	Cutting	Cleaning	Lifting
1965		2	0.2	26
1966		3	0.5	44
1967		2	7	53
1968		3	13	61
1969		2	15	65
1970		1	25	83
1971		2		
1972	42	7		
1973	42	12		90
1974	45	19		
1975	53	26		
1976		33		
1977		35[a]		
1978		39		
1979		42[a]		95
1980	100[b]	60−80[b]		100[b]

[a]Author's estimates.

[b]Goals of the 1976−80 plan. The 1981−85 plan set as a target for 1985, 60 to 65 percent of mechanization in cutting.

Sources: 1965−70 Sergio Roca, *Cuban Economic Policy and Ideology: The Ten Million Ton Sugar Harvest* (Beverly Hills: Sage Publications, 1976), p. 54. 1966−80 "Cuba: Cane Mechanizations," *Direct from Cuba,* no. 173, 5 July 1977, pp. 5−6; "The KTP-1 Cane Harvester Plant in Holguín," *Granma Weekly Review,* 24 July 1977, p. 10; *Anuario 1974,* p. 58; *Anuario 1975,* p. 70; "Día del trabajador azucarero," *Granma,* 4 August 1979, p. 1.

by 1980. Each harvester apparently does the work of 50 canecutters and cuts sugarcane to produce about 1,670 tons of sugar. In 1978 Cuba reportedly had about 1650 harvesters of various types (including 350 KTPs), which cut 39 percent of the harvest to produce about 2.8 million tons, while 143,000 men cut sugarcane to produce 4.5 million tons of sugar.[11]

As seen in Table 12, sugar output declined in 1971−72 by almost one-half, as a result of the reorganization in the sugar sector and the failure of the Australian system. Since 1973 sugar output has steadily increased—except for the drought in 1976 and for the plague in 1980—as mechanization progressed. Industrial efficiency improved in 1973−75 with the industrial yield of 1975 almost equal to that of 1958 and 1961; however, the extension of the harvests in 1976−79 resulted in yields declining again.[12] The sugar harvests of 1978 and 1979 produced respectively 7.35 and 7.99 million tons, thus becoming the third and second largest harvests in history.[13] This feat was accomplished by expanding mechanization, but the latter has progressed at a slower pace than planned thus forcing an extension of the harvest by more than two months and reducing industrial yields further.[14]

The goal for the 1980 sugar plan was to produce 8.7 million tons, but the rapid spread of a sugarcane blight (roya, cane smut or rust) affected both the amount of cane available and the industrial yields.[15] This pathology is caused by a fungus that houses in the roots of the cane, dries its leaves, and paralyzes the growth of the plant. The blight hit one of the best varieties of sugarcane ("Barbados 43-62" introduced in the early 1960s by the Revolution), which was planted on about one-third of sugarcane land. It was officilly reported that at least one million tons of sugar were lost in 1980. Western estimates for that harvest fluctuate from 6.4 to 6.6 million tons, while the Cuban figure is 6.8 million tons. The 1981 harvest will also be affected since all the infected cane has to be burnt, fields disinfected, and a new variety planted. This job is supposed to be completed in the spring of 1981.[16]

The Cubans have postponed for the early 1980s the 8.7 million-ton target, originally set for 1980—the target for 1985 is ten million tons. To fulfill such an ambitious target, an investment of 600 to 700 million pesos in improvements is planned. Four new sugar mills will be built to raise installed capacity by 500,000 tons, twenty-one existing mills will be rebuilt, others will be modernized to increase capacity by another one million tons. There will also be expansion in the cultivated and irrigated area of sugarcane, replanting of all sugarcane area with higher yielding seed, augmented use of fertilizers and pesticides, and full mechanization of canecutting. Nine thousand five hundred kilometers of railway track catering for the sugar industry will be repaired; full mechanization of cart transport will be completed; fifteen port terminals to automate fully sugar bulk-loading for exports (seven of them had been completed by 1979) will be constructed; and sixteen sugar refineries will be built.[17] It is impossible to judge the feasibility of these plans, but it is clear that after two decades of revolution sugar remains at the center of the Cuban economy.

Sugar monoculture is more pronounced now than before the Revolution. In 1962, harvested sugarcane in state land was 30.4 percent of the agricultural-cultivated state land; the proportion increased to 34.9 percent in 1974.[18] The United Nations reported that sugarcane took 63.7 percent of major cultives (including grains, tubers, tobacco, coffee, and beans) in 1960; sugarcane took 71.6 percent in 1975.[19] According to Table 12, the amount of raw sugar refined in Cuba was about the same in 1952 and 1976. The percentage of refined sugar increased from 11 percent in 1958−62 to 19 percent in 1963−69 but declined to 12 percent in the 1970s. When in 1976 declining sugar prices in the international market negatively affected the goals of the 1976–80 plan forcing a curtailment in imports and food rations, Castro stated that no return to an "antisugar attitude" would occur. Cuba would "stick to sugar" because of the comparative advantages of that product.[20]

NONSUGAR AGRICULTURE, LIVESTOCK, AND FISHING

Nonsugar agriculture generated 35 percent of the agricultural product in 1962 but only 29 percent in 1976 (see Appendix 2A). The decline in nonsugar agriculture is surprising in view of the substantial progress achieved in irrigation, mechanization, and fertilization. Yet most of these technological advances have been concentrated in a few crops, such as citrus fruits and rice, mainly cultivated in state farms. Most nonsugar agriculture, including coffee and tobacco, remains labor intensive, difficult to mechanize, and requires specialized manpower. The role of the private sector has been important in the outcome: in some of the specialized crops difficult to mechanize, private farmers are still the major producers, but incentives have been poor and the percentage of private land has been gradually reduced. In a few cases the state has tried to take over these troublesome crops with rather negative results.[21]

Production of tobacco, Cuba's second export crop, reached a record high in 1961 (57,600 tons). It then gradually declined to less than one-half that amount in 1971, recuperated in 1972–76, but in the latter year output was still at the same level of 1958 and 12 percent below the 1961 peak. In 1978, the "need to recuperate and raise the historical record tobacco crops reached under capitalism" was publicly acknowledged. The output goal for 1980 was 60,000 tons, but a plague of blue mold affected 27 percent of Cuba's tobacco plantations by the end of 1979 and practically had wiped out all plantations by March of 1980. The blue mold is a fungus which can destroy a plantation in 72 hours: it starts with a yellow stain under the leaf and soon the leaf dries and falls off. According to Cuba's Ministry of Agriculture, the epidemic probably spread from Georgia and the Carolinas through the Florida Strait to the Caribbean. Fungicides can kill the infestation but they were in short supply in Cuba and too much rain made their application ineffective. Furthermore, the mold seems to have developed a resistance to fungicides and the plants saved are often unacceptable for manufacturing. Cigar factories were shut down in January 1980 and Cuba pulled out of the tobacco export market for the entire year; in fact the island had to import tobacco leaf to fulfill some export commitments. The reported loss in 1979 was $100 million and it should surpass $300 million in 1980.[22] Most Cuban tobacco is produced by private farmers who, in spite of a reduction in their land (from 92 percent of total tobacco land in 1963 to 77 percent in 1976), managed in 1976 to still produce 82 percent of the crop as compared to 88 percent in 1963. The decline in tobacco output has negatively affected the exports of this product as well as the production of cigars and cigarettes, forcing the rationing of the latter since 1968.

Coffee output reached a peak in 1962 (52,000 tons) and steadily declined thereafter; in 1976 output was one-third of the 1962 mark and production in 1979–80 was affected by plant rust. Here the output share of the private sector dramatically declined from 82 percent in 1967 to 48 percent in 1976. The state sector was incapable of increasing coffee output, and the result was overall decline in production. In the late 1950s and early 1960s Cuba's domestic production of coffee satisfied its demand, but rationing had to be imposed in 1965. It was necessary to import about 40 percent of coffee to meet the rationed needs in the 1970s. Skyrocketing prices of coffee in the international market in 1976 resulted in a cut in both imports and the rationed quota of this product.

Production of tubers has been mixed. Potato plantations are mostly in the state sector and largely mechanized. While the output share of the private sector declined in 1967–76, its level of output was maintained, and the state sector increased its output. As a result, the level of production in 1976 was 50 percent above the 1957 level. The production of malanga and yuca—two tubers popular in the Cuban diet—has not been mechanized. The private sector has done better than the state sector, but still output of both tubers steadily declined since 1961. The trough was in 1970, then their output recuperated but by 1976 it was below the 1960 peak: 66 percent below in yuca and 82 percent below in malanga.

Output of rice, a principal staple in the Cuban diet, reached a peak in 1959–60 (325,000 tons), declined in 1961–63, and dropped further in 1964–65 when rice fields were converted into sugar plantations. The Cubans then alleged that they could earn much more cultivating sugar and trading it for rice from China; however, the 1966 quarrel with China resulted in a reduction of rice imports and rice fields were again expanded. By then, the state produced almost one-fifth to one-fourth of the crop and gradually increased its share to 93 percent in 1976. Aided by mechanization and fertilizers, rice output rose, although with oscillations, and by 1975–76 had recuperated the 1959–60 level. Domestic production of rice satisfied two-thirds of the consumption needs in 1960, and less than two-thirds of rationed needs in 1975–76. Cuba now imports about 200,000 tons of rice and the expectations of self-sufficiency for 1980 will hardly be realized.

Two highly successful agricultural ventures are eggs and citrus, in both of which the state is the main producer and has made a substantial investment. Output of eggs steadily increased, even during the Mao-Guevarist stage, and by 1976 was almost sixfold the prerevolutionary level. Production of citrus steadily increased until the Mao-Guevarist stage when it declined. It quickly recovered and by 1976 was almost three times the 1959 level. Yet visitors to Cuba have reported deficiencies in citrus production, such as lack of adequate care in the plantations and of selection and quality control for exports. If these problems are corrected in the 1980s, citrus fruits would replace tobacco as Cuba's second export crop.[23]

Livestock generated 41 percent of the agricultural product in 1966 but only 31 percent in 1976. The dramatic reduction in head of cattle is seen in Table 14. The average annual rate of increase in head of cattle in 1952−58 was 6.8 percent, it declined to 0.4 percent in 1959−61, increased to 3.5 percent in 1962−66, and jumped in 1967 to 5.9 percent; however, it still remained below the prerevolutionary rate. Since 1967, data have not been released on head of cattle. This is intriguing because Cuba's statistical yearbooks report systematically on the number of bulls and cows in the artificial insemination program, as well as on the head of horses, mules, donkeys, sheep, and goats (sometimes even by sex and province!). No reference was made to the fulfillment of the 1970 planned goal of eight million head of cattle, and it is safe to infer that it was not met. Indirect data confirm that the cattle stock was significantly reduced in the last decade: the acopio of cattle declined by 39 percent in 1968−75 (from 361,000 to 219,000 tons) while acopio of milk declined by 31 percent in 1966−71 (from 329,000 to 227,000 tons); on the other hand, the annual imports of beef increased by almost eight times in 1965−75 (from 5,700 to 43,000 tons).[24] In 1975, Fidel Castro stated that cattle raising "grew in the early years and later declined through excess slaughter. The cattle population is now somewhat larger than before the Revolution, which is not much of an achievement."[25] If we estimate the number of cattle in 1975 at 6 million head ("somewhat larger"—300,000 head—than the 5.7 million existing in 1958), then a decline of more than one million head has occurred since 1967. Furthermore when the increase of Cuba's population is taken into account, the number of head of cattle per capita in 1975 appears to be considerably less in relation both to 1967 and 1958: 0.83 in 1958, 0.87 in 1967, and 0.58 in 1975. This explains the reduction of the rationed quota of meat by the mid-1970s and the statement of the President of JUCEPLAN in 1979 that rationing of meat will not disappear for a long time even if other products will eventually be taken out of rationing.[26]

The bad performance in cattle raising has been attributed to complications with breeding, fodder, artificial insemination, illnesses, and administration. An ambitious plan in the second half of the 1960s attempted to develop a new cattle breed by mating

TABLE 14. Livestock, Poultry, and Fishing in Cuba, 1952, 1958, and 1961–78

Years	Cattle	Pigs[a]	Poultry	Fishing
	(thousand head)			(thousand metric tons)
1952	4,042	1,258		
1958	5,700	1,780		22.0
1961	5,776	827	15,380	30.4
1962	5,975	1,358	18,600	35.4
1963	6,378	1,539	19,500	35.6
1964	6,611	1,746	21,900	36.4
1965	6,700	1,810	21,400	40.4
1966	6,774	298	11,016	43.5
1967	7,172	343	12,468	63.4
1968		276	12,436	65.2
1969		318	13,526	79.8
1970		280	13,581	106.4
1971		320	13,346	126.1
1972		377	16,435	139.7
1973		382	15,873	150.2
1974		489	18,328	165.2
1975	6,000	599	18,130	143.5
1976		673	19,946	194.0
1977		662	19,686	184.4
1978		698	22,376	211.1

[a]1961–65 all; 1966–76 state and private-connected sectors.

Sources: The 1958 cattle figure comes from Raúl Cepero Bonilla, "Los problemas de la agricultura en América Latina y la reforma agraria cubana," *Cuba Socialista*, 3 (January 1963): 91; the 1975 cattle figure is an estimate based on Fidel Castro, "Main Report Presented to the 1st Congress of the Communist Party of Cuba," *Granma Weekly Review*, 28 December 1975, p. 6. Other data from *Boletín 1966*, p. 63; *Boletín 1971*, pp. 83, 90–93; *Anuario 1976*, pp. 71–72; *Compendio 1976*, p. 27; *La economía cubana 1977*, p. 3, and *1978*, pp. 8, 11; and *Anuario 1978*, pp. 76–77.

Cuban native stock (mostly Cebu, a poor milk producer) with imported Holstein and Brown Swiss, directly or through artificial insemination. The new breed—F-1 and F-2—was expected to increase milk output by four to eight times over the Cebu milk output; however, at the First Congress of Animal Science held in Havana in 1969, a team of British advisors to the Cuban government reported that the milk output of the F-1 was only 16 percent of that of the Holstein and that F-1 cows dried out after 100 days of nursing their calves. This report generated a violent controversy at that time, but in recent years nothing has been reported on the F-1 and F-2 milk yields. The team of British advisors also opposed, in their 1969 report, the use of pastures and sugar molasses as cattle feed, asserting that corn was the best fodder and insinuating that political reasons had been an obstacle to choosing the proper fodder in Cuba. Castro personally criticized this report arguing that it was very expensive to produce corn in Cuba, whereas it was cheap to produce pastures and sugar molasses. But one year later he acknowledged that it was difficult to increase the output of beef because pasture lands had not received the necessary care and hence cattle had lost weight.[27] In 1978 a technical report published in Cuba's top economic journal stated that the traditional cattle fodder was not sufficiently cheap or nutritious, resulting in high production costs and nonprofitability of cattle raising, thus imposing a heavy burden on the nation. This report labeled as inaccurate another one, published in 1975, because it had considered only traditional fodder methods as alternatives to those then in use. The 1978 report concluded that if the optimal fodder alternative was used, substantial gains in nutrition and cost reduction would be achieved.[28] In the same year, a high Cuban official acknowledged "serious problems in cattle raising" due to "the disorganization and underfeeding of the cattle, its bad handling and lack of care."[29] Another technical report, prepared by one of the British geneticist advisors to the Cuban government, indicated the following causes for the bad performance in cattle raising: poor pastures; spread of cattle illness that increases morbidity and mortality; administrative flaws such as poor files on cattle; and failures in the application of the artificial insemination program— this being most surprising because of the wide publicity given to this program. According to this report, the introduction of large-scale artificial insemination in 1966–67 had a "marked negative effect" upon fertility. It also forecast that even if the planned improvement for 1970 occurred, the rate of fertility in that year would be below that of the early 1960s.[30] Unfortunately no data exist for the early 1960s, but the fertility rate declined from 65 percent in 1965 to 51 percent in 1968, then gradually increased to a peak of 75 percent in 1972, to decline again to 71 percent in 1975. In the meantime the number of stud bulls in the insemination program was reduced by 47 percent between 1969 and 1976, while the number of cows decreased by 33 percent in the same period.[31]

Performance in pig raising has also been poor—and beseiged by epidemics—but better than in cattle. According to Table 14, the number of pigs declined by more than one-half in the early years of the Revolution due to slaughtering and disorganization, but the number steadily increased in 1962–65. Beginning in 1966, data are given only for state farms and acopio (state buyings) from private farms, but it appears that the number of pigs declined in 1968–70 largely due to an epidemic of pig cholera or African swine fever. There was a recuperation in 1971–73 and vigorous increase thereafter, but comparisons between 1978 and 1958 are not possible. In 1979–80 pig raising suffered another serious blow, particularly in Cuba's eastern provinces, from a second widespread epidemic of African swine fever.

Attempts to analyze poultry-raising performance present the same difficulty as with pigs—data reporting changed after 1965. And yet, as seen in Table 14, a steady increase within the state sector occurred in 1966–78, although at a smaller annual average rate (8 percent) than in 1961–65 (10 percent). About half of the poultry stock has been devoted to egg production with considerable success.

In sharp contrast with livestock, fishing is the success story of the Revolution. As seen in Table 14, the total catch of fish (including shellfish and amphibians) increased from 22,000 tons in 1958 to 211,100 tons in 1978 for an impressive tenfold jump in the two decades of the Revolution. And yet the catch declined sharply to 156,000 tons in 1979.[32] Until 1962, the 2,300 boats in the fishing fleet were rather small, mostly made of wood, fished in Cuban waters, and were organized into cooperatives. All of these vessels are now part of in-shore fleets that caught about one-third of the total catch in 1976. The state fishing fleets began to be developed in 1962 and by 1976 had imported 262 modern deep-sea vessels.[33] Cuban shipyards were significantly expanded in the 1960s and by 1975 had built some 6,000 small and medium wood vessels, plus 400 ferrocement medium vessels, and 90 steel large vessels. Cold storage, canning, freezing facilities, and fishmeal processing have also been expanded significantly. As a result of these developments, Cuba, a net importer of fish in 1958, has now become a net exporter and the seventh largest fishing country in Latin America. And yet the value of fishing is relatively small; it contributed only 0.5 percent of GSP in 1976, a slight increase over 1962.[34]

NICKEL, MANUFACTURING, AND ENERGY

Besides fishing and tourism, the greatest potential for Cuba's economic diversification lies in the industrial sector—particularly in nickel. The share of mineral output in GSP gradually declined from 1.1 percent in 1962 to 0.5 percent in 1976, and the minerals' output share in the industrial product also diminished from 2.5 percent in 1963 to 1.3 percent in 1976 (see Appendix 2B). Nickel currently accounts for two-thirds of total mineral output, with the other one-third mainly made up of oil, copper, chrome, and salt. The potential of nickel is higher than its current contribution to GSP suggests. Cuba has the fourth largest world reserves of this mineral—about 9 percent of the total—and its production puts it fifth in world output behind Canada, USSR, New Caledonia, and Australia. Yet Cuba is the third largest exporter, accounting for

15 percent of world exports. If current plans for expansion of the nickel industry are met, then Cuba could become the fourth largest nickel producer and perhaps the second largest exporter in the mid-1980s. The value of nickel production could be equal to 30 percent of the value of sugar production and generate the equivalent to 50 percent of the hard currency value of sugar exports. Nickel has the potential to make Cuba less vulnerable to price fluctuations in the international market and more economically independent. But as the U.S. specialist Theodore H. Moran has pointed out, three serious problems will have to be solved to reach that goal. Most Cuban deposits are laterite ores with low nickel content, which because of high energy consumption associated with extraction are eight to ten times more costly to process than sulfides; however, to make the extraction of the mineral competitive in world markets will require a technology that neither the Cubans nor the Soviets seem to have. The international marketing of nickel presents an additional problem because of the world oligopoly of nickel and the current U.S. embargo imposed on Cuba. Finally there is a time constraint: as time passes by and price of oil rises, the costly processing of Cuban ores makes them less attractive in relation to other Caribbean ores, which are cheaper to process.[35]

Cuba's existing nickel plants were actually developed prior to the Revolution. The first plant, Nicaro Nickel Company, was built by U.S. Freeport Sulphur Company in 1943 to assure U.S. supply during World War II. The plant closed in 1947 due to high costs but reopened and expanded during the Korean War. The second plant, Moa Bay Mining Company also built by Freeport, was completed on the eve of the revolutionary takeover and began operations on an experimental basis in 1959. The low-grade nickel ore extracted by this plant was to be processed in a new plant in Louisiana. The nationalization of the two plants in 1960 seriously affected output because U.S. technicians fled. The Nicaro plant was temporarily closed at the end of that year, and the Moa plant faced innumerable difficulties delaying it being put into full operation until the late 1960s. Soviet writers claim that it was with their help that the two plants were put back in operation (the USSR is also processing the ore that was sent previously to Louisiana), but other observers assert that it was the Cubans themselves with some British equipment who accomplished the task.[36] Nickel output was 18,000 tons in 1958–59 but declined by one-fifth in 1960–61. There was a recuperation and increase of the previous output level in 1962–77, but output was stagnant at an average of 36,000 tons in 1968–78—twice the output at the eve of the Revolution. Yet output is about 25 percent below full capacity of the two nickel plants, which is reported to be 49,000 tons.[37]

Plans to increase output include modernization of the two existing plants. Soviet aid was agreed upon in 1972, but it still has not come through. The goal was to have a combined output of 47,000 tons for 1980 but it has been postponed for 1983. The Soviets also agreed in 1972 to build a third plant in Punta Gorda, close to Nicaro, that was expected to produce 30,000 tons in 1980; however, the target has also been postponed until 1984 and reduced to 23,000 tons. In 1975, COMECON agreed to build a fourth plant, of Soviet design, scheduled to produce an additional 30,000 tons by the early 1980s, but that plant will not start until the second half of the decade. There were reports of a commitment to build a fifth plant in the second half of the 1980s with an output of 50,000 tons, but this apparently has been discarded. If the first four projects come through, then output in 1985 should be 69,000 tons—about three times current output—and 100,000 by 1990.[38] Yet, in 1979, output was 32,500—the lowest in the decade.[39] The Cubans have acknowledged that the modern technology they need cannot be supplied by the USSR but rather by the West. They have shown interest in acquiring such technology, but the cooling in U.S.-Cuban relations due to the African ventures has impeded such transactions.[40] At the end of 1979, Moran's arguments were officially confirmed when Castro said that Cuba's nickel industry was "ruined" because of its obsolete technology: while nickel prices had increased 40 percent, oil prices had jumped fifteenfold.[41]

The GSP share of manufacturing declined in the 1960s and 1970s. The share of most manufacturing lines to the industrial product declined—oil, electricity, beverages, sugar, and leather—while only a few lines increased—food, chemistry, metallurgy and metallic products, and construction materials. Food production was and still is the major contributor to the industrial product, but it is directly linked to the agricultural product. The leading food lines are: dairy products (with a substantial expansion in yogurt and ice cream); wheat flour and wheat products (mainly bread and other bakery items, and pastas); rice processing; canned fruits and vegetables; and frozen fish and seafood. The rise in chemistry is also partly the result of the development or significant expansion of products destined for agricultural use—including a twofold increase in the output of fertilizers in 1963−76[42] and a tenfold increase in ammonium nitrate in 1970−76. On the other hand, chemical products such as tires, paints, and soap for direct consumption have mostly declined or been stagnant. The most significant increase in manufacturing output is in metallurgy and metallic products. Steel production increased almost fifteen times, from 24,000 tons in 1958 to 350,000 tons in 1978, and installed capacity is now reported at 440,000 tons. Preliminary work has begun, with Soviet help, to build a steel plant with an annual capacity of 1.3 million tons.

Significant increases have been made in the output of steel derivatives, machinery (for example, harvesters), electronics (for example, digital computers), spare parts, transportation equipment (like vessels and buses), and a few domestic appliances. Yet, Castro has acknowledged the limitations that the steel industry faces: "Cuba's iron abounds in laterite form and not in iron oxide, which is the one used traditionally by the steel industry. . . . The lack of a raw material basis [coal, oil] for the development of the steel industry and petrochemistry, two crucial industries in any modern economy, has up to now been a great disadvantage."[43] Within the construction material sector, cement is the most important line. Cement production peaked in 1961, became stagnant and then dipped in 1969, recuperated in the 1970s, and by 1978 production was 2.7 million tons—almost fourfold the prerevolutionary output. Two new cement plants scheduled to be in operation in the next quinquennium should increase total output to five million tons.

Cuba's oil production of 45,000 tons in 1958 declined in the early years of the Revolution but by 1977 had increased sixfold (255,800 tons). The expansion is the result of the discovery of some ten oil deposits, but none has supported large-scale output. The small domestic output satisfied only about 3 percent of the nation's needs in the 1970s, and practically all of the rest was imported from the USSR (see Table 23 in chapter 5). Most of the crude oil Cuba produces and imports is refined in two refineries dating from the prerevolutionary era. In 1976, oil and derivatives supplied almost 58 percent of total energy consumption; sugarcane bagasse and alcohol supplied another 36 percent; and the remaining 6 percent was met with hydroelectric energy, coal, and gas. Output of electricity has increased threefold throughout the Revolution, from 2.6 billion kw/h in 1958 to 8.4 billion kw/h in 1978, and the 1980 goal of 9 billion kw/h was easily met.[44] And yet, per capita electricity consumption rose in 1959–78 at half the average rate of 1950–59, while overall energy consumption rose at only one-sixth of the prerevolutionary rates.[45] This explains why both the oil and electricity shares of the industrial product declined in 1963–76 (see Appendix 2B). The population increase and the nation's economic expansion combined with bad maintenance of the old equipment and waste have resulted in electricity shortages, disruptions, and blackouts. In 1976 alone there were 295 days in which some part of Cuba suffered a power shortage. This problem compounded with spiraling costs of oil and the probable inability of the USSR to continue supplying Cuba in the future forced a decision to shift from oil to nuclear energy. It seems that, with Soviet aid, Cuba will build a nuclear power plant near Cienfuegos with four reactors, each one with a generating capacity of 440 MW, for a total of 1,760 MW. Construction was scheduled to begin in 1979, with the first reactor entering into operation in 1984, the second in 1986, and the last two in the 1990s, but construction is two years behind schedule because geologists discovered that the chosen locale is in a seismic region. When and if this project is completed, Cuba should have one-and-one-half times as much electric generating capacity as the country had in 1976.[46]

TOURISM: THE SECOND HARVEST?

Prior to the Revolution, tourism was called "the second sugar harvest." Some 300,000 tourists annually visited the island, most of them from the United States. The break in U.S.-Cuban relations and the austerity of the 1960s reduced the flow of tourists to 3,000 in 1968, most of them from Eastern Europe. In the 1970s, however, Cuba once again began to attract substantial numbers of tourists. A campaign to draw Canadian tourists was successful, and the reestablishment of relations with several Latin American and Caribbean countries allowed their citizens to visit Cuba. The lifting of U.S. barriers to tourists and Cuba's willingness since 1979 to permit visits by exiles resulted in an influx of Americans. Hence the number of tourists increased systematically: 15,000 in 1974, 50,000 in 1975, 60,000 in 1976, 75,000 in 1977, 100,000 in 1978, and probably 130,000 in 1979. [47]

Cuba hoped to be back to the prerevolutionary figure of 300,000 tourists in the 1980s, most of them coming from the United States.[48] One-week package tours to Cuba cost $500 to $800; however, because of the overvaluation of the Cuban peso in relation to the U.S. dollar, tourist hotels are expensive ($40 to $50 daily in Havana) and the same is true of meals ($8 a lunch; $15 a dinner). If indeed 300,000 tourists go to Cuba in the 1980s, they should be spending from $150 to $250 million, equivalent to 7 to 12 percent of Cuba's GSP in 1976, about twice the value of the fish catch and three times the value of nickel production in that year. Many tourists coming from the United States may be Cuban exiles who have been allowed to return to their homeland for short visits since 1979. In that year more than 100,000 exiles reportedly visited the island. Although they spend a minimum of $850 for a week, most of them did not use the accommodations they paid for. Instead, they stayed with relatives for whom they bought expensive gifts in tourist shops. Cubans exiles alone contributed $100 million to the island's economy in 1979.[49]

To accommodate the increasing flow of tourists, Cuba began to build new hotels in 1975: six were finished in 1976; nine in 1977; eight in 1978; and thirteen more were scheduled for inauguration in 1980. The Cuban domestic tourist season—especially in beach resorts—is in the summer; thus tourist facilities are practically empty during the rest of the year. Even with these arrangements it is expected that current and planned facilities will be insufficient to meet the demand of foreign tourists. Hence the state is shifting investment from domestic to international tourism, and Cubans have been warned by Castro that in case of need, rooms in hotels for domestic tourism may have to be assigned to foreign tourists and vacation programs cut back in order to get the needed foreign currency.[50] Cuba has also expressed interest in entering joint ventures with foreign corporations to develop tourist facilities in the island. One of these ventures was apparently completed with Club-Méditerranée for a 200-bed club in Bacuranao beach and another is being explored by a U.S. corporation to convert the Cayo Sabinal island into a $250 million tourist center.[51]

Some foreign observers—and undoubtedly Cuban nationals— have expressed concern over the ideological impact that the foreign tourist flow may have on the frugal Cuban society: the demonstration effect of clothing, cameras, and other symbols of the consumer society; the take-over of hotels and restaurants by foreign tourists; the tourist access to special hard-currency shops barred to nationals; and the potential for ill will between those relatives and friends who receive Cuban exiles' gifts and others who do not have visiting relatives.[52] These potential risks were discounted by Castro, at the end of the 1970s, when he asserted that Cuba had to take advantage of its natural resources to generate needed foreign currency and added that the chance of corrupting the Cuban population was quite small.[53] And yet, the massive exodus of Cubans in the spring of 1980 has been partly blamed on the demonstration effect of exile visitors in the midst of a year of economic crisis in the island. The subsequent wave of criticism against the United States, violent denunciation of those who wanted to leave, and some change in attitude toward the exiles resulted in a sharp decline in Cuban-American tourists in 1980 and may have a negative effect on the tourist industry at least in the short run.

5

External Economic Independence

THE NATURE OF DEPENDENCY

External economic independence is defined in this study as a country's capability to self-satisfy its domestic needs for capital, technology, energy, capital goods, manufactures, and so forth without resorting to the external or international economic system. The concept is relative rather than absolute, because in today's highly interdependent world, no country, developed or developing, is completely self-sufficient. The higher the degree of independence, however, the less vulnerable a country is to the influence of another country or the international economic system. A country heavily dependent on another country to meet its basic economic needs runs the risk of falling under the economic and political influence of the supplier.

This interpretation of external economic independence should not be confused with the views of the so-called Dependency Theory, which attempts to explain underdevelopment in Latin America based on the concept of *dependencia*. Actually that theory is advanced by a heterogeneous group of social scientists who often disagree on both the causes of dependency and the prescriptions for its cure. For example, two leading dependencia writers do not accept that all forms of dependency have common features and the same effects and hence that there are universal causal laws and a theory of dependency.[1] Most dependencia ideologues divide the world into dichotomous parts: developed, central, dominant or nondependent countries; and underdeveloped, peripheral, dominated or dependent countries. The international capitalist system produces both types of economies—one being fed by the other—and preserves the asymmetric situation. The economy of the dependent country is conditioned and responds to the needs of both the international capitalist system and the dominant country rather than to its own domestic needs. Economic growth or decline in the dependent country is primarily a result of international forces over which national actors have little or no control. The dominant countries predominantly produce capital and manufactured goods and export these to dependent countries, which in turn produce and export raw materials. A long trend of stagnant or declining prices of raw materials and increasing prices of capital goods results in deteriorating terms of trade against the dependent countries. Hence an economic surplus is transferred from the dependent to the dominant countries through trade, as well as capital amortization and interest payments, expatriation of profits, and so forth. The dependent country does not generate its own capital accumulation and expansion and its capital-good production sector is not strong enough to ensure continuous growth and technological advances. To promote economic growth, the dependent country has to borrow from dominant countries and becomes increasingly in debt. Dependency also results in a concentration of wealth and substantial income inequalities.[2]

For the most radical dependencia writers, the only escape from dependency is the substitution of a command for a market economy and the break away from the world market economy. They also assume that economic relations are different within the socialist economic system in which countries are nondependent. A divergent point of view is that dependency arises in any type of economic system—both capitalist and socialist—that includes countries with different levels of development and power.[3]

This study is not the place to contest the general premises of dependencia. My objective here is to explore whether Cuba has reduced its external economic dependency through the substitution of a market economy and an economic relationship with the USA by a command economy and an economic relationship with the USSR.[4] In order to analyze the quantitative and qualitative changes, if any, that have taken place in Cuba in the last two decades, several mechanisms of external economic dependency will be considered: overall dependency on trade; sugar export predominance; dependency on imports and their mix; terms of trade; trade partner concentration; dependency on foreign energy and merchant-marine; and capital and foreign debt dependency.[5] The combination of several of these mechanisms—rather than the presence of a single one even in an exacerbated form—is what determines the degree of external economic dependency in a country.

OVERALL DEPENDENCY ON TRADE

The more a country relies on foreign trade to obtain goods and services that are not produced domestically and the larger and more dominant the external (export) sector is, the more vulnerable the economy of the country may become to external forces.[6] Traditionally Cuba, a monoculture economy, has concentrated its efforts in producing a few commodities for export and has produced very few of the goods that it consumes. Naturally, foreign trade has been fundamental to Cuba's economy. In 1946–58 the average ratio of Cuba's exports to GNP was 30.6 percent (and declining), that of imports was 25.7 percent (but increasing), and that of the total trade was 56.3 percent (stagnant). A comparison with similar averages following the Revolution suggests at first glance a reduction of Cuba's overall trade dependency. As seen in Table 15, in 1962–78 the average proportion of exports in relation to GMP declined sharply (as compared to 1946–58) to 21 percent; but the average ratio of imports/GMP was slightly higher at 27.4 percent; and the average ratio total trade/GMP declined to 48.5 percent.

A more careful examination of Table 15 indicates, however, that throughout 1962–78 there were increasing trends in all three proportions and by 1975 they were substantially above the averages of the prerevolutionary period and also above the 1958

TABLE 15. Trade Dependency of the Cuban Economy, 1962–78
(in percentages of GMP)

Years	Exports	Imports	Total Transactions
1962	14.1	20.5	34.6
1963	14.6	23.2	37.8
1964	17.5	25.0	42.5
1965	16.7	20.9	37.6
1966	14.9	23.2	38.1
1967	17.3	24.4	42.7
1968	14.9	25.2	40.1
1969	16.0	29.2	45.2
1970	24.9	31.2	56.2
1971	17.8	28.7	46.6
1972	12.7	19.7	32.4
1973	17.2	21.8	39.0
1974	30.0	30.0	60.0
1975	33.2	35.0	68.2
1976	30.3	35.8	66.1
1977	31.5	37.1	68.6
1978[a]	33.8	35.1	69.0
Average 1962–78	21.0	27.4	48.5

[a]Preliminary.

Sources: Carmelo Mesa-Lago, "The Economy and International Economic Relations," *Cuba in the World,* Cole Blasier and C. Mesa-Lago, eds. (Pittsburgh: University of Pittsburgh Press, 1979), p. 182, corrected and updated with *Anuario 1976,* p. 146, and Tables 3 and 16 infra; and statistics supplied by the State Committee on Statistics to the author in July 1979.

proportions. The table also suggests a deepening of Cuba's trade dependency in the 1970s. Average percentages increased in the 1970s over the 1960s as follows: exports from 16 to 26 percent; imports from 24 to 31 percent; and total trade from 40 to 56 percent. In 1978, the value of total trade was equivalent to 69 percent of the nation's GMP, twice the proportion of 1962. Notice also that import/GMP percentages are consistently and substantially higher than export/GMP percentages, revealing another mechanism of Cuban dependency: increasing trade deficits, which are shown in Table 16.

Throughout the prerevolutionary Republic (1902–58), a trade deficit was recorded for three years (1907, 1921, and 1958). Their total deficit in those three years was 118 million pesos. In the remaining fifty-three years, the value of exports was substantially higher than that of imports, generating a cumulative trade surplus of more than two billion pesos.[7] During the first two decades of the Revolution, a trade surplus was generated only in two years (1960 and 1974) for a total of 39 million pesos. In the remaining years, trade deficits resulted in a cumulative deficit of 5.5 billion pesos. What are the reasons for this dramatic change?

In 1959–61 the value of Cuban exports was roughly similar to that of imports, but from 1962 to 1973, the value of exports either declined or was stagnant (with the exception of 1970) while that of imports increased. The main causes of decreasing value of exports were the decline in sugar output, which restricted the amount of sugar available for export, combined with low prices for this product in the international market. Reasons for the incremental value of imports were the step-up in importing capital and intermediate goods, rising prices of imported goods, the expanding demand of an increasing population, and all at a time of stagnant or declining domestic output of many consumer goods, which forced the importation of basic foodstuffs and selected manufactures. As a result of these trends, trade deficits climbed steadily, reaching records of a half-billion pesos in 1969 and 1971. The huge sugar crop of 1970, although boosting exports to a record one billion pesos, was accompanied by an even higher level of imports, which resulted in a deficit. The increase in sugar prices in 1973–74 set new historical records in value of both exports and imports and, in 1974, a small trade surplus. In spite of the decline of sugar prices in the international market, in 1975 the value of exports increased to almost three billion pesos; however, the value of imports increased even more—both setting new records—and a deficit ensued. [8] In 1976, when the impact of the dip in sugar prices was felt, the value of exports declined sharply and to a lesser extent that of imports, creating an acute increase in the trade deficit. Consequently, planned imports from market economies had to be cut by half because Cuba did not have enough foreign exchange to pay for them. Determined not to default, Cuba asked several Western suppliers (Argentina, Japan, Canada, and Spain) to postpone delivery of imports contracted and to accept delayed payments of a total sum over close to one billion pesos. This decision nevertheless involved a substantial economic loss for Cuba since most sellers requested payment of interest, insurance, and warehouse fees for stockpiled goods.[9] As a result of higher sugar prices paid by the USSR, the value of exports increased in 1977 with a higher increase in the value of imports, hence enlarging the trade deficit. In 1978, the second largest sugar harvest in Cuban history, helped by international price stabilization, pushed exports up substantially, while imports increased moderately with a sharp reduction in the trade deficit.[10]

An analysis of Tables 15 and 16 reveals the role sugar plays in Cuban foreign trade dependency. Low export/GMP percentages are related to poor sugar crops (from 4 to less than 5 million tons), mostly compounded by low prices in the international market. High export/GMP percentages are the result of fair or good sugar harvests (from 5 to 8 million tons), mostly with fair and, in some cases, record sugar prices in the international or

TABLE 16. Foreign Trade of Cuba; 1957–1978 (in million pesos)

Years	Exports (f.o.b.)	Imports (c.i.f.)	Total Transactions	Trade Balance
1957	807.7	772.9	1,580.6	+34.8
1958	733.5	771.1	1,510.6	− 37.6
1959	636.0	674.8	1,310.8	− 38.8
1960	608.3	579.9	1,188.2	+ 28.4
1961	626.4	638.7	1,265.1	− 12.3
1962	522.3	759.3	1,281.6	−237.0
1963	545.1	867.3	1,412.4	−322.2
1964	714.3	1,018.8	1,733.1	−304.5
1965	690.6	866.2	1,556.8	−175.6
1966	597.8	925.5	1,523.3	−327.7
1967	705.0	999.1	1,704.1	−294.1
1968	651.4	1,102.3	1,753.7	−450.9
1969	666.7	1,221.7	1,888.4	−555.0
1970	1,049.5	1,311.0	2,360.5	−261.5
1971	861.2	1,386.6	2,248.7	−526.3
1972	770.9	1,189.8	1,960.7	−418.9
1973	1,153.0	1,462.6	2,615.6	−309.6
1974	2,236.5	2,225.9	4,462.4	+ 10.6
1975	2,946.6	3,113.1	6,059.7	−166.5
1976	2,692.3	3,179.7	5,872.0	−487.4
1977	2,912.2	3,432.7	6,344.9	−520.5
1978[a]	3,416.7	3,557.6	6,974.3	−140.9

[a]Preliminary.

Source: Same as Table 15.

Soviet market. This phenomenon is also evident in the prerevolutionary period: the least trade dependency occurred in 1933, probably the worst in the century in terms of low sugar prices; trade dependency increased during sugar booms—the 1920s Dance of the Millions, the post-World War II period, the Korean War, and the Suez Canal crisis. Thus fluctuations in sugar prices and harvests are the key to understanding Cuba's economy. When there is a good performance in sugar trade, dependency seems to increase and vice versa. Furthermore, low export/GMP percentages, particularly in the 1960s, push down the total trade/GMP averages reinforcing the illusion of reduced trade dependency. But there is no delusion in Cuba's high percentage of import/GMP and on the magnitude of the trade deficit resulting from stagnant exports and increasing imports. Castro has recently complained about this problem: "[We must] develop an exporter's mentality because at the moment we have an importer's mentality. . . . Exports must be increased with [capitalist countries] and with the socialist region as well. . . ."[11]

COMPOSITION OF EXPORTS: SUGAR PREDOMINANCE

Cuba is an exporter of a few raw materials and relies overwhelmingly on sugar as the fundamental source of exports and foreign exchange. This export concentration makes the nation's economy more vulnerable to price fluctuations in the international market than if it had more diversified exports. From the 1920s to the 1950s, the share of sugar exports over total exports ranged from 70 to 92 percent, with an overall average of 81 percent. As seen in Table 17, the share of sugar oscillated in 1959–76, with a range of 74 to 90 percent and an average of 82 percent, slightly above the prerevolutionary average. The share of tobacco exports in total exports declined from an average of 8 percent in the 1940s to 6 percent in the 1950s. It increased slightly to 5.4 percent in the 1960s because of stagnation in the nickel industry and subsequent drop in its exports. But in the 1970s tobacco dipped to an average of 3 percent due to the increase in the sugar share. The export of minerals was not significant until the 1940s, with the development of the nickel industry, and averaged 7.5 percent in the 1940s and 1950s. Mineral exports declined sharply in the early years of the Revolution, recuperated in the 1960s, increased to a record average of 14.5 percent of total exports in 1968–73, and declined again to less that 6 percent in 1974–76. In any event, mineral exports (basically nickel) have replaced tobacco as Cuba's second export. Other exports are mainly fish, citrus fruits, vegetables, and rum; their combined share of total exports seems to have declined in the 1960s and 1970s, with fishing products now taking the lead generating from 2 to 3 percent of exports. Fluctuations in the percentage

TABLE 17. Percentage Distribution of Cuban Exports by Product, 1957–76

Years	Sugar	Tobacco	Minerals[a]	Others[b]	Total
1957	78	6	6	10	100
1958	78	7	3	11	100
1959	77	9	2	12	100
1960	80	10	1	9	100
1961	85	6	6	3	100
1962	83	5	7	5	100
1963	87	4	6	3	100
1964	88	4	5	3	100
1965	86	5	6	3	100
1966	85	4	7	4	100
1967	86	4	8	2	100
1968	77	6	12	5	100
1969	76	6	13	5	100
1970	77	3	17	3	100
1971	76	4	16	4	100
1972	74	5	15	6	100
1973	75	5	14	6	100
1974	87	3	6	4	100
1975	90	2	5	3	100
1976	88	2	6	4	100

[a]Mainly nickel.

[b]Mainly fish, shellfish, fruits, and rum.

Sources: Same as Table 15, infra and *Anuario 1976*, p. 147, and Banco Nacional de Cuba, 1977, p. 19.

distribution in Table 17 are mainly determined by the sugar harvest physical output and value. In most cases reduction in the share of sugar over total exports is associated with a decline in sugar output combined with declining or stagnant prices, while an increase in the sugar share over total exports is associated with increases in output and prices. It should be noticed that Cuba was somewhat protected from fluctuation of sugar prices in the international market in prerevolutionary times by the U.S. annual sugar quota and premium price. Since 1960 it has had a buffer in the medium-range agreements signed with the USSR, which have guaranteed both the buying of a certain amount of sugar at premium prices which, with very few exceptions, have been above the international market price.

The close relationship between the value of sugar exports, total exports, and GMP in 1962–75 can be seen in Graph 1.[12] Cuban dependency on sugar exports has not been reduced in the first two decades of the Revolution.

GRAPH 1. GMP, Total Exports, and Sugar Exports in Cuba, 1962–75.

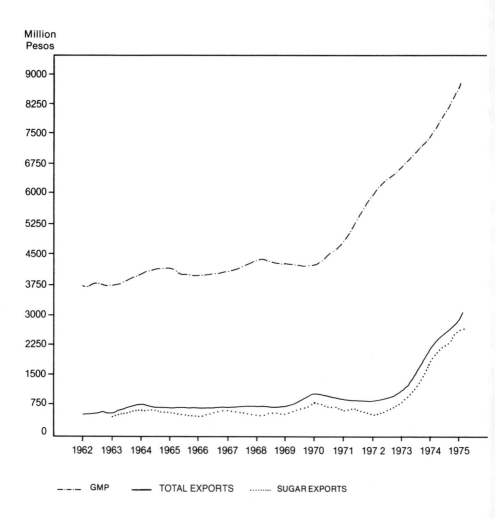

Sources: GMP from Table 3 infra; total exports from Table 16 infra; sugar exports from *Anuario 1968,* p. 150; *Anuario 1973,* p. 192; and *Anuario 1975,* p. 164.

COMPOSITION OF IMPORTS

The more a country relies on imports of basic goods instead of producing them domestically, the more dependent the country may become. The composition of imports is also important: a high percentage of manufacture imports indicates continued dependency, while a high proportion of capital good imports such as machinery suggests a process of import substitution that may eventually allow the country to produce consumer goods domestically and reduce dependency. A quick glance at the section on foreign trade in Cuba's statistical yearbook indicates the degree of that nation's dependency on imports: while the list of Cuba's total exports occupies two pages, that of the reported imports—less than two-thirds of the total value of imports—extends for ten pages.

The composition of imports in 1959 and 1963–75 (data for 1960–62 are not available) is given in Table 18, but an accurate comparison is not possible because the category of "others," almost insignificant in 1959, increases to an average of 23 percent in 1963–75. This category has not been disaggregated in spite of the fact that it is the most important, and several reasons suggest themselves. One possibility is that it includes strategic goods. Soviet weaponry was apparently supplied free of charge to Cuba at least in 1962–71, but this is not true of other countries and perhaps other periods. Another possibility is that part of "others" is manufactures. We know that Cuba imports durable consumer goods from Japan and the USSR that are not listed among imports.

In spite of comparability problems, the proportion of most imports given in Table 18 has not changed significantly, except for the apparent decline in manufactures. Foodstuffs continue to be, as an average during 1963–75, the most important import, although they declined dramatically in the frugal Mao-Guevarist stage, when consumption was sacrificed. Since 1971 new policies have improved foodstuff consumption somewhat. Most foodstuffs imported are produced in Cuba but not in sufficient amount to satisfy demand—for example, meat, dairy products, rice, corn, beans, coffee, lard, and oils. Cuba also imports foodstuffs that she exports but in a different variety; for instance she exports high quality seafood and imports low quality fish. Second in importance in the proportion of total imports are machinery and transportation. Their proportion declined in 1963–66, increased dramatically in 1967–70—as the proportion of foodstuff and manufactures declined due to the emphasis on capital accumulation over consumption—but regressed in 1972 to the 1959 level with a new increase thereafter, although at lower levels than in the peak years. Most important machinery imports are for agriculture, mainly in the sugar sector—tractors, harvesters, sugarcane lifters, and carts. Other items are spare parts and industrial equipment.

TABLE 18. Percentage Distribution of Cuban Imports by Product, 1959 and 1963–75[a]

Years	Food & Fats	Raw Materials	Fuel & Minerals	Chemicals	Manufactures	Machinery & Transportation	Others[b]	Total
1959	27	4	9	9	31	19	1	100
1963	24	3	9	6	15	14	29	100
1964	24	4	9	6	15	14	28	100
1965	24	3	10	4	17	15	27	100
1966	23	4	10	7	16	14	26	100
1967	24	5	9	9	11	24	18	100
1968	21	5	8	9	10	27	20	100
1969	19	4	9	6	10	31	21	100
1970	20	4	9	6	10	28	23	100
1971	23	5	9	4	10	28	21	100
1972	25	4	12	5	12	19	23	100
1973	24	4	11	5	12	21	23	100
1974	25	4	9	4	13	21	24	100
1975	19	4	10	6	12	24	25	100

[a]Years 1960–62 are not included in the table due to lack of data.

[b]Not disaggregated in the original source.

Sources: Same as Table 17 infra. updated from *Anuario 1978*, p. 164.

Transportation imports consist of vessels for two successful revolutionary ventures—the merchant-marine and the fishing fleets—as well as locomotives, aircraft, and railway and port equipment. Cars are also imported but in a proportion considerably reduced from the level in 1959. Third in importance are manufactures, whose proportion of total imports in relation to the 1959 level appears to have declined to one-half in 1963–66 and one-third in 1967–71 with some recuperation thereafter. Listed imported manufactures are tires, paper, textiles, steel and metallic products, and auto parts. Imports of fuels—oil, gasoline, coal, and coke—took a larger share of total imports in 1972–75 than previously. Cuba has not been as affected by skyrocketing oil prices as have other nonoil producing countries due to Soviet subsidized prices. Most imported chemicals—which show some decline over the period—are fertilizers, herbicides, and pesticides for agricultural use. Imports of pharmaceutical products are also significant. Finally, the smallest share of imports—held almost constant—are raw materials, among them wood and pulp, cotton, and natural fertilizers.

TERMS OF TRADE

The barter or commodity terms of trade measure the amount of imports that a country can obtain with a unit of its exports. A deterioration in the terms of trade means that a country can buy fewer units of imports with a given quantity of exports, while an improvement in the terms of trade implies the opposite. For almost two decades, Western specialists on international trade have discussed whether the USSR has taken advantage of its socialist trade partners by exporting to them at higher prices and importing from them at lower prices than the USSR does with trade partners from market economies. Most of the accumulated evidence answers that question affirmatively: in the second half of the 1950s and most of the 1960s the USSR's terms of trade with COMECON countries were more favorable to the USSR than those with Western market economies. [13] Cuba, however, was not included in that comparison since she did not enter COMECON until 1972. (COMECON or CMEA is the Council for Mutual Economic Assistance formed by the USSR, Bulgaria, Cuba, Czechoslovakia, GDR, Hungary, Mongolia, Poland, Rumania, and Vietnam; with North Korea and Yugoslavia as observers.)

The only reference that we have for a Cuban analysis of its terms of trade with the USSR is unfortunately unidentified. Reportedly it was done by the National Bank and asserted that the total costs of the Soviet goods supplied to Cuba were 50 percent above what Cuba would have paid if it had been able to purchase the same type and quality of goods from market economies.[14] Two studies conducted in the United States reach a similar conclusion, although with different estimates on the loss suffered by Cuba.

The Central Intelligence Agency—without identifying its sources or explaining its methodology—has compared Cuba's terms of trade with socialist economies and market economies for 1968–75.[15] Those calculations suggest a deterioration in Cuba's terms of trade with socialist economies in 1971–72 followed by an improvement thereafter, with a 200 percent increase of the terms of trade in 1975 over 1968. There was a steady improvement in Cuba's terms of trade throughout the period with market economies, with a total increase of 395 percent in 1975 over 1968. Therefore Cuba's terms of trade with market economies was 95 percentage points better than with socialist economies.[16]

A second study, which carefully states sources and explains its methodology, has been done by Jorge Domínguez. He used changes in unit values of all Cuba's 20 export goods and 114 import goods (accounting for 60 percent of the value of imports) in 1968–74 to calculate Cuba's terms of trade, globally and with the USSR. According to Domínguez' findings, prices for Cuban exports to the USSR rose more slowly than overall export prices (except for two years), while prices for Cuban imports from the USSR were substantially higher than Cuban prices for overall imports except for one year. Thus Cuba's *overall* terms of trade was 22 percentage points better in 1974 over 1968 than Cuba's terms of trade with the USSR.[17]

One problem with the CIA and Domínguez studies, at least concerning exports, is that both chose the year 1968 as a base and ended the comparison in 1974–75, which introduces a bias in favor of market economies. As seen in Table 19, the world price of sugar in 1968 was the second lowest in 1960–76, but in 1968 the USSR was paying Cuba three times the world price. Conversely in 1974, the Soviet Union was paying one-third of the world price, and this was the year in which Cuba lost most to the USSR in her sugar deals. Thus the world price of sugar increased fifteen times in 1968–74, moving from a trough to a peak year, while the Soviet price increased only three times because it started with a year of Soviet overprice and ended with a year of Soviet underprice.

Cuba's two major exports are sugar and nickel, and for both there seems to have been favorable price treatment in trade with the USSR. Based on the figures in the third column of Table 19, the price paid by the USSR for Cuba's sugar was above the world price except for the years 1963, 1972, and 1974. The world market price for sugar almost tripled between 1962 and 1963; yet while the USSR increased its price in 1963 to 6 cents per pound, this was still more than 2 cents below the market price. In 1964 the USSR paid about the same as the world price, but in 1965–70 it paid a price of 6.11 cents per pound, an average of 3.7 cents above

TABLE 19. Prices of Sugar and Oil in the World Market and the Soviet-Cuban
Market, 1960–76 (sugar in U.S. cents/lb.; oil in U.S. $/bbl)

| Years | Raw Sugar | | | Oil and Derivatives | | | Ratio[a] |
	World	USSR	Difference	World	USSR	Difference	Sugar/Oil
1960	3.14	3.20	0.06	1.92	1.74	−0.18	5.53
1961	2.91	4.07	1.16	1.86	1.66	−0.20	7.36
1962	2.98	4.14	1.16	1.80	1.60	−0.20	7.76
1963	8.50	6.23	−2.27	1.80	1.81	0.01	10.32
1964	5.87	6.04	0.17	1.80	1.77	−0.03	10.21
1965	2.12	5.90	3.78	1.80	1.78	−0.02	9.92
1966	1.86	6.17	4.31	1.80	1.77	−0.03	10.44
1967	2.03	6.14	4.11	1.80	1.76	−0.04	10.47
1968	1.98	6.12	4.14	1.80	1.78	−0.02	10.31
1969	3.37	6.12	2.75	1.80	1.75	−0.05	10.50
1970	3.75	6.11	2.36	1.80	1.74	−0.06	10.52
1971	4.53	6.23	1.70	2.19	1.74	−0.45	10.77
1972	7.43	6.61	−0.82	2.46	2.19	−0.27	9.07
1973	9.63	12.34	2.71	3.29	2.82	−0.47	13.12
1974	29.96	19.70	−10.20	11.58	3.19	−8.39	18.52
1975	20.50	28.60	8.10	11.53	5.82	−5.71	14.72
1976	12.70	27.90	15.20	12.38	6.01	−6.37	13.92

[a]Value of a metric ton of sugar in rubles divided by value of metric ton of oil in rubles.

Sources: Based on Jorge F. Pérez-López, "Sugar and Petroleum in Cuban-Soviet Terms of Trade," *Cuba in the World,* pp. 282–283, 289, and private correspondence 2 May 1979.

the world price. In the first half of the 1970s, a series of factors pushed sugar prices up: world demand for sugar increased; sugar harvests in the United States declined; Cuba's output was low and world inflation reached unparalleled heights. By the end of 1971, the world price of sugar had surpassed the Soviet price and the gap expanded in 1972. The Soviet price was raised to 11 cents per pound at the end of 1972, but the world price soon overtook it. In 1974 the average world price was about 30 cents per pound, and in November it peaked at the record of 65.5 cents. The Soviet price was then increased to 20 cents per pound, still 10 cents below the average world price. Finally in 1975 the Soviets raised the price to 30 cents of peso per pound and agreed to pay it in the period 1976–80. In the meantime world demand for sugar slowed down, there was a significant increase in world output and stocks of sugar, and the production of sugar substitutes also expanded. Hence sugar prices began to decline in the second half of the 1970s to a low of about 7 cents per pound in 1977. A new International Sugar Agreement signed in the fall of 1977, and which provisionally came into force in 1978, recommended a minimum price of 11 cents per pound and a high of 20 cents.

Although the agreement has not been ratified by the United States and the European Common Market—the largest consumers—it has helped at least to stabilize the sugar price. In any event, the USSR has been paying to Cuba at least three times the world price of sugar in 1976–78.[18]

While the USSR has paid prices above the world price for Cuba's sugar, other COMECON countries have often paid a price below the Soviet price. In 1973, all COMECON countries paid half of the Soviet price and in 1979 they paid 43 percent of the Soviet price. Furthermore in 1973–75 most market economies paid more for Cuban sugar than did COMECON countries—excluding the USSR. On the other hand most COMECON countries buy refined sugar from Cuba—which is sold at higher prices than raw sugar—while the USSR buys only raw sugar, which is refined in the USSR and partly resold to other countries.[19] But refined sugar is only a small fraction of Cuba's exports of raw sugar, and it does not offset the fact that Cuba receives more favorable price treatment from the USSR than from other COMECON countries. This difference may explain why the CIA estimates of Cuba's terms of trade, which embrace all socialist countries, are worse than Domínguez' estimates, which apply only to the USSR.

The USSR has also subsidized the price of Cuba's second export, nickel. In 1972–75 the Soviet price was set at $5,450 per ton while the international price was set at $3,500 per ton; and in 1976–80 the Soviet price was $5,980 per ton while the world price was $4,000 per ton. No statistics exist on prices paid by the USSR for other Cuban exports such as citrus fruits, rum, and cigars, but Moscow economists told a U.S. scholar in 1979 that Soviet price subsidies are paid only for sugar and nickel.[20]

The analysis of the value of Cuban imports is complicated by the lack of information on quality, which is crucial in machinery, transportation equipment, manufactures, and chemicals. However, data are available on one significant Soviet export, oil, whose quality is homogeneous; the value of its import by Cuba is about one-tenth of her total imports and one-fourth in relation to Cuba's imports from the USSR. It can be seen from the sixth column of Table 19 that until the 1973 oil crisis, Cuba paid a price in line with the world price for her imports of Soviet oil. The big jump in the world price of oil in late 1973 and 1974 was followed by a modest increase in the Soviet oil price to Cuba in 1974 and a more significant (80 percent) raise in 1975, when a new formula for pricing Soviet oil exports based on a moving average of world market prices in several previous years was implemented. Despite this change, the Soviet price in 1975 was about one-half of the world price. The Soviet increase in oil prices to developed COMECON countries and to Cuba has been comparable and higher than the Soviet increase to North Korea, North Vietnam, and Mongolia.[21] Cuban prices for Soviet oil have continued to climb in 1976–78 and are expected to continue to do so if the current pricing formula is used and world market prices continue to rise.

An estimate of Cuba's sugar/oil terms of trade with the USSR prepared by Jorge Pérez-López (reproduced in the last column of Table 19) shows slight changes in 1963–72, an improvement in 1973–74, and deterioration in 1975–76. Pérez-López concluded that the sugar/oil terms of trade in the rest of the decade will most likely continue to deteriorate because Soviet oil export prices can be expected to rise faster than Soviet import prices for Cuban sugar.[22] And yet there is no doubt that at least in 1974–77 Cuba bought oil from the USSR at prices substantially below the world price. The CIA has estimated the combined value of Soviet subsidies to Cuba on sugar, nickel, and oil in 1961–76 at $3.6 billion.[23]

I have already explained why both the CIA's and Domínguez's export indices overestimate the worsening of Cuba's terms of trade with the USSR in relation to market economies. Both indices also show worse terms concerning imports from the USSR in spite of Cuba's substantial gains in Soviet oil imports. This apparent contradiction would be resolved if the prices charged by the USSR for other goods imported by Cuba (for example, machinery, transportation equipment, manufactures, chemicals, foodstuffs, and raw materials) are higher than prices prevailing in the world market.[24] In private conversations with U.S. businessmen, politicians, and journalists, Cuban officials have hinted that their effort to import Soviet technology has not been very successful. The top Cuban economic official, Carlos Rafael Rodríguez, has publicly stated that the socialist camp lacks a whole range of technology that is only available from the West.[25] And Castro has candidly proclaimed that "the United States is the most advanced country in the world in technology and science; Cuba could benefit from everything America has."[26] Another indication that either Soviet prices or the technological level of Soviet capital and intermediate good imports are not satisfactory to Cuba can be found in the latter's dramatic shift of trade towards market economies in 1974–75. For those two years, Cuba had plenty of sugar-generated foreign exchange to choose trade partners. This issue will be discussed in the next section; suffice it to say that the percentage of agricultural and industrial machinery, transportation and construction equipment, and chemical products imported by Cuba from the USSR in 1972–73 sharply declined in 1974–75. Concerning imports of foodstuffs from the USSR, U.S. grain producers who visited Cuba in 1977 asserted on their return that the cost of soybean imports could be reduced by 30 percent if Cuba bought this grain from the United

States, and that large savings could also be made on wheat, rice, and beans.[27]

Since 1976 the price of Cuban sugar exports to the USSR is apparently being indexed with the prices of certain Soviet imports such as oil, steel, machinery, food and other "basic goods." The President of JUCEPLAN has said in reference to this: "[Cuban] sugar is sold to the USSR at a price which, beginning at 30 cents [of pesos] a pound in 1976, has gradually climbed every year at the same rate as prices of the basic goods that Cuba purchases from the USSR have gone up." [28] According to the Soviet yearbook of foreign trade of 1977, the USSR paid Cuba in that year an average of 35 cents of peso for the pound of sugar, an increase of 16 percent over the 1976 price. This yearbook, however, does not report the price paid by Cuba for Soviet oil in 1977, but it is known that the USSR increased the price to other COMECON countries by more than 22 percent over 1976. [29] Castro has reported that at the end of 1979 the USSR was paying Cuba 44 cents of peso for the pound of sugar (almost threefold the world market price) while the Soviets charged 70 pesos for the ton of oil (almost one-fourth the world market price).[30] This scattered information seems to confirm that the price of sugar exported to the USSR is being indexed now by a basket of Soviet goods imported by Cuba. If this information is correct, Cuba should be able to reduce its trade deficit with the USSR at least until the current trade agreement between the two countries ends in 1980, a significant Soviet concession to Cuba.

TRADE-PARTNER CONCENTRATION

Heavy reliance of a country on one or a few trading partners implies a high degree of dependence, while a large diversity of trade partners makes a country less vulnerable to political influence. Prior to the Revolution, about two-thirds of Cuba's total trade was with the United States, with a higher proportion of imports than exports. This high degree of trade-partner concentration was still present in 1959, as can be seen in Table 20. Conflicts between the two countries at the beginning of the 1960s—including from the Cuban side the nationalization without compensation of U.S. property and from the U.S. side the elimination of the sugar quota and the imposition of the embargo—resulted in trade declining sharply and becoming negligible by 1962. Cuba then claimed that she had eliminated her traditional trade dependency on the United States.

By 1961, however, socialist countries (mainly the most industrialized) had substituted for the U.S. trade, absorbing an average of 73 percent of total Cuban trade in 1961–78. The USSR has become Cuba's main trade partner, taking an average of half of total Cuban trade in the same period and—as with the United

TABLE 20. Percentage Distribution of Cuba's Total Trade by Socialist and Market Economies, 1959–78

Years	Socialist Economies			Market Economies		TOTAL
	USSR	Rest[a]	Total	Main Partner	Total	
1959	1.0	0.1	1.1	68.7[b]	98.9	100.0
1960	15.5	6.3	21.8	50.5[b]	78.3	100.0
1961	44.8	27.2	72.0	4.1[b]	28.2	100.0
1962	49.4	33.1	82.5	2.8[c]	17.5	100.0
1963	44.2	31.6	75.8	2.6[d]	24.2	100.0
1964	39.5	24.8	64.3	6.2[d]	35.7	100.0
1965	48.2	28.6	76.8	5.2[d]	23.2	100.0
1966	52.2	28.0	80.2	7.1[d]	19.8	100.0
1967	55.6	24.4	80.0	3.6[d]	20.0	100.0
1968	54.8	23.2	78.0	4.7[c]	22.0	100.0
1969	47.6	23.8	71.4	4.7[d]	28.6	100.0
1970	51.7	19.8	71.5	6.0[c]	28.5	100.0
1971	46.0	22.2	68.2	7.1[c]	31.8	100.0
1972	47.9	20.4	68.3	9.3[c]	31.7	100.0
1973	49.3	19.4	68.7	10.1[c]	31.3	100.0
1974	41.3	17.9	59.2	12.4[c]	40.8	100.0
1975	48.0	11.5	59.5	9.6[c]	40.5	100.0
1976[e]	53.2	14.1	67.3	4.6[d]	32.6	100.0
1977[e]	61.8	13.2	75.0	5.1[c]	25.0	100.0
1978[e]	69.0	13.3	82.3	3.5[c]	17.7	100.0

[a]COMECON (excluding USSR) plus China, Albania, North Korea, and Yugoslavia.
[b]USA. [c]Japan. [d]Spain. [e]Preliminary.
Sources: Same as in Table 15 infra updated with *Anuario 1976*, pp. 148–51; and data supplied to the author by the State Committee on Statistics, July 1979.

States before—selling more to than buying from Cuba. The other socialist trade partners have been, by order of importance: China (an average of 8 percent of Cuba's total trade); Czechoslovakia and East Germany (4 percent each); Bulgaria (2 percent); Poland, Rumania and Hungary (one percent each); and Yugoslavia (half of one percent). It could be argued that Cuba has diversified its trade partners in the 1960s and 1970s, since trade-partner concentration has been reduced from two-thirds (with the United States) to one-half (with the USSR). However, in 1978, Cuban trade with the USSR alone reached a record of 69 percent and, because of the close economic and political relationship of Eastern European countries to the USSR, it can be reasonably maintained that in terms of trade-partner concentration, Cuba today is as vulnerable to external economic and political influence as it was before the Revolution.

The remainder of Cuban foreign trade in 1961–78—an average of 27 percent of total transactions—was with developed market economies. As is indicated in Table 20, Japan was one of Cuba's two main trade partners outside of the socialist camp, with an increasing percentage of trade, from 3 percent in 1962 to 12 percent in 1974. Spain has alternated with Japan as Cuba's second major trade partner but with a lower average (4 percent) for the whole period. The average combined percentage of trade with Western Europe (14 percent) in the period has been higher than those of Japan and Spain. The main trade partners in Western Europe are the Federal Republic of Germany, United Kingdom, France, Italy, Holland, Sweden, Austria, and Belgium. Trade with Canada has been about 2 percent for the whole period. Trade with Latin America, mostly in the 1970s, has been below 2 percent with major partners being Argentina and Mexico (Chile in 1971–73 under the socialist government of Salvador Allende). A tiny fraction of trade was carried on with a few African, Middle Eastern, and Asian countries.

The fluctuations in the distribution of Cuban trade between socialist and market economies are apparent in Table 20. Trade with all socialist economies was at its lowest point in 1964 (64 percent) and in 1974–75 (59 percent) when the world price of sugar was very high. In those years trade shifted toward market economies, reaching peaks of 36 and 41 percent. The lowest percentage of trade with the USSR was also in 1964 and 1974. On the other hand, in 1966–67 and 1978 when the world sugar price was at low points, Cuba's dependency on socialist trade reached peaks of 80 percent and above, while trade with market economies declined to 20 percent or less.

In those years when Cuba had sufficient foreign exchange to choose trade partners, trade shifted from socialist to market economies. In an official report from Cuba's National Bank, it was noted that the island's trade with market economies "has allowed Cuba to import large amounts of up-to-date technology and to expand and diversify its export market."³¹ Early in 1976, a high Cuban official in the Ministry of Foreign Trade told Business International that a desirable distribution of future Cuban trade should be 40 percent with socialist countries, 30 percent with the United States, and 30 percent with other market economies. One year later, however, facing declining sugar prices, the Cuban Director of Commercial Policy for North America told a group of visiting U.S. businessmen that Cuba's trade breakdown would be 60-40 percent in favor of socialist countries and that U.S. firms would have to carve their share from the nonsocialist 40 percent.³²

The five-year Cuban-Soviet agreements signed in 1976 on trade and economic-technical cooperation have locked Cuba into the greatest trade dependency to date on the USSR. Carlos Rafael Rodríguez, Cuban Deputy Prime Minister of Foreign Affairs, has forecast that the level of Cuban-Soviet economic cooperation will be 2.5 times greater in 1976–80 than in 1971–75 and the level of trade two times greater.³³ The President of JUCEPLAN has announced as a future planning goal "a greater integration of our economy to that of the socialist countries particularly with the USSR," and a reduction of imports from market economies.³⁴

In the period 1962–74 Cuban trade with the USSR always ended in a deficit. An average of 78 percent of Cuba's trade deficit was with the USSR, and in the years 1972–73 the deficit with the USSR alone was higher than Cuba's total trade deficit (see Table 21). In 1975–78, however, Cuba's trade with the USSR resulted, for the first time, in a surplus, due to the concessionary prices offered by the USSR. Cuban-Soviet cumulative trade balance in 1959–78 resulted in a deficit of 2.6 billion pesos against Cuba, equivalent to 48 percent of Cuba's cumulative trade deficit in that period. On the other hand, the deficit with other socialist countries has been small, peaked in 1964, but then declined sharply. Surpluses were generated through most of the 1970s when these countries imported considerably more than they exported to Cuba. China has been the socialist country outside of the USSR having mostly a deficit trade with Cuba. Trade with Rumania and Hungary has also ended in deficits most of the time. The cumulative trade balance between Cuba and other socialist countries for the whole period ended in a deficit of 178 million pesos, only 3 percent of the cumulative deficit. Cuban trade with market economies as a whole has also ended in deficits except for a few years; however, trade with Japan and Spain has normally resulted in surpluses. Deficits with western countries reached peaks in 1975–77 because Cuba overcommitted herself on her imports and because of the decline in world sugar prices. Cuba's 1959–78 cumulative trade balance with market economies reached -2.7 billion pesos while this represented 49 percent of

TABLE 21. Cuba's Balance of Trade with Socialist and Market Economies, 1959–78 (in million pesos)

Years	Overall Trade Balance	Socialist Economies				Market Economies	
		USSR		Rest			
		Amount	%[a]	Amount	%[a]	Amount	%
1959	−39	13	0	1	0	− 53	100
1960	28	23	0	18	0	− 13	100
1961	−12	38	0	− 27	54	− 23	46
1962	−238	−190	80	− 12	5	− 36	15
1963	−322	−297	88	− 40	12	15	0
1964	−305	−135	44	−134	44	− 36	12
1965	−175	−105	60	− 16	9	− 54	31
1966	−327	−247	76	− 9	3	− 71	21
1967	−294	−216	73	− 1	1	− 77	26
1968	−451	−382	85	− 9	2	− 60	13
1969	−555	−436	79	− 22	4	− 97	17
1970	−262	−161	58	13	0	−116	42
1971	−527	−427	78	21	0	−121	22
1972	−419	−490	99	− 3	1	74	0
1973	−310	−334	95	43	0	− 19	5
1974	11	−214	100	134	0	91	0
1975	−166	411	0	− 15	3	−562	97
1976	−488	148	0	78	0	−714	100
1977	−521	205	0	− 92	13	−634	87
1978	−141	178	0	−106	33	−213	67
Totals	−5,513	−2,618	48[b]	−178	3[b]	−2,719	49[b]

[a]Percent of Cuba's annual trade deficit.

[b]Percent of Cuba's cumulative trade deficit.

Sources: Same as Table 15 infra; updated with *Anuario 1976*, pp. 148–51; and Banco Nacional de Cuba 1977, p. 24.

Cuba's total cumulative deficit, 78 percent of that deficit was accumulated in 1975–78 alone.

The USSR and other socialist countries are the principal buyers of most of Cuba's exports—sugar, nickel, citrus, and rum—and the sellers of most of Cuba's imports—mostly foodstuffs, raw materials, fuel and metallic products, and to a lesser extent chemicals and machinery. In 1962–76 Cuba exported an average of 45 percent of her sugar to the USSR, about 10 percentage points less than what Cuba exported to the United States prior to the Revolution. But an additional average of 13 percent of Cuban sugar exports went to the GDR, Bulgaria, and Czechoslovakia—the three COMECON countries that have closest relations with the USSR. An additional 2 percent went to the rest of COMECON, about 5 percent to China, and 4 percent to Vietnam, North Korea, and

Yugoslavia; thus almost 70 percent of Cuba's sugar exports went to socialist countries. China cut sharply both her imports of Cuban sugar and exports of rice in 1966 and 1975—with significant economic impact upon Cuba—when the two countries collided on political issues: in 1966 on the leadership of the Latin American revolutionary movement and in 1975 on the Angolan war. In spite of Soviet subsidized prices, Cuba needs to export sugar to the international market because this is how she generates her major source of hard currency. The International Sugar Agreement assigns a quota of two million tons of sugar for Cuba to sell in the world market. The principal importers are Japan and Spain. They have bought averages of 12 and 4 percent respectively in the last decade, although their purchases declined sharply in 1976–77.[35]

Until 1971, the USSR bought about one-fifth of Cuba's exports of nickel-cobalt sinter and oxide but stopped purchases altogether after 1972. On the other hand, Soviet buying of Cuba's nickel sulfide steadily increased from 84 percent in 1968 to 100 percent in 1973–75. Czechoslovakia is the second major buyer of Cuban nickel exports, taking an average of 22 percent of the oxide and 10 percent of the sinter. Hungary, the GDR, and Rumania take another 17 percent of the sinter. The remaining exports of nickel are bought by Western European nations, mainly Italy and Holland.

In 1967–75 exports of citrus fruits went entirely to COMECON countries: 40 percent to the GDR, 24 percent to the USSR (increasing from 5 percent in 1968 to 34 percent in 1974), and the rest to Czechoslovakia, Hungary, and Poland. About 80 percent of Cuba's rum exports also went to COMECON: 47 percent to the USSR (increasing from 32 to 86 percent); 14 percent to Rumania, and the rest to Czechoslovakia, Poland, the GDR, and Hungary. Cuba's most diversified exports markets are for tobacco and fish products, almost all of which are bought by market economies. In 1967–75, one-third of Cuban cigar exports were bought by Spain (which also took about four-fifths of tobacco leaf); United Kingdom, France, and Switzerland bought another one-third; the Soviet Union one-tenth (although Soviet buyings steadily increased from 3 to 16 percent); and the rest went to other European countries and Canada. Fish and seafood—fresh, frozen, and canned—were bought by France, Canada, Spain, Holland, Italy, and Japan.

To measure Cuba's dependency on imports from the socialist countries, I followed some 50 imports that were systematically reported by Cuba's statistical yearbook in 1967–75, in quantity and value (in pesos), showing the major suppliers.[36] The results presented in Table 22 indicate that between 1967 and 1975 the share of imports supplied by socialist economies declined. The smallest reductions occurred in raw materials (a decline of 6

TABLE 22. Percentage Distribution of Cuban Imports Supplied by Socialist and Market[b] Economies, 1967–75

Imports[a]	1967	1968	1969	1970	1971	1972	1973	1974	1975
Foodstuffs									
Socialist	82.5	86.8	85.4	75.2	71.1	75.7	73.6	71.7	66.6
Market	17.5	13.2	14.6	24.8	28.9	24.3	26.4	20.3	33.4
Raw Materials									
Socialist	86.4	90.4	83.2	80.4	84.6	89.1	91.8	76.8	80.0
Market	13.6	16.7	16.8	19.6	15.4	10.9	8.2	23.2	20.0
Fuel									
Socialist	99.3	98.6	97.9	97.6	98.0	97.5	99.3	97.6	98.3
Market	0.7	1.4	2.1	2.4	2.0	2.5	0.7	2.4	1.7
Chemicals									
Socialist	46.1	37.2	28.4	33.0	51.5	40.4	38.4	40.8	31.0
Market	53.9	62.8	71.6	67.0	48.5	59.6	61.6	59.2	69.0
Manufactures									
Socialist	81.2	89.0	71.7	53.9	54.8	57.6	27.8	39.0	33.5
Market	18.8	11.0	28.3	46.1	45.2	42.4	72.2	61.0	66.5
Machinery									
Socialist	75.1	69.9	72.3	64.3	52.0	65.8	69.1	58.9	39.2
Market	24.9	30.1	27.7	35.7	48.0	34.2	30.9	41.1	60.8
Transportation									
Socialist	68.4	56.9	42.9	46.0	45.8	75.1	43.9	29.1	35.2
Market	31.6	43.1	57.1	54.0	54.2	24.9	56.1	70.9	64.8
Total									
Socialist	77.1	75.2	71.7	66.4	65.3	75.4	68.7	63.0	55.6
Market	22.9	24.8	28.3	33.6	34.7	24.6	31.3	37.0	44.4

[a]Selected imports representing an average of two-thirds of all imports in the period.
[b]Market economies and "others" presumably nonsocialist countries.
Sources: Computations based on *Boletín 1971*, pp. 246–63 and *Anuario 1976*, pp. 170–85.

percentage points), chemicals (15 percentage points), and foodstuffs (16 percentage points). The highest declines were in transportation equipment (33 percentage points), machinery (36 percentage points), and manufactures (48 percentage points). Also seen in Table 22 is that in 1967–68, when the world sugar price was depressed, Cuba bought from socialist economies 80 to 90 percent of her imports of foodstuffs, raw materials, and manufactures, as well as from 60 to 75 percent of machinery and transportation. In 1974–75, when sugar prices were booming in the international market, Cuba bought from market economies from 60 to 70 percent of her imports of chemicals, manufactures, and transportation equipment and about half of the machinery.[37] In these years, however, socialist countries still supplied from 70 to 80 percent of Cuban imports of foodstuffs and raw materials.

The relative decline of Cuban imports from the USSR (except for oil) in 1975 over 1967 is illustrated by the following averages: foodstuffs from 79 to 51 percent, raw materials from 85 to 78 percent, chemicals from 41 to 23 percent, manufactures from 58 to 27 percent, machinery from 37 to 32 percent, and transportation from 56 to 19 percent. Between 1972 and 1975, when Cuba had the widest choice for buying, specific industrial imports from the USSR dipped even more dramatically: bulldozers by 98 percentage points; tractors by 89 points; loaders by 51 points; trucks by 43 points; diesel engines by 45 points; steel sheets and tubes by 41 points; and fertilizers by 45 points.[38] These data are additional evidence supporting my previous assumption that Cuba does not get a good deal either in price or quality, or both, in Soviet industrial goods.

DEPENDENCY ON FOREIGN ENERGY

Since the world oil crisis of 1973, dependency on foreign supply of energy sources has become a painful and costly reality even for industrialized countries, and much more so for developing ones. A world power such as the United States has become vulnerable to economic and political influence of the oil cartel of the Organization of Petroleum Exporting Countries (OPEC). Cuba is not well endowed with energy: it apparently does not have coal; its hydro potential is very low (its rivers have low heads, carry relatively small volumes of water, and show an uneven flow during the year); and the known oil and gas deposits are very limited. Solar energy is a possibility, but Cuba lacks the technology to develop it on a relatively cheap large-scale basis. They do not seem to be interested in the production of gasohol out of sugar. The project to construct a nuclear power plant will not be completed at least until the second half of the current decade, and even after completed, Cuba will depend on the importation of enriched uranium from the USSR. Sugarcane bagasse has been used in Cuba for many years as a fuel for the sugar harvest, but it declined in 1968–76 as a source of energy from 43 to 36 percent while the share of oil products increased from 51 to 58 percent. Other sources of energy—coal, hydro, and gas—were stagnant at about 6 percent in that period.[39] In 1974 Cuba was ranked among the least able of eighty-eight developing countries to meet current and projected energy needs from domestic sources.[40]

In spite of Cuba's increase in domestic output of oil, current production meets less than 4 percent of domestic consumption; hence the bulk of the oil has to be imported (see Table 23). In 1967–76 the USSR supplied an average of 98 percent of Cuban oil imports. This oil comes from Black Sea ports 6,400 miles away, and in 1972 required a flotilla of 150 medium-sized Soviet tankers—practically one tanker every other day to keep Cuba

TABLE 23. Crude Oil Production, Imports, and Supply in Cuba, 1963–76[a]
(in thousand metric tons)

| | | | | Percentage of | |
| | | | | Supply domestically produced | Imports supplied by USSR |
Years	Production	Imports	Supply		
1963	31	3,709	3,740	0.8	
1964	37	3,469	3,506	1.0	
1965	57	3,483	3,540	1.6	
1966	69	5,826	3,895	1.8	
1967	116	3,713	3,829	3.0	99.3
1968	197	3,851	4,048	4.9	98.6
1969	206	4,156	4,362	4.7	97.9
1970	159	4,261	4,420	3.6	97.6
1971	120	4,757	4,877	2.5	98.0
1972	112	4,749	4,861	2.1	97.5
1973	138	5,243	5,381	2.6	99.3
1974	168	5,875	6,043	2.8	97.6
1975	226	5,797	6,023	3.7	98.3
1976	235	5,783	6,018	3.9	—

[a]Crude oil only, does not include oil products such as gasoline.

Sources: The basic idea and some data from this table come from Jorge Pérez-López, "Sugar and Petroleum in Cuban-Soviet Terms of Trade," Cuba in the World, p. 276. Additional data from Boletín 1966, p. 132; Boletín 1971, pp. 250–51; Anuario 1973, pp. 128,198, 216–17; Anuario 1976, pp. 88, 156, 174–75; Anuario 1978, pp. 92, 173.

supplied.[41] That was in 1972 when oil consumption was 20 percent below that in 1976, and if consumption continues to increase at the current rate it will be at least 20 percent higher in 1985. Possibilities for reducing consumption are almost nil since most conservation measures have already been taken: few cars are driven; bus service is at a minimum; gasoline rationing was introduced in 1968; and electricity is also rationed through periodic shutdowns of service on a rotating basis.[42]

In 1976 Cuba bought almost 6 percent of total Soviet oil exports, ranking the island seventh among major importers, behind Czechoslovakia, GDR, Poland, Italy, Bulgaria, and Finland, and receiving more than Hungary. The level of Cuban imports of oil puts her with nations much more industrialized and with larger populations.[43] Transportation costs are quite high because the oil tankers have to travel an average of forty-two days per tanker. In the mid-1970s, these costs were equivalent to 7.3 percent of the total cost of Soviet oil imports or $43 million.[44] Since 1974 the potential for triangular agreements among the USSR, Mexico, or Venezuela, and Cuba have been explored in hopes that one of those Latin American countries would supply part of the oil that Cuba consumes in exchange for similar amounts that the USSR would provide to Venezuelan or Mexican clients in Western Europe. Such an arrangement would save Cuba a considerable sum in freight costs, but only a small amount was supplied by Venezuela in 1977–80 with a cut in half in 1981. It seems that any further deal must await full normalization of U.S.-Cuban relations.[45]

The Cuban leadership is painfully aware that a cut in the oil supply will paralyze the country almost immediately. This danger was made very real in 1968 when the USSR slowed down the supply of oil to the island, forcing gasoline rationing, and drawing down the island's oil reserves including those of the armed forces. At the same time the USSR publicly announced an increase in its oil output and of its oil exports to Brazil, one of Cuba's archenemies at the time. This was a clear example of coercion from the USSR to force Cuba to change some of its Mao-Guevarist policies.[46] Many observers believe that Castro's subsequent endorsement of the Soviet invasion of Czechoslovakia was a yielding to USSR pressure. A more speculative hypothesis recently advanced tries to explain Cuba's involvement in Africa in the second half of the 1970s (when Soviet oil reserves began to decline, world oil prices skyrocketed, competition for Soviet oil exports became stronger, and Cuban oil consumption needs increased) as an outcome of Cuba's oil dependency.[47]

DEPENDENCY ON FOREIGN MERCHANT MARINE

Cuba's dependency on foreign trade and the long distance that the merchandise has to be transported impose a heavy burden on the island's economy. Almost 85 percent of Cuban trade is with the USSR, Eastern Europe, Japan, and China, hence shipping distances are from 6,000 to 9,000 miles. In 1964 when trade with the USSR was at a low point, the average distance of a ton of merchandise transported by international maritime freight was also at a low of 5,321 miles; but as trade with the USSR and Japan increased, so did the average distance: 7,650 in 1966 and 9,886 in 1970. In 1974, when the Soviet share of trade declined and that of Western Europe and Canada increased, the average distance declined to 6,762.[48] It has probably risen again in the second half of the 1970s as trade with the USSR expanded significantly.

In hopes of reducing somewhat the cost of transportation, Cuba has developed in the two decades of the Revolution what is now the fourth largest merchant marine in Latin America. The total tonnage of Cuba's international merchant marine fleet increased almost tenfold in 1958–75. In spite of this dramatic expansion,

the island's own fleet was only able to increase its handling of
Cuba's total trade from 3 percent in 1963 to 10 percent in 1975
(see Table 24). Another 9 to 15 percent of foreign trade was
carried by ships rented by Cuba (mostly from socialist countries)
and 75 to 81 percent by other ships. Even if the planned goal for
expansion of the Cuban fleet is met, its ships would be carrying
only from 13 to 15 percent of the nation's trade in 1980.

Cuba's significant reliance on foreign merchant marine vessels,
most of them from socialist countries, adds to the island's
vulnerability and dependency. If Cuba were able to diversify its
trade and deal mostly with Canada and the United States,
merchant ship's voyages would be reduced from 20 to 90 days to
voyages of 2 to 3 days. Moreover, the current merchant marine
fleet could handle 3.5 times the freight it carried in 1974. Besides
savings in freight Cuba would ameliorate problems such as lack
of sufficient warehouses and port facilities, rotation of ships, and
payments for delays in ports due to concentration of ships.[49]

DEPENDENCY ON EXTERNAL CAPITAL:
THE FOREIGN DEBT

Any developing country, regardless of its economic system,
needs foreign capital in its process of development—be it nonrepayable grants, medium or long-term loans, direct investment,

TABLE 24. Capacity of Cuba's International Merchant Fleet, 1963–75

Years	Number of Ships[a]	Tonnage (Thousand metric tons)	Percent of foreign trade carried		
			Cuban Ships	Rented Ships	Others
1963	15	64	3		
1964	13	73	3		
1965	18	106	4	15	81
1966	25	177	6		
1967	32	223	7		
1968	34	237	7		
1969	38	265	7		
1970	37	282	6	13	81
1971	32	311	6	14	80
1972	34	322	7	12	81
1973	38	392	9	9	82
1974	50	483	9	14	77
1975	52	544	10	15	75

[a]Excludes coastal vessels.

Sources: Carmelo Mesa-Lago, "The Economics of U.S.-Cuban Reapprochement,"
Cuba in the World, p. 208, corrected and updated with *Anuario 1975*, pp. 130–33
and *Anuario 1976*, pp. 108–11.

and so forth. The extent to which a country relies on one or a few countries to obtain the needed capital determines its degree of capital dependency. Until the Revolution, the United States was the fundamental source of foreign capital for Cuba, mainly through direct investment; however, since the nationalization of U.S. property in 1959–60, no foreign direct investment has been allowed in the island.

The USSR replaced the United States as Cuba's main supplier of capital after 1961. But the Soviets do not have direct investment or own property, factories, land, or utilities as the Americans did. Instead Soviet aid has come in four ways. The first two are loans that must be repaid, and the last two are nonrepayable grants: provisions of annual credits to finance the Soviet-Cuban trade deficit (the most significant source of Soviet aid, estimated at more than $4 billion in 1976); direct aid for economic development (estimated at $860 million in 1976); subsidies to the price of the imports of Cuban sugar, particularly since 1965, and nickel since 1973, and to the export of Soviet oil since 1974 (estimated at $3.6 billion in 1976); and military equipment (estimated at $1.5 billion for the 1960s alone). Therefore, by the end of 1976, Cuba had received from the USSR a total of at least $10 billion (about $600 million annually), but only half of it ($4.9 billion) has to be repaid.[50] The repayable loans granted to Cuba by both the USSR and other socialist countries are listed in Table 25. The latter have apparently given Cuba only one type of economic aid—$267 million in medium-term development loans, mostly in the early 1960s. The exception to this was Rumania—the most independent Eastern European country and allegedly sympathizer with the Chinese in the late 1960s—which gave Cuba a grant in the midst of the Mao-Guevarist stage. Socialist countries have not shown the economic favoritism toward Cuba that the USSR has. They have not provided credits to finance trade deficits, they have not supplied military equipment free (for example, in the early 1960s Czechoslovakia sold obsolete weapons to Cuba), nor have they systematicaly or substantially subsidized prices of Cuban exports. The average loan from the USSR and other socialist countries has had an amortization period of ten years and charged an interest rate of 2.5 percent.

According to Cole Blasier, Cuba has received more economic assistance from the USSR than any other developing country outside the USSR's Eurasian orbit, and that aid took about 4 percent of total Soviet assistance in 1966–74. Blasier also quotes a Soviet scholar as stating that in the 1970s, 80 percent of Cuba's capital investment was on the account of socialist countries.[51] This last statement requires some qualification. With the exception of about one billion dollars provided by the socialist countries for specific development projects mostly in the early 1960s, most socialist economic aid has not gone into investment but to keep

TABLE 25. Selected Credits Extended to Cuba by Socialist and Market Economies, 1960–77

	Million U.S. Dollars	Year Granted	Amortization Period (Years)	Interest Rate (%)
Socialist Economies				
USSR	459[a]	1960–64	10–12	2–2.5
	402[a]	1973–76	25	2.5 starting 1976
	4,050[b]	1962–76	25[a]	2.5 starting 1986
Rumania	75[a]	1961, 1968–69	10–12	2.5
China	60[a]	1960	10	none
GDR	60[a]	1960–63	10–12	2.5
Czechoslovakia	40[a]	1960	10	2.5
Hungary	15[a]	1961	10	2.5
Poland	12[a]	1960	8	2.5
Bulgaria	5[a]	1961	10	2.5
Sub-total	5,178			
Market Economies				
Agentina	1,200[c]	1973	8	
Spain	900[c]	1974		
United Kingdom	580[c]	1975	5	7.5
Eurocurrency	537[d]	1973–77	5	1.75 over LIBOR
France	350[c]	1975	10	
Japan	400[c]	1973–77	5	
Canada	155[c]	1974–75	10–30	3 to current rates
Sweden	33	1973–75		
Italy	35[c]	1975		
Mexico	20[c]	1975		
Switzerland	15			
Sub-total	4,225			
Total	9,403			

[a]Development loans; used.
[b]Credit to finance trade deficits; used.
[c]Export credit facilities; not totally used.
[d]Borrowings to finance trade deficits; used.
[e]In 1972 the Cuban debt to the USSR was postponed with no earned interest until 1986.
Sources: Archibald Ritter, *The Economic Development of Revolutionary Cuba* (New York: Praeger, 1974), p. 89; CIA, *The Cuban Economy: A Statistical Review, 1968–76* (Washington, D.C., 1976), pp. 14–15; Banco Nacional de Cuba, 1977, p. 25; Jorge I. Domínguez, *Cuba: Order and Revolution* (Cambridge: Harvard University Press, 1978), pp. 151–52; and Carmelo Mesa-Lago, *Cuba in the World*, p. 210.

the island's economy going—foodstuff supplies, fuel, and raw materials—and for military aid. The USSR has also largely absorbed the social costs of the Cuban Revolution. Soviet aid has allowed the island to develop its costly programs of social services, as will be discussed in chapter 7. Even taking into account the considerable waste in investment that took place in the 1960s, if four-fifths of the ten billion dollars in socialist help had indeed gone into agricultural, industrial, and transportation investment, Cuba today would be exporting a large number of goods that it currently imports and rationing would not be necessary.

By the early 1970s, the impossibility of Cuba repaying the colossal external debt accumulated with the USSR was apparent. The island's compliance with the introduction of the political and economic reforms desired by the USSR prompted that country in 1972 to defer for thirteen years the payment of the Cuban debt—both principal and interest—accrued since 1960. Payments are expected to be in rubles, to begin in 1986 and end by 2011.[52] The USSR also loaned Cuba—for the first time since 1964—300 million rubles (about $400 million) for development purposes, to be repaid in 1976–2000. Finally, a credit was also granted (to be repaid in 1986–2011) to finance the expected Cuban-Soviet trade deficits in 1973–75. Since 1976 the price of Cuban sugar exports to the USSR has been tied to the price of Soviet oil and other basic imports, an arrangement that has resulted in a slow down in the deterioration of Cuban terms of trade with the USSR. Several western scholars, including myself, have accumulated substantial evidence to prove that Cuba was at a dead-end in 1970 because of the combined failure of its development strategy and model of economic organization. To obtain the needed financial aid to save her economy, Cuba accepted a higher degree of dependency with the USSR.[53]

Since 1972, Cuba has also had access to capital financing from market economies in two basic forms (see Table 25); medium-term (five year) loans borrowed from Eurocurrency markets to finance Cuba's trade deficits with the West, particularly since 1974; and long-term credits—only partly used—for the purchase of capital and intermediate and consumer goods from Western Europe (Spain, United Kingdom, France, Sweden, Italy, and FRG), Japan, Canada, and Latin America (Argentina and Mexico). Accessibility to Western capital has been possible for various reasons: the island's economic boom of the mid-1970s and the resulting buying spree in the West; political changes in Latin America—such as the brief return of Peronism in Argentina and reestablishment of relations with Cuba; Cuba's good record of repaying early debts promptly and without trouble (for example, in 1976 the Cubans faced the possibility of default, and they preferred to suspend imports and absorb the loss); and the assumption among international bankers that the USSR and COMECON banks will

provide assistance to any member country facing financial difficulties. Cuba's net hard currency debt with the West has been
estimated at $1.3 billion for 1976—$400 million in outstanding
loans with Eurocurrency markets plus $900 million in used
credits.[54] This suggests that Cuba has used only one-fourth of the
credits opened by market economies for purchasing of merchandise, probably because of the island's economic recession of
1976–77. As Cuba increases its debt with market economies, the
burden of debt repayment will worsen because of shorter maturity
periods and higher interest rates. In mid-1979 Cuba's external
debt with commercial banks from industrialized market economies
totalled $1.8 billion, the majority with a maturity of one year or
less, and paying at least 19 percent interest.[55] This burden,
combined with skyrocketting loan interest rates and the grave
deterioration of the Cuban economy in 1979–80 induced a halt in
loans from nonsocialist sources. From an estimated $300 million
in 1978, loans declined to $40 million in 1979 (mostly used by
Cuba for debt service), and practically to zero in 1980.[56]

Cuba does not publish data on total indebtedness, but estimates
can be derived by adding the repayable debts to both the USSR
($4.9 billion) and the West ($1.3 billion). Cuba's foreign debt
should conservatively be estimated at $6.2 billion in 1976. This
assumes that the $267 million debt to other socialist countries
initiated largely in 1960–61 with a ten-year amortization period
has been paid, and that new credits from socialist countries
outside the USSR have not come through in the 1970s; otherwise,
Cuba's foreign debt should be higher. In 1959, Cuba's foreign debt
stood at $45.5 million; it increased 136 times in the first seventeen
years of the Revolution and was certainly much higher in 1980.
I have compared Cuba's foreign debt with that of other Latin
American countries in 1975 and found that in absolute figures
Cuba's debt was the third largest in Latin America, surpassed
only by those of Brazil and Mexico. Yet Cuba was the Latin
American nation with the highest debt per capita—fourfold that
of Brazil and threefold that of Mexico. Concerning the capacity to
service the debt of Cuba within the Latin American context, the
proportion of the debt in relation to the GNP for the largest
countries in the region was 18 percent and for the rest was 26
percent, while the debt/GSP proportion for Cuba was 36 percent.
Cuba's debt/export proportion was 198 percent, compared with
averages of 122 percent for Latin America and 110 percent for all
developing countries.[57] A U.S. specialist on international trade has
calculated the proportion of the hard-currency debt (that is, loans
from market economies) in relation to the GSP of most COMECON
countries and found that Cuba's proportion was the highest—12.3
percent as compared to an overall average of 3.5 percent.[58] Cuba's
capital amortization of her public debt in the 1979 budget, when
most of the debt was not due, possibly increased 639 percent over

1963. This was the largest increase in any category of the budget except for the "reserve." Moreover, the other budget categories increased by an average of 310 percent.[59]

The year 1986 will be critical for Cuba because most of the debt with the USSR matures then. In chapter 3 it was shown that the probability of Cuba fulfilling most of the 1976–80 planned goals is remote, and thus the 1981–86 plan will start handicapped. It is unlikely that the Cuban economy will go into a boom like the one of 1973–75, but unless it does the island's capacity to repay the Soviet debt will be insufficient. Cuba will probably have, therefore, to renegotiate and it would be hoped postpone its debt with the USSR. It is true that the USSR has provided a capital pipeline to Cuba under exceptionally generous financial conditions and without owning any property on the island, but from this it should not be inferred that Cuba's dependency has been reduced. What would happen to Cuba if the USSR cut the capital pipeline or simply refused to renegotiate the debt in 1986?

6

Full Employment

The Marxist theory of full employment in a socialist economy argues that with collectivization of the means of production employment is systematically and rationally expanded, unemployment eliminated, and economic growth promoted. This theory was apparently confirmed with the Soviet experience of the late 1920s and early 1930s when industrialization rapidly absorbed the labor surplus from agriculture. But in more recent times, other socialist countries, with overpopulation problems and a significant labor surplus in the agricultural sector, have found that the theory has not worked as well. Technological progress has made industrialization more costly and less absorbent of the labor surplus. China tried in the Great Leap Forward to utilize fully its agricultural labor surplus in construction and industrial activities of a low technological level, under the assumption that there would not be any loss but a net gain. The plan failed because the Chinese neglected to recognize key factors such as material inputs, transportation costs, managerial and organizational skills, and productivity. Yugoslavia is the only socialist country that has suffered from and reported high rates of open unemployment since the late 1950s, probably because within the market-socialism framework it tried to expand employment without significantly sacrificing productivity. Other socialist countries, however, do not report open unemployment, and yet many of them endure severe problems of underemployment and disguised unemployment. These countries have often solved the social angle of unemployment partly by creating artificial jobs: the jobless no longer bear alone the heavy cost of unemployment and are provided with a guaranteed job and income. And yet since the national product does not increase parallel with the expansion of demand, because of the bureaucratic nature of many of the new jobs or their very low productivity, the result is either price increases or physical rationing. Therefore, the economic cost of this employment policy is spread to the population as a whole.[1]

Reviewed in this chapter are Cuba's revolutionary policies to eliminate open unemployment and their consequences in terms of labor productivity. To provide the necessary framework, such analysis is preceded by a study of the evolution of the labor force and its composition by age, sex, race, economic activity, and states versus private employment.

THE LABOR FORCE: STATE VERSUS PRIVATE EMPLOYMENT

Cuba does not regularly publish data on the total labor force or unemployment. The available data are only on the state civilian employment and private employment, leaving out the armed forces, the police, and security personnel.[2] I have tried to fill this vacuum by reconstructing, in Table 26, the overall composition of the labor force.[3]

Cuba's labor force experienced growth rates of 1.5 percent in the 1960s and 2 percent in the 1970s and is expected to maintain the latter rate through most of the 1980s. These rates, while substantially lower than the average rates for Latin America, are higher than those of the most advanced countries such as Argentina, Chile, and Uruguay. The labor force participation rate—that is, labor force as a proportion of the total population—stood at 32.8 percent in 1962 but steadily declined to 30.2 percent in 1971. Reasons for this decline were the increasing absorption of youngsters by the expanding educational system, which kept them away from the labor force, the exodus of hundreds of thousands of disaffected (some 200,000 in the labor force), and the liberalization of retirement laws, all of which more than offset labor force increases due to labor mobilization campaigns, particularly the incorporation of females into the labor force. Since 1972 there has been an increase in the labor force participation rate, which reached 32.2 percent in 1978—back to the levels of the late 1950s and early 1960s. Reasons for the increase were the sharp reduction in the emigration, the acceleration in the female incorporation into the labor force, and the entrance into the labor market (since 1977) of the baby boom of the 1960s.[4] Cuba's labor force participation rate in 1978 was slightly above the 1975 average rate for Latin America (31.5 percent) but below that of more developed countries such as Argentina (38.7 percent) and Uruguay (38.5 percent).[5]

State employment prior to the Revolution (1953 census) was 9 percent of total employment but probably increased to more than one-half by the end of 1960 following the nationalization waves of the fall of that year. The nationalization of the educational system in 1961 and the transformation of private cooperatives

TABLE 26. Estimates of the Labor Force in Cuba; 1962–78 (in thousands)

Years	Total Population	Labor Force[a]	Percent	Employment			Unem-ployment
				State		Private[c]	
				Civilian	Military[ab]		
1962	7318	2401	32.8	1083	363	740	215
1963	7512	2431	32.4	1238	382	613	198[a]
1964	7712	2456	31.8	1369	386	516	185[a]
1965	7907	2490	31.5	1452	367	508	163[a]
1966	8063	2508	31.1	1517	360	476	155[a]
1967	8215	2549	31.0	1604[a]	350	460[a]	135[a]
1968	8352	2579	30.9	1760	325	384[a]	110[a]
1969	8489	2608	30.7	1895	275	363[a]	75
1970	8613	2638	30.6	2064	200	340	34
1971	8768	2657	30.2	2082	195	320	55[a]
1972	8773	2680	30.5	2126	190	300	64[a]
1973	9035	2795	30.9	2246	185	280	84[a]
1974	9266	2869	31.0	2313	185	260	111[a]
1975	9405	2923	31.1	2391	210	232	90[a]
1976	9537	2974	31.2	2469	220	200	85[a]
1977	9649	3075	31.8	2608	225	182	60[a]
1978	9765	3140	32.2	2695[a]	230	175[a]	40[a]

[a]Estimated by the author.

[b]Militarymen, policemen and intelligence personnel; excludes militiamen, paramilitary bodies doing construction and agricultural work, and unmobilized reserves. In the second half of the 1960s, total personnel under the Ministry of the Armed Forces was higher than the table indicates but part of that personnel was involved in productive activities. In the 1970s, the Youth Labor Army falls not under military but under productive activities also.

[c]Mostly farmers, and a small number of fishermen, taxi drivers, and cargo movers. There is a possibility that the number of people in nonagricultural activities is larger than estimated in 1978; if this is so military personnel should be smaller.

Sources: Column 1 from Table 6 infra. Column 2 estimated as explained in the text. Columns 4 and 6 from Boletín 1966, p. 24; Boletín 1968, pp. 18–22; Boletín 1970, p. 24; Jorge Risquet, "Comparecencia sobre problemas de la fuerza de trabajo," Granma, 1 August 1970, pp. 2–3; Anuario 1975, p. 44; Banco Nacional de Cuba 1977, p. 9 and 1978, p. 9. Column 5 partly based on estimates by Jorge Domínguez's private correspondence 16 March 1979. Column 7 is mostly a residue but is based also in scattered data.

into state farms in 1962, increased state employment to 66 percent of total employment. The second agrarian reform of 1963 (with full impact in 1964) resulted in a transfer of more than 200,000 jobs from the private to the state sector. This pulled up employment in the latter to 77 percent. The nationalization of 55,600 businesses (trade shops, personal services, and handicrafts) during the Revolutionary Offensive of 1968 induced another significant transfer of employment from the private to the state sector, which reached almost 85 percent. Finally the gradual reduction of private agriculture has further expanded state employment which, by 1978, was close to 95 percent of total employment (percentages of state versus private employment are based on Table 26). All remaining private employment is in the small private farms, which basically are worked by the farmer and his family. Part-time wage earners in private farms were almost eliminated in 1971 by the law against loafing, which established the obligation to work full-time for all men from seventeen through sixty. There are about 1,300 private fishermen and an unknown number of private taxi drivers and cargo porters. The data in Table 26, however, probably do not take into account the total number of self-employed, who have been rapidly rising in the second half of the 1970s.

LABOR FORCE AND EMPLOYMENT BY ECONOMIC ACTIVITY

All available data on the distribution of the labor force by economic activity are presented in Table 27.[6] The Agricultural labor force increased slowly in the prerevolutionary years, probably stagnated in 1960–61 and declined thereafter so that by 1970 it was below the prerevolutionary level.[7] The industrial labor force increased in 1953–57 and probably continued growing, although at a lower rate, in 1959–60. This occurred "not as a result of an expansion of productive capacity but by a higher use of the existing capacity."[8] But in the early 1960s, there were a large number of shutdowns and slowdowns in factories and mines because of the lack of spare parts, raw materials, and chemicals that used to be imported for industry from the United States, as well as the significant exodus of technical and managerial personnel. To compound this problem, all nationalized state factories of the same production line were merged into *consolidados* or trusts to achieve economies of scale. And contrary to expectations, no significant expansion of industrial plants occurred in the first half of the 1960s. Hence by 1964 the industrial labor force had contracted, but it seemed to have significantly increased by 1970 (more on this later).

The construction labor force increased in 1953–58 and probably continued growing in 1959 and the first part of 1960, but it declined in the rest of 1960 and 1961 due to the paralysis of private construction. The latter was caused by the urban reform laws, which seized all rental houses and buildings and prohibited all future rental of real estate and abolished all mortgages. A slowdown of state construction was apparent also in 1963, but reportedly the labor force in this activity increased in 1964 and 1970 probably due to state construction of schools, hospitals, military installations, and agricultural facilities. Housing construction, though, significantly declined during the 1960s.

TABLE 27. Distribution of the Labor Force by Economic Activities, Selected Years 1953–70 (in thousands)

Economic Activities	1953	1956–57	1960–61	1964	1970	Average yearly change (%)	
						1953–56/57	1956/57–1970
Agriculture and fishing	819	855	862	838	786	1.2	−0.6
Industry and Mining	345	384	412	376	519	3.2	2.7
Construction	65	84	72	119	148	8.3	5.8
Transport and communication	104	105	86	90	167	0.3	1.5
Commerce	232	268	266	252	312	4.4	1.3
Services	396	418	[573	[833	603	1.6	3.4
Not Specified	11	90			71		
Labor Force	1,972	2,204	2,270	2,508	2,606	3.4	1.4

Sources: 1953 census and 1956–64 surveys reproduced in Mesa-Lago, *The Labor Force*, pp. 17 and 44. 1970 from JUCEPLAN, *Censo de Población y Viviendas 1970: Datos Fundamentales de la Población* (La Habana: Instituto Cubano del Libro, n.d.), pp. 100–101.

In transportation and communication, the labor force was stagnant in the prerevolutionary period and probably declined or was stagnant through most of the 1960s. This decline resulted from import restrictions, lack of spare parts, and wearing out and poor maintenance of buses, railroads, and taxi cabs. The merchant marine was the only sector expanding in this period. However, the labor force in transportation and communication apparently increased sharply in 1970.

The labor force in commerce increased in the prerevolutionary period but declined in 1960–64 because of rationing and the mergings and closing of numerous department stores, groceries, and other commerce shops. The 1970 census, however, reported a significant increase of trade workers in 1970.

The service sector is the one in which the largest increase of the labor force took place. It probably doubled between 1957 and 1964 for an addition of some 400,000 workers. This was a result of the significant expansion of the armed forces in the first half of the 1960s, as well as in the social services (education, health, and social security), and the booming bureaucracy in planning, central ministries, and other state agencies. The luxuriant bureaucracy, however, was trimmed in the second half of the 1960s through a series of measures to be discussed later, and hence the labor force in this activity had probably declined by some 200,000 workers in 1970.

The comparison of average annual labor force growth rates in 1953–57 and 1957–70 (last column of Table 27) shows for the Revolution a sharp increase in the rate of services, a moderate increase in transportation-communication, a slight decline in industry-mining, a moderate decline in agriculture, and sharp declines in commerce and construction. In absolute figures the economic activity growing most in 1957–70 was services (200,000 workers) and to a lesser extent industry (130,000)—the latter concentrated in 1970. Moderate increases were recorded in construction and transportation-communication (60,000 each) and even less in commerce (44,000), while agriculture contracted (-70,000). In comparison with 1970 overall averages for the region, Cuba's labor share of agriculture was substantially lower, that of industry moderately higher, and that of services considerably higher, but this was also true of the 1950s comparison.[9]

No information exists on the distribution of the labor force by economic activity for the 1970s; instead, only the distribution of state civilian employment is reported. The latter excludes military and private employment as well as unemployment. The series on state civilian employment is available for 1962–66 and 1971–76; the missing period in between would have allowed a comparison with the labor force in 1970. The complete series available on the distribution of state civilian employment by economic activity (reproduced in Table 28) show some surprising changes in the

TABLE 28. Distribution of State Civilian Employment by Economic Activity, 1962–66 and 1971–76 (in thousands)

Economic Activity	1962	1963	1964	1965	1966	1971	1972	1973	1974	1975	1976
Agriculture[a]	297	305	386	433	450	604	637	670	674	685	685
Industry[b]	267	289	303	309	323	440	438	453	467	472	477
Construction	104	97	108	117	118	133	154	177	184	208	243
Transportation[c]	74	83	82	84	83	175	177	182	186	187	199
Commerce[d]	132	207	220	220	242	168	166	177	184	179	179
Services[e]	209	257	270	289	301	562	554	587	618	660	686
Total	1,083	1,238	1,369	1,452	1,517	2,082	2,126	2,246	2,313	2,391	2,469

[a]Agriculture (sugar and nonsugar), cattle raising, fishing, and productive services.

[b]Manufacturing (sugar, food, construction materials, beverages and tobacco, chemistry, metallurgy), mining (including oil), electricity.

[c]Includes communications

[d]Domestic trade, acopio and distribution, foreign trade, restaurants, and similar services.

[e]"Nonproductive services": education, culture and research; health and social security; housing; sports and recreation; public administration and financing.

Sources: Boletín 1970, p. 34; Anuario 1975, p. 44; Anuario 1976, p. 53; and Banco Nacional de Cuba 1977, p.9.

figures between 1966 and 1971. Significant differences are evident also for 1962−70 in comparison to the labor force data reproduced in Table 27. Some of the differences between state civilian employment and labor force data can be explained by the exclusion from the former of private employment; part of the increases in the state civilian employment simply resulted from the absorption of private employment, thus as private employment is eliminated (except for agriculture), figures of state civilian employment and the labor force come closer. Still state civilian employment in services is substantially below the labor force in services because the latter adds military men, policemen, and security personnel. Unemployment also accounts for some differences as will be seen later.

In agriculture, differences between the labor force and state civilian employment can be fully explained by the transfer of jobs from private to state farms—probably with no net increase in employment since 1960−61. In industry, however, all remaining private employment was transferred to the state sector in 1968 during the Revolutionary Offensive. Hence since 1969, state and total industrial employment are equal and should be equal to the industrial labor force (minus unemployment). The increase in the industrial labor force reported in 1970, therefore, must have been short-lived employment expansion in the industrial-sugar sector during the gigantic harvest of that year. But state industrial employment in 1971 was 79,000 jobs below the 1970 industrial labor force, and declined again by 2,000 jobs in 1972. State industrial employment increased again in 1973−76 but in the last year was still 42,000 jobs below the 1970 industrial labor force mark.

In construction and transportation-communication, the differences are less significant and can be explained mostly by the transfer of jobs from the private to the state sector. In construction, nevertheless, there seemed to be a decline of some 15,000 jobs between 1970−71, although employment rapidly increased thereafter. Commerce presents an intriguing puzzle: the decline from 312,000 jobs (in the 1970 labor force) to 168,000 jobs (in the 1971 state civilian employment). As in industry, private commerce employment was reportedly eradicated in 1968, hence the difference of 144,000 jobs in one year was either a drastic cut of jobs in commerce or reveals that in spite of official rhetoric there were thousands of private merchants doing business in 1970, probably in the black market. Finally, in the service sector, both the labor force and the civilian employment data show an increasing trend, with the difference between the two resulting from changes in the size of the armed forces.

CHARACTERISTICS OF THE LABOR FORCE: AGE, SEX, AND RACE

Data on the distribution of the labor force by age and sex under the Revolution are available only from the 1970 census, although female participation rates have occasionally been given. Data on race, although collected, have not been published.

The distribution of the 1970 labor force by age and sex is reported in Table 29. Almost 53 percent of the labor force was concentrated in the 20–39 age bracket; more than 30 percent was in the 40–59 age bracket; and a combined 17 percent was either less than 20 or over 60. The female distribution shows a younger structure than the male one, as there are proportionally more women than men in the lower age brackets, this being the result of the increasing female participation in the labor force under the Revolution. The age distribution of the labor force in the 1953 census showed slightly higher proportions in the tails of the labor force. Expansion of compulsory education for children in elementary and secondary-school age, and of social security to all the population, accounts for the difference.

The incorporation of females into the labor force did not happen suddenly. It has been a long process that accelerated under the Revolution, particularly since the late 1960s (see Table 30). The rate of female participation in the labor force gradually increased from 10.3 percent in 1943 to 12.6 percent in 1956–57 and to 13.1 percent in 1958 (the 1953 census reported a rate of 17.1 perhaps an overestimation).[10] No data are available for 1959–67, but probably the rate in the latter year was only slightly above that of 1958. The manpower deficit in agriculture and the preparation for the 1970 sugar harvest induced a mobilization by the Federation of Cuban Women that resulted in an incorporation of

TABLE 29. Labor Force Distribution by Age and Sex, 1970

Age	Total		Males		Females	
	Thousands	Percent	Thousands	Percent	Thousands	Percent
10–14	7	0.3	5	0.2	2	0.4
15–19	254	9.7	192	9.0	63	13.1
20–29	782	30.0	613	28.9	168	34.9
30–39	594	22.8	480	22.6	113	23.5
40–49	454	17.4	376	17.7	79	16.4
50–59	334	12.8	290	13.6	44	9.2
60 and over	182	7.0	170	8.0	12	2.5
Total	2,607	100.0	2,126	100.0	481	100.0

Source: JUCEPLAN, *Censo de Población y Viviendas 1970*, p. 79.

TABLE 30. Female Incorporation in the Labor Force, 1956-58 and 1968-78

Years	Number of Females Employed (thousands)	Percentage of	
		State Civilian Employment	Labor Force
1956-57	277	—	12.6
1958	290	—	13.1
1968	407	23.1	15.8
1969	435	23.0	16.7
1970	474	23.0	18.0
1971	475	22.8	17.9
1972	479	22.5	17.9
1973	535	23.8	19.1
1974	590	25.5	20.6
1975	647	27.0	22.1
1976	705	28.5	23.7
1977	735	28.2	23.8
1978	761	28.1	24.2

Sources: Number of employed females in 1956/57 from Mesa-Lago, "The Labor Force," p. 22; 1958 *La población de Cuba (La Habana: Editorial Ciencias Sociales, 1976)*, p. 176; 1968 Rodríguez, *Cuba, ejemplo de América*, p. 61; 1969–72 *Anuario 1972*, pp.21, 34; 1973 and 1978 Roberto Veiga,"Informe Central al XIV Congreso de la CTC," *Granma*, 1 December 1978, p. 5; 1974 F. Castro, "Speech in the Closing Session of the 2nd Congress of the FMC," *Granma Weekly Review*, 8 December 1974, p. 271; 1975 F. Castro, "Main Report to the 1st Congress of the PCC," *Granma Weekly Review*, 4 January 1976, p. 5; 1976 *Anuario 1976*, p. 54; 1977 and 1978 author's estimates. State civilian employment and labor force from Table 26 infra.

some 84,000 females in the labor force in 1968-69,[11] and possibly 40,000 more in 1970. Hence, female participation rates rapidly increased from 15.8 percent in 1968 to 18 percent in 1970. However in 1971-72 the employment of females was stagnant, with declining rates in relation to 1970. A new campaign for the incorporation of females began in 1973, resulting in a rapid increase in the participation rate to 24.2 percent in 1978. The goal for 1980 was a rate of 33 percent, but it was not fulfilled.[12] The average annual rate of growth of female participation in the labor force in 1943-1956/57 was 0.28 percent. It increased to 0.33 percent in 1958, stagnated at 0.34 percent in 1959-72, and increased to 1.05 percent in 1973-78. In terms of civilian employment, the increase in the female rate of participation is less impressive—from 23 percent in 1968 to 28 percent in 1978. This difference is due to the fact that total state civilian employment expanded much faster than the labor force because of the absorption of the private sector.

As the first segment of Table 31 demonstrates, in 1970 more than two-thirds of the female workers were concentrated in the tertiary sector: 42 percent in services and 24 percent in commerce as compared to 19 and 9 percent for males. About one-fourth of females were in industry, a similar proportion to males, but less than 8 percent were in agriculture, as compared to 35 percent for males. A comparison with the percentage distribution of the female labor force by economic activity in 1953 does show slight increases for 1970 in the shares of agriculture, industry, construction, transportation, and communications, but an increase of almost 16 percentage points in commerce and a decline of 23 percentage points in services. The share of services in 1943, however, was similar to that in 1970. Prior to the Revolution, about one-fifth of employed females were domestic servants; their number sharply declined thereafter, although the occupation has not disappeared altogether. Female additions to the labor force and most former domestic servants found jobs under the Revolution mainly in the social services and commerce. The second segment of Table 31 shows that the highest rate of female participation by economic activity in 1970 was in commerce (37 percent) and services (33 percent), with a much lower rate in industry (19 percent) and even less in other economic activities (from 2 to 5 percent). Within certain social services, the rate of female participation was even higher—for example, 57 percent in education and 60 percent in health, and the same is true of the garment industry where the rate was 78 percent.[13] Significant improvement has occurred under the Revolution in overall incorporation of females into the labor force and abandonment of domestic service chores, but the female in Cuba makes up less than one-fourth of the labor force and continues to be concentrated

TABLE 31. Distribution of the Labor Force by Sex and Economic Activity, 1970

Economic Activities	Males		Females		Percent of participation		
	Thousands	Percent	Thousands	Percent	Male	Female	Total
Agriculture	748.2	35.3	38.0	7.9	95.2	4.8	100.0
Industry	419.8	19.7	99.8	20.7	80.8	19.2	100.0
Construction	145.3	6.8	3.0	0.6	97.9	2.1	100.0
Transport	147.3	6.9	4.2	0.9	97.2	2.8	100.0
Communication	9.0	0.4	6.9	1.4	56.6	4.4	100.0
Commerce	197.7	9.3	114.2	23.7	63.4	36.6	100.0
Social Services	404.0	19.0	199.3	41.5	67.0	33.0	100.0
Others	54.8	2.6	16.0	3.3	77.4	22.6	100.0
Totals	2,126.1	100.0	481.4	100.0	81.5	18.5	100.0

Source: JUCEPLAN, *Censo de Población y Viviendas 1970*, pp. 100–101.

in activities associated with conventional women's roles such as nursing, teaching, child care, restaurant services, garment industry, and the like. Various obstacles exist to a more rapid incorporation of females into the labor force and ascension to more male-dominated occupations: the increasingly difficult task of creating new jobs in the late 1970s and in the 1980s; the still traditional family roles played by Cuban females in relation to males; the difficulties of getting to work because of insufficient day-care centers and transportation problems; and the smaller probabilities of being promoted due to widespread perception that family obligations would interfere with performance and duties required by upper-level positions.[14] The guidelines for the 1981–85 plan set as a goal the maintenance of the current proportion of female participation in the labor force.[15]

The questionnaire for the 1970 census included a section on race, to be filled in by the census taker choosing from four categories—white, black, mulatto, and yellow.[16] The various publications coming out of the census, however, have not included any information on race, not even for the population as a whole. A study published in 1976 by the Center for Demographic Studies analyzed the Cuban population and included a section on race and ethnicity that compared race in all Cuban census except for that of 1970.[17] A Cuban-born scholar, who had access in Havana to the complete census report, noticed that the section dealing with race had been extracted and could not get any Cuban officials to discuss this issue.[18]

Prior to the Revolution only the 1943 census provided data on employment and unemployment by race. From such data it was apparent that blacks were overrepresented in domestic service and manual jobs while underrepresented in occupations requiring advanced training. It also showed that blacks suffered from a higher unemployment rate than whites.[19] Through the expansion of education and employment opportunities for all, particularly among the low-income strata where blacks were also concentrated, the Revolution significantly improved the job situation of blacks. Yet traces of employment inequality persist. One U.S. black militant and one U.S. white scholar who lived several years in Cuba in the second half of the 1960s reported that very few blacks held top positions in the government, the party, and the administration of state enterprises; however, a disproportionate number of blacks still performed menial jobs as maids, street cleaners, garbage collectors, and ditchdiggers.[20] Domínguez has also argued that the Revolution has had little impact in increasing the black share of the elite. Only nine of the one hundred members appointed to the Central Committee of the party in 1965 were black or mulatto, about one-third of what should be a proportional representation in terms of the number of blacks in the population. In the armed forces, he reported that in the early

1970s blacks were overrepresented at the troop level and under-represented at the officer level.[21] Very few blacks occupy positions in the top government hierarchy such as the presidency, deputy vice-presidents, ministers, and directors of state committees. On the other hand, according to official sources, 28.4 percent of the delegates elected to the municipal assemblies in 1976 were either black or mulatto, and Lourdes Casal has reported that 36.2 percent of the delegates to the National Assembly in 1978 were black.[22] It seems that in elected positions for the Organs of People's Power established in the second half of the 1970s, a conscious effort has been made to raise black representation.

UNEMPLOYMENT AND UNDEREMPLOYMENT: FACTS AND POLICIES

The 1943 population census estimated unemployment at 21.1 percent of the labor force, but this census was taken in the midst of the sugar dead season when unemployment was at its highest; however, the 1953 population census, taken in the midst of the sugar harvest, calculated the unemployment rate as only 8.4 percent. A weekly sample taken from May 1956 to April 1957, checking for seasonal fluctuations, showed that unemployment declined from a high of 20.7 percent, in the midst of the dead season, to 9 percent in the midst of the harvest, these proportions being similar to those respectively given by the 1943 and 1953 census. The average annual unemployment rate was estimated at 16.4 percent and the underemployment rate at 13.8 percent. The latter was roughly measured by adding unpaid family workers and paid workers employed less than 30 hours per week. Additional monthly samples taken in 1957 and 1958 reported average annual unemployment rates of 12.4 and 11.8 percent (see Table 32) and underemployment rates of 7.6 and 7.2 percent. These figures suggested a decline in both phenomena in relation to 1956–57.[23]

Under the Revolution, the monthly samples of unemployment and underemployment were continued from January 1959 until March 1961, when they ceased. The average unemployment rate increased to 13.6 percent in 1959 but declined to 11.8 percent in 1960, while the underemployment rate rose to 12.1 percent for both years. And yet a labor census conducted by the Ministry of Labor in April of 1960 (toward the end of the harvest) registered a very high unemployment rate of 20.4 percent, a proportion similar to that recorded in 1943 and in 1956–57 in the midst of the dead season; however, this census probably overestimated unemployment somewhat. The Ministry of Labor calculated the underemployment rate in 1960 at 16.3 percent, higher than the annual averages derived from the monthly sample taken in 1960 and 1956–57. But the monthly samples taken in January-March

TABLE 32. Open Unemployment in Cuba, 1957–78

Years	Labor Force (thousands)	Unemployment (thousands)	Percent
1957	2,214	275	12.4
1958	2,218	262	11.8
1959	2,251	307	13.6
1960	2,276	269	11.8
1961	2,338	242	10.3
1962	2,401	215	9.0
1963	2,431	198	8.1
1964	2,456	185	7.5
1965	2,490	163	6.5
1966	2,508	155	6.2
1967	2,549	135	5.3
1968	2,579	110	4.3
1969	2,608	75	2.9
1970	2,638	34	1.3
1971	2,652	55	2.1
1972	2,680	64	2.4
1973	2,795	84	3.0
1974	2,869	111	3.9
1975	2,923	90	3.1
1976	2,974	85	2.8
1977	3,075	60	2.0
1978	3,140	40	1.3

Sources: 1957–61 based on Carmelo Mesa-Lago, *The Labor Force, Employment, Unemployment and Underemployment in Cuba: 1899–1970* (Beverly Hills: Sage Publications, 1972), pp. 27, 36. Rest from Table 26 infra.

1961 suggested a decline in both unemployment and underemployment rates in relation to the same months in 1959 and 1960. In the next ten years no census and possibly no systematic surveys of unemployment were taken. Figures on underemployment have not been published again, while only occasional, unofficial estimates of unemployment have been released—and these are often contradictory.[24]

The 1970 population census registered a low number of unemployed (33,855) for a rate of only 1.3 percent of the labor force, probably the lowest in Latin America. The National Bank reported a lower figure of 0.6 percent for the same year, perhaps because it only took into account those unemployed not seeking jobs for the first time.[25] Since 1970 no figures have been released on unemployment. Trying to fill this vacuum, I have developed in Table 32 rough estimates of the number of unemployed and the corresponding rates over the labor force. These figures suggest that unemployment sharply increased in 1959, steadily dipped since 1961, reached a trough in 1970, then rose slowly in 1971–74 to decline again in 1975–78.

Who were the unemployed at the beginning of and during the first decade of the Revolution? This question is partly answered by assembling and comparing all available data in Table 33. Most of the unemployed both before and after the Revolution were males, but as the proportion of the male labor force declined so did the proportion of the male unemployed; unemployment rates, higher among males than among females prior to the Revolution, declined in size and became almost equal in 1970. Distribution by age, only available for 1970, shows that 63 percent of the unemployed were concentrated in the 17–24 age brackets, with

TABLE 33. Characteristics of the Unemployed in Cuba, 1956–57, 1960, and 1970 (percentage distribution in each category)

Characteristics	1956–57	1960	1970
Sex			
Male	88.2	64.8	80.8
Female	11.8	35.2	19.2
Age			
17–19			20.8
20–24			42.1
25–34			20.4
35–60			16.7
Length			
Searching job for first time			44.6
Other			55.4
Occupation			
Agriculture		16.5	
Industry and mining		30.7	
Transport and communication		3.6	
Commerce		9.3	
Services		14.0	
Others		25.9	
Location			
Urban	68.7		74.2
Rural	31.3		25.8
Provinces			
Pinar del Río	4.8	7.8	2.9
Havana	21.5	39.4	38.5
Matanzas	8.9	4.9	4.7
Las Villas	22.9	15.9	14.8
Camagüey	12.0	7.6	8.2
Oriente	29.0	24.4	30.9

Sources: 1956–57 and 1960 from Mesa-Lago, *The Labor Force*, pp. 22, 38. 1970 computations based on Junta Central de Planificación, *Censo de Población y Viviendas 1970: Datos Fundamentales de la Población* (La Habana: Instituto del Libro, n.d.), pp. 74–97.

the remaining 37 percent in the 25–59 bracket. No unemployment rates were reported in 1970 below 17 years or above 60 years (this, again, a result of universalization of education and social security). Composition by race, although collected in 1970, has not been released. Close to half of the unemployed in 1970 were searching jobs for the first time, suggesting that unemployment was largely frictional in nature. The distribution of unemployment by occupation, only available for 1960, detects the highest concentration in industry, followed by services-commerce, and agriculture (despite the fact that the sugar harvest was still underway). Under the Revolution, the unemployed became more concentrated in urban areas and in the old province of Havana where the capital city is. Declines were registered in other provinces—except perhaps for Oriente. In summary the typical unemployed under the Revolution is a male, between 17 and 24 years of age, searching for a job for the first time, an urbanite possibly living in Havana, and with an occupational orientation in industry or services.

Massive and chronic open unemployment, a socioeconomic plague of the prerevolutionary era, was practically eradicated in the first decade of the Revolution. Although unemployment increased in the first half of the 1970s, its magnitude did not even approximate the levels of the late 1950s and early 1960s. This significant feat was accomplished through four means: the exportation of part of the labor force abroad, which opened about 200,000 jobs in Cuba in the 1960s; the removal from the labor market of those below 17 and above 62 years of age through expanding education and social security; the elimination of seasonal unemployment in the countryside through a combination of rural-to-urban migration with overstaffing in state farms, which guarantee jobs throughout the year; and the expansion of employment in social services, the armed forces, and the bureaucracy coupled with overstaffing in industry and subsidies to redundant urban workers, which avoided open unemployment in the cities. In the early 1960s open unemployment was basically transformed into underemployment and disguised unemployment concentrated in urban areas, but the revolutionaries hoped to absorb the surplus through productive jobs generated by rapid industrialization. When the development strategy shifted in 1964 in favor of agriculture and industrialization was postponed, the leadership attempted to transfer the urban labor surplus to the countryside, particularly the sugar sector, which by then suffered from an acute artificial manpower deficit. In the 1970s several problems combined to create a resurgence of unemployment: the new concern for raising productivity, which brought into the open disguised unemployment and underemployment; the reduction in the size of the armed forces and the attempt to slow down the growth of social services—two major absorbers of unemployment in the 1960s; the entering into the labor market of increasing numbers of females as well as the young adults from the baby boom of the 1960s; and the sharp reduction in the number of emigrants in the 1970s (from 56,000 in 1970 to 3,000 in 1975). A detailed explanation of these policies follows and three stages are distinguished: 1959–63, 1964–70, and the 1970s.[26]

1959–63 Policies

In agriculture, seasonal unemployment was rapidly absorbed through various means. A large rural-to-urban migration occurred that was encouraged by peasant mobilizations to the city and recruitment by the armed forces, thus the population of Havana increased in 1960 more than twice the average annual growth of the 1950s. Many of the migrants found employment in the army, state security, the police, unions and other mass organizations, public works, and personal services; others joined the number of unemployed and underemployed in the cities. Thousands of young peasants received scholarships, which precluded their entry into the labor force. Land ownership granted by the agrarian reform did not increase employment because most of the new farm owners worked the same land before as sharecroppers, lessers, and so forth. State farms, however, gave stable employment throughout the year to many peasants previously affected by seasonal unemployment. Private farmers increased their own consumption and bartered or marketed a small agricultural surplus and relaxed. State farmers no longer feared unemployment, received a minimum wage and state services, and were not under strict labor discipline. Lacking incentives and checks, they reduced their labor effort; productivity declined and absenteeism grew. An investigation conducted in 1963 on 136 state farms revealed that employees only worked an average of 4.5 to 5 hours daily but were paid for 8 hours. The slackened labor effort created an artificial manpower deficit, particularly acute in the sugar harvest, which previously was handled by the seasonally unemployed. In a typical vicious circle, managers of state farms reinforced overstaffing by hiring new employees. As the vice-chairman of INRA acknowledged, "The explanation of the labor shortage in agriculture is very easy; if a worker does not work eight hours and, in addition, his productivity is very low, then two or three men must be employed instead of one."[27] Bureaucratic jobs in state farms also rose significantly, something Castro revealed in a personal anecdote: "The place where I was born and brought up, which was a latifundia, had one or two office clerks; now it is a state farm and has twelve office clerks. . . ."[28]

The labor surplus accumulated in the cities could not be productively employed in the early 1960s by the industrial sector because the contraction in the old industry—mostly U.S. made—

was not compensated by the small expansion of new industries bought from socialist countries; hence overstaffing and subsidies also occurred. But shutdowns and slowdowns in mines and factories were not followed by massive lay-offs. While many idle workers were kept on the payroll as *excedentes* or surplus, a good number were fired—a decision apparent in the high concentration of unemployment in industry registered in the 1960 labor census. The policies of merging of factories, elimination of unnecessary jobs either because they were no longer needed (such as advertising) or because they were duplicated, and promotion of mechanization in such areas as cigar making, sugar packing, and transportation and bulk-loading also generated a labor surplus. Instead of being laid off, these workers joined the ranks of the *excedentes* waiting for a transfer to productive jobs. By mid-1961 thousands of *excedentes* were kept on the payroll of the enterprises; Castro gave as a typical example a factory whose payroll had 200 workers but only 30 were really needed. Several laws were passed to train the *excedentes* and get them productively employed, but in 1963 the problem persisted—as a government economist acknowledged: "It is not a mystery that we are living today in the midst of an environment of disguised unemployment, having a large number of unnecessary personnel."[29]

Cuban leaders and planners had great expectations of absorbing the urban labor surplus through installation of a number of factories to be provided by socialist countries. But in 1962, Minister of Industry Ernesto Guevara acknowledged that in the four-year period ending in 1965 "none of the basic industries acquired from socialist countries will be in operation yet" hence "we cannot say yet that the new industries are reducing unemployment."[30] The new factories finally installed in Cuba were highly mechanized and generated little employment, in fact the industrial labor force in 1964 was smaller than in 1960 (see Table 27). Thus Cuban planners discovered in the early 1960s what the Chinese had realized a few years before—that because of technological progress in the thirty years since the Soviet "miracle" of rapid unemployment absorption through industrialization, it was difficult to replicate that experience. "The tendency toward a relative abundance of labor in the cities is going to increase in response to the elimination of redundant personnel and the degree of technology of the new factories. This is a problem that Cuba will have to cope with in the years to come."[31] The Economic Commission for Latin America has noted that the existence of a large manpower surplus made it unadvisable to introduce mechanization techniques that replaced manpower; nevertheless, the Cubans have tried to incorporate the most advanced technology available.[32]

Only a few of the unemployed could find jobs in state construction in 1959, but employment dwindled in 1960–61, and probably did not expand again until 1964. The situation was even worse in transportation-communication and commerce where the labor force contracted in 1960–64. Personal services were also sharply reduced for these reasons: the disappearance of thousands of jobs in insurance, real estate, and legal offices as a result of the nationalization wave of 1960; the eclipse of jobs in casinos, hotels, and resorts emptied by the absence of 300,000 foreign tourists; and the sharp decline in domestic service. On the other hand, self-employment in services such as repair work, seamstresses and tailors, hairdressers, and so forth increased when the black market boom began in 1962.

Most of the unemployed found jobs in the state service sector, which increased twofold (some 400,000 jobs) between 1958 and 1964 (see Table 27). Many were employed by the armed forces, which reached 386,000 jobs in 1964. Another large group got employment in state administered social services while a significant contingent became employed in state administration. The bureaucratic inflation reached such alarming size in 1964 that Castro acknowledged and criticized it in a series of speeches:

> Where there is one bureaucratic employee in excess in an unnecessary position, there is a man living at the expense of the workers. . . . In small enterprises where the former capitalist owners maintained few employees, we now see three to four times that number. . . . It is necessary that we avoid the inception of a parasite class living at the expense of productive work. . . . We have accomplished nothing if previously we worked for the capitalist and now we work for another type of person who is not a capitalist, but who consumes much and produces nothing. . . . The standards of living of the people cannot be raised while what one produces must be divided among three.[33]

1964–70 Policies

When in 1963–64 the industrialization program was postponed and the development effort shifted to agriculture, the Cuban leaders faced a manpower surplus in urban areas composed of the unemployed, subsidized laid-off workers in industry, and excessive bureaucracy in services along with an artificial manpower deficit in agriculture. Thus a vigorous effort was undertaken in 1964–70 to correct the labor unbalance by curtailing rural-to-urban migration, measuring the maximum labor force to be efficiently employed, dismissing redundant employees, and transferring the urban labor surplus to the countryside.

In 1964 Castro announced that rural-to-urban migration would be stopped because "there are more than enough workers in the cities to provide manpower for any new industry or service that is created."[34] The state monopoly of employment was the key for migration control. Three measures were mainly used: issuance of a compulsory identification labor card indispensable to request employment followed later by a labor booklet with a complete file of the workers' activities; the need to have authorization from the Ministry of Labor for employment transfers; and the restriction of ration cards for one specific location thus limiting labor mobility. The effectiveness of these steps is seen in the decline in the rate of growth for the city of Havana. While in 1960–61 Havana grew by an average rate of 4.4 percent, that rate declined to 2.1 percent in 1964, 1.5 percent in 1965, and 0.9 percent in 1966.[35]

Real manpower needs were to be measured by Soviet-style work quotas introduced in 1964–65 that fixed the quantity of labor each worker must produce in physical or time units.[36] It was then estimated that 2.4 percent of the labor force (some 60,000 workers) were unnecessary. Protests in some factories badly hit by lay-offs prompted a reaction from the Minister of Labor: "It is necessary to dispose of the redundant manpower now because as the factories belong to the workers these must be placed where they are most needed."[37] But enforcement of work quotas was weakened in the Mao-Guevarist stage, and reportedly by 1970 levels achieved in 1965 had been lost.[38]

The task of reducing the number of administrative jobs was entrusted to Commissions for the Struggle Against Bureaucratism established in 1965–67 throughout the country, especially in Havana. Laid-off workers were sent to a "labor reserve" and paid their salary until they could be retrained and transferred to other jobs. Approximately one percent of the labor force (22,000 workers) was determined to be redundant and laid off, half of them in Havana; however, only one-third were reemployed (mostly shifted from one bureaucratic job to another) and the rest kept waiting or studying while paid by the state. Thus at the end of 1966 Castro denounced the bureaucratization of the Commission of Struggle Against Bureaucratism, announced harsh sanctions for the violators, and appointed an investigative committee. This group found that 43 percent of all laid-off employees since 1965 had been reemployed in enterprises that had just been cleared of bureaucrats. A new wave of lay-offs followed reaching 31,500 or 1.2 percent of the labor force by the end of 1967. At that time one-third were still waiting or studying while two-thirds were reemployed, although no information was provided on where they got the new jobs. I suspect that many of the laid-off workers in the late 1960s were recruited into the gigantic mobilization for the 1969–70 sugar harvest or in construction activities—much of which was also linked to the harvest in activities like building new roads or repairing old ones to facilitate transportation of sugar cane. Another part may have stayed in urban areas, going into commerce (black market activities) or working their way back to the bureaucratic haven. This may explain the big jump in industrial and commerce activities reported by the 1970 census.

The transfer of part of the urban surplus to the countryside was attempted through three measures: introduction in 1964 of the Compulsory Military Service, which recruited an annual average of 100,000 youngsters using most of them in agricultural work throughout the three-year draft; organization of labor brigades integrated by some 50,000 young people recruited in nonproductive jobs who signed three-year contracts to work in agriculture; and increase in the mobilization of voluntary labor (mostly urbanites in nonproductive jobs) for the sugar and other harvests from 106,000 in 1966 to 302,000 in 1968 to 700,000 in 1970. Poor organization of voluntary work and the lack of skills of the volunteers resulted in considerable waste of time and resources. Voluntary labor was often used without real need for it, in other cases the volunteers spent hours waiting to be transported to the fields only to remain idle when arriving because of the lack of needed tools. A final liability was that the cost of mobilizing, feeding, and providing the volunteers with seeds and tools was higher that the meager product created by that inefficient labor force.[39] The fizzle of the 1970 harvest mobilization and the subsequent increase in workers' absenteeism to 20 percent of the labor force made evident the failure and induced a revision of the employment policies of the second half of the 1960s.

1970s Policies

The fundamental change in the employment policy of the 1970s was that, for the first time, productivity took priority over employment creation. In other words, new jobs should be productive or not created at all. In 1971 it was initially estimated that the nation needed 300,000 additional jobs, but that figure was soon reduced to 48,000. The Soviet system of work quotas began to be reintroduced after 1971, and hence "tens of thousands" of unnecessary workers began to be released again. Samples taken nationally in 1972 showed that employment had been cut by one percent. To compound the problem, the size of the armed forces was cut down from 200,000 men in 1970 to 185,000 in 1973. In 1972, then president Osvaldo Dorticós reported unemployment pockets in the provinces of Las Villas and Oriente.[40] By the end of 1973, Castro acknowledged that the employment pendulum was swinging the other way and announced "the time may come when we will have a headache finding jobs for all those who want to work." He promised, however, that solutions would be found to avoid the return of an army of the unemployed.[41] As indicated in Table 32, unemployment probably increased from 33,855 in 1970 to some 111,000 men in 1974, raising the unemployment rate from 1.3 to 3.9 percent.

To cope with the problem, several steps were taken. Retirement became more flexible in 1971, and the number of those retiring sharply increased in 1972–76, thus opening new jobs (see chapter 7). In November 1973 the Confederation of Cuban Workers (CTC) agreed to modify regulations passed in 1967, when the manpower deficit was acute, which reserved certain types of service jobs for females in order to force males into fields in which their physical strength was necessary. Since conditions had changed, such service jobs were reopened to male workers. In 1976 the number of jobs from which women were barred due to health or safety reasons was expanded, which in effect opened these positions for males.[42] In 1974 the government announced that future industrial plants would be concentrated in Havana and two other heavily urbanized provinces because there was an "abundant labor supply" in those provinces.[43] The 1976–80 five-year plan also called for a significant increase in construction, a good part of it in the beautification of the city of Havana and housing mainly in urban areas, thus opening new jobs.

Agriculture continues to be plagued by underemployment due to the difficulties in implementing work quotas in this sector. In the sugar sector "underemployment still subsists because the seasonal nature of the industry forces the maintenance year around of a high number of workers who are not fully utilized in [the dead season]."[44] At the end of 1979, Raúl Castro referred to "a good many instances today, especially in agriculture, of people . . . working no more than four or six hours [instead of the expected eight]."[45]

Released workers from the application of work quotas (called *disponibles* or available, a similar name to the *excedentes* of the 1960s) were expected to be retrained and rapidly transferred to productive jobs. And yet, in 1975, the Secretary General of the CTC, Roberto Veiga, complained that many of them had been assigned to "superfluous activities as an underutilized labor force" or were not transferred and received a salary without working.[46] A decree enacted in 1976 established a time limit for payment of a sort of unemployment compensation, as well as the obligation of the *disponible* to accept an adequate job, and decentralized the task of transferring the jobless. But in 1978, Veiga repeated the charges he had voiced in 1975, adding that many disponibles had received several job offers but turned them down as inadequate. "All this," he said, "has put a heavy burden on the economy; part of the resources we save on one hand are wasted on the other."[47] As in the 1960s, the redundant worker has apparently found ways to cheat the system and keep collecting his salary without working.

In 1976 a law was enacted legalizing the private practice of hairdressers, manicurists, gardeners, taxi drivers, photographers, electricians, carpenters, auto mechanics, laundresses, tailors, seamstresses, bootblacks, and even professionals such as physicians and dentists. Candidates for these jobs have to register, request a license, and pay a monthly self-employment tax that ranges from 5 to 58 pesos. In occupations in which manpower is hard to find, workers should have a regular state job and are allowed to exercise their private activity only after work hours and on week-ends. In other cases, however, people can be working full-time for the private sector, although they cannot hire workers as employees. In the first month the law was enforced, 2,000 received licenses to be street peddlers in the city of Havana alone. In 1979, a high planning-official said that there were 100,000 private workers outside of agriculture although he did not specify if these were working full or part-time. Although the official reason given for this dramatic change of the 1968 ban against these private activities was the improvement of service to the people, one cannot but see it also as a way to provide new jobs.[48]

Cuba's involvement in Africa provided the justification for a new expansion of the armed forces from an estimated 185,000 men in 1974 (when unemployment peaked) to 230,000 in 1978. And Castro also announced that certain professionals in abundant supply, such as physicians and dentists, will be exported both as a way to help underdeveloped nations and to generate revenue for the state. One could add a third reason—to siphon off surplus labor.

As a result of the above-mentioned policies, estimated unemployment steadily declined in 1975–78, which in the latter year possibly reached the low rate registered in the 1970 census of 1.3 percent. And yet since 1977 the baby boom of the 1960s began to enter the labor market and will go on through the 1980s. The deterioration of the Cuban economy in 1979–80 and the stabilization of the military force abroad aggravated unemployment again. In late 1979 Castro and Humberto Pérez acknowledged that the increase in the labor force combined with slow economic growth, insufficient resources for development, and the emphasis in productivity would generate a labor surplus until the end of the 1980s, when the decline in the birth rate of the 1970s will be felt.[49] Castro, estimated that "tens of thousands of youth [will be] out of work." Besides thousands of construction workers, from 60,000 to 70,000 factory workers became temporarily laid off due to a shortfall in raw materials.[50] In March 1980, Castro reported that "the employment problem [was] a real, objective one" and that the highest labor surplus was located in the eastern provinces, the ones where "the population explosion was the greatest." He indicated that the exportation of the surplus was a way to tackle the problem and gave as examples the thousands of technicians and construction workers who were abroad; earlier he had suggested that 10,000 workers could be sent to Siberia to cut lumber.[51] In the great exodus of April-August 1980, males in productive ages were predominant and many reported they were unemployed, hence the labor surplus may have been cut by 30,000 to 40,000 workers. Other measures to cope with unemployment have been to relax the vagrancy law allowing even more people to work in the private sector, to give administrators of state enterprises and agencies more freedom to hire manpower including part-time workers, to permit those who have land to cultivate anything they want and raise animals, and to sell the agricultural surplus in the free market. Those temporarily laid off are paid 70 percent of their wages and can work in marginal shores and keep the extra income.[52]

LABOR PRODUCTIVITY: FROM UNCONSCIOUS NEGLECT TO NATIONAL CONCERN

The Economic Commission for Latin America has summarized the negative impact on productivity of the Revolutionary employment policy, particularly that of the 1960s, as follows: "The generalized absorption of the unemployed, necessary under a social viewpoint, provoked various distortions in the economy. One was the decline in productivity [because] it was not possible initially to create all the needed jobs to absorb, in a productive manner, all that manpower."[53] Guevara was one of the few Cuban leaders who became aware, early in the Revolution, of the trade-off between underemployment and productivity. He asked in a labor meeting in 1962: "What is better for the nation, to maintain the absurd inefficiency of our industries so that everybody works and receives a disguised subsidy, or to increase productivity to the maximum?" He answered: "It is much better to increase labor productivity even if it brings about the problems of lay-offs."[54] It was not until 1970, however, that productivity became a national concern and was raised from bottom to first priority as an economic goal. Castro called attention to the problem using as an example the manufacturing sector of the sugar industry where employment increased by 38 percent in 1970 over 1958 (from 91,655 to 126,643 workers) without any substantial increase in output. After complaining that this, typical of many other industries, was no way to create wealth he candidly acknowledged:

> At the time [of the triumph of the Revolution] we practically had to invent jobs in order to give all those [unemployed] people work. . . . Nobody ever mentioned the matter of productivity as a fundamental thing. . . . Our population [and labor force] has increased, and yet, in some items, production is no higher; in fact it's lower. . . . What is this bottomless pit that swallows up this country's human resources . . . the country's wealth, the material goods that we need so badly? It's nothing but inefficiency, nonproductivity, and low produc-

tivity. . . . Everybody, every branch of the economy and practically every work center, is guilty of the same crime.[55]

This policy resulted in obvious gains for the former unemployed (about 16 percent of the labor force) in the way of a stable job and guaranteed annual income. The former unemployed became a steady consumer of goods and services but, in most cases, did not contribute significantly to an increase of output. Since demand increased and supply was stagnant or lagged behind, the cost of "eliminating" open unemployment was borne by the majority of the population, the formerly employed, in the way of "socialist inflation" and reduced consumption (more on this in chapter 7).

Lack of data in socialist Cuba precludes a formal analysis both of total factor productivity as well as any serious discussion of questions such as the amount of capital per worker, economies of scale, technological change, and the like. In Table 34, I roughly estimated labor productivity by dividing GSP by employment in the productive sector. However, the series starts in 1962, the worst economic year of the Revolution, when productivity probably had declined. Moreover, the methodology used overestimates productivity in some sectors, particularly agriculture.[56]

When the policy of full employment was pushed largely by artificial job creation in the first half of the 1960s, labor productivity declined steadily and dramatically in three major sectors (agriculture, industry, and commerce) and increased in three minor sectors (communications, construction, and transportation). In overall terms, productivity only rose significantly in 1964 and to a lesser extent in 1965 possibly as a result of the introduction of work quotas. But these never worked well in agriculture as the vice-chairman of INRA recognized in 1966: "Labor productivity is very low. . . . Output standards have not attained a substantial increase in productivity. . . . "[57] In 1967–70, under the Mao-Guevarist philosophy, enforcement of work quotas was neglected due to the belief that everybody would spontaneously work in an efficient manner. This, combined with overstaffing, the significant increase in the use of low-productive or unproductive voluntary labor, and slackened labor effort due to poor economic incentives, resulted in a catastrophic decline in labor productivity. As seen in Table 34, all lines of production— except for transportation and commerce— sharply declined between 1966 and 1970. The slight increase in those two sectors may have been the result of inflation, which as explained in chapter 3, mostly affects commerce and transportation.

The reintroduction of work quotas began in 1971 and gradually expanded to 65 percent of state civilian employment in 1976. In the following year, the connection between wages and labor productivity had also been established for 26 percent of the

TABLE 34. Labor Productivity by Economic Sectors and Overall Rates; 1962–66 and 1970–76 (1962–66 in constant prices; 1970–76 in current prices)

Years[a]	Index Numbers: 1962 = 100[b]						Overall Productivity Rate[c]
	Agriculture	Industry	Construction	Transport	Communication	Commerce	
1962	100.0	100.0	100.0	100.0	100.0	100.0	
1963	93.6	90.8	100.9	89.7	106.6	65.2	0.1
1964	78.4	90.2	109.8	102.2	117.7	67.6	6.0
1965	78.3	91.6	125.4	102.0	124.2	67.9	1.3
1966	73.1	86.0	123.3	110.6	134.4	61.8	−2.1
1970	68.3	76.2	87.6	112.4	111.0	84.2	
1971	60.2	92.3	121.1	105.3	90.5	102.3	
1972	60.2	98.9	146.7	104.1	86.2	143.1	
1973	59.9	107.0	169.8	105.9	84.0	164.0	
1974	62.2	112.2	180.1	111.7	84.5	195.0	5.0
1975	64.2	124.9	190.1	131.8	90.0	254.5	7.1
1976	67.6	127.3	172.5	126.2	92.2	240.9	

[a]The years 1967–69 are missing because of the lack of the distribution of state civilian employment for those years. I estimated the distribution of 1970 using data from the 1970 census and the 1971 distribution of civilian employment.

[b]Value of GSP in each sector divided by the number of state civilian workers employed in each sector.

[c]Official figures; labor productivity growth rates.

Sources: Productivity in economic sectors calculated by the author as explained in footnote 56 based on data for Tables 11 and 28 infra. Official rates from *Boletín 1966*, p. 20; "Comportamiento de la economía en 1974," *Economía y Desarrollo*, 34 (March-April 1976): 5; and Osvaldo Dorticós, "XV Aniversario del Ministerio de Comercio Exterior," *Economía y Desarrollo*, 35 (May-June 1976): 12.

civilian labor force.[58] In addition, voluntary labor was drastically cut: in the 1960s, enterprises did not absorb the cost of voluntary labor and hence were not concerned with the waste of time of the volunteers, but now they have to pay both wages and transportation of the volunteers hence they became very careful in using it.[59] Finally, economic incentives were reintroduced and labor discipline tightened somewhat. As a result, labor productivity rose in all sectors except in communications and agriculture, the latter partly due to difficulties with implementing work quotas. In 1973 Raúl Castro reported that in many state farms, labor costs alone exceeded the value of production, giving as an example a farm in which the wage bill was 48,000 pesos, while the value of output was 8,000 pesos thus resulting in a loss of at least 40,000 pesos.[60] The average annual rate of productivity increase for 1971–74 was officially reported at 9 percent.[61] The highest productivity increases were registered in commerce (largely due to inflation), construction, industry and transport. In agriculture, productivity increased after 1974, but still the level of 1976 was two-thirds that of 1962, which had been an awful economic year. In 1976 productivity declined in construction, transportation, and commerce. Probably the overall productivity rate was stagnant. The situation worsened in 1977–78 resulting in significant declines in productivity. The difficulties stemmed from slowdowns in the process of connecting wages and work quotas, problems created by the introduction of the new economic system (SDPE), declining yields in the sugar sector, and "easy going" attitudes that in some cases resulted in a "relaxation of the labor effort" and a "deformation in the measurement of labor costs." In the agricultural sector, other problems pinpointed were waste of the labor force, lack of controls, overlooking of the work quotas, and alteration of the figures of fulfillment of the work day.[62] The situation further deteriorated in 1979 when Raúl Castro said that "problems of indiscipline, lack of control, irresponsibility, complacency and negligence [aggravated Cuba's] notorious lack of efficiency [and] generated justified irritation on the part of broad sectors of the population." Some of the problems he reported were labor absenteeism and deliberate slowdowns to avoid overfulfilling an already low work quota. Other problems included deals among foremen and workers to meet the quota in half a day and then go off and work for the other half for a private farmer or fulfillment of two or three work quotas in a single day to have free days to do nothing or do something else that brought in more money.[63] The 1976–80 plan set as a goal an average increase of overall productivity of 7 percent per year. The rates of 1976–77 were probably below that target, the reported rate of 1978 was 4 percent, the rate in 1979 sharply declined to 0.8 percent, and the planned productivity rate for 1980 was 3 percent.[64] At best the average productivity rate in 1976–80 was below 4 percent.

I have discussed some factors that explain the divergent productivity performance of various economic sectors: enforcement of work quotas and inflation are two of them. Another important factor is the amount and modernity of the technological equipment that each sector has. An industrial study conducted in 1965 showed that the lowest levels of productivity—in relation to the industrial average equivalent to 100—were often in the least capital intensive sectors (for example, wood products, 41) while as the technological level increased so did labor productivity (such as minerals, 76, and most manufactures from 80 to 100). The highest productivity was recorded in the most technologically-advanced lines (like chemicals, 239, and oil, 557). It is interesting to note that of the 141 industrial lines reported in the study, almost two-thirds were below the national average.[65] Data for 1977 confirm that highest labor productivity gains have been in the most technologically advanced sectors—electricity, metallurgy, chemicals, and mining.[66]

Variations in productivity can also be explained by causes attributable to labor or management or to external factors beyond the control of both. Among the first group of causes, I have already discussed overstaffing of enterprises and state farms, subsidies paid to redundant employees kept on the payroll, labor absenteeism, the use of inefficient voluntary labor, and slackened labor effort due to poor controls (work quotas) and lack of economic incentives (more on incentives in chapter 7). Among the second set of causes are plant shutdowns or slowdowns due to lack of spare parts or inputs, repairs, and electrical blackouts, breakdown of equipment, transportation problems, and natural phenomena particularly important in agriculture, such as drought or flood. A survey, systematically conducted among 146 enterprises from November 1968 to November 1969, analyzed differences among various production lines concerning percentage of the workday lost. The results, reproduced in Table 35, showed that agriculture was the worst sector with the time lost ranging from 40 to 75 percent. Tractor operators lost most time due to breakdowns, followed by administrative problems, and to a lesser extent because of rain and repairs. Although labor related causes seemed minor factors, information gathered elsewhere indicates that most tractor breakdowns resulted from lack of skills of the operators, poor maintenance, or use of the equipment for nonproductive tasks. Among lift operators the most common cause of time lost was lack of transportation, followed by breakdowns; among drivers of carts and other vehicles, the administration was blamed as the most important cause. Surprisingly fishing also was affected by a high percentage of time lost and so were petroleum and food, while the sugar industry had the lowest reported percentage. Perhaps the tremendous pressure in 1969 to achieve

TABLE 35. Loss of the Workday in Selected Production Lines, 1968-69

Production Lines	Percent of Workday Lost	Caused by Workers	Other Causes[a]
Agriculture			
Tractors	74.8	7.9[b]	66.9
Lifters	49.4	9.2[b]	40.2
Transport	40.0	7.9[b]	32.1
Fishing	35.5		
Mining			
Petroleum	30.6		
Overall	24.8	9.6	15.2
Construction	30.0		
Industry			
Food	31.2	12.8	18.4
Metallic products	22.0	7.9	14.1
Tobacco	20.1		
Manufactures	16.2	8.1	8.1
Sugar	14.3		

[a]Shutdowns, breakdowns of equipment and repairs, rain (in agriculture), administrative flaws, lack of transportation.

[b]Lack of labor discipline and other causes.

Sources: Based on a survey conducted among 146 state enterprises from 11 November 1968 to 11 November 1969 as reported by Jorge Risquet, "Comparecencia sobre problemas de la fuerza de trabajo y productividad," *Granma*, 1 August 1970, pp. 2-6.

the gigantic sugar crop of 1970 accounted for the low rate of lost time.

In measuring labor productivity at the macro level, Cubans are expected to take quality into account. But in the Fourteenth Congress of the CTC held at the end of 1978, it became obvious that quality is very poor and apparently not a real concern to the workers. Secretary General Veiga reported numerous cases of poor quality in construction, textiles, garments, shoes, cigars, cigarettes and so forth. To correct this situation, he suggested that each product should have a mark identifying the enterprise and work shift that produced it so that the consumer could identify those responsible for a defective product. Veiga also reported multiple cases of bad quality of services in health, communications, transportation, commerce, and restaurants. Among the instances he cited were "bad treatment and lack of human sensitivity" as well as "abuse and insults" to the public, "abandonment and filthiness of businesses," "unnecessary queues due to administrative laziness," "irritating delays in services," "deficiencies in repair work" and "stealing the public by cheating in the weight."[67] Official criticism of the bad quality of services escalated in 1979 when Castro referred to the problems in transportation: "We have fostered the idea that [under socialism] everything will function perfectly in a spontaneous way, when in fact [it] may well function disastrously. . . . Why has discipline on the railroads collapsed? Under capitalism there was discipline on the railroads. . . . The educational level of the workers on the railroads is three times greater now. . . ; however, the discipline under capitalism functioned better."[68] A new salary system was being studied at the end of 1979 whereby salaries will be more closely connected with and stimulate output increases, quality, efficiency, and savings.

Finally, the economic system itself is an important factor in productivity. Private ownership of production is mainly restricted to agriculture. Although private farms in Cuba do not operate fully under the market system, they are the closest to that system that can be found in that nation. State and private farms are compared in Table 36 in terms of sugarcane yields in 1962–76. In 1962–64 state farm yields were slightly higher than those in private farms, but the latter closed the gap in the next three years and in 1968–77 showed consistently higher yields over the state sector. Yields in the private sector in 1977 were almost twelve percentage points higher than in the state sector. These findings are not limited to the sugar sector alone; for instance, private tobacco farms controlling 77 percent of the tobacco land

TABLE 36. Sugarcane Yields in State and Private Farms, 1962–76

	Yield per Hectare	
Years	State	Private
1962	35.3	30.8
1963	30.8	28.6
1964	38.5	34.4
1965	48.2	47.3
1966	37.7	37.4
1967	49.2	48.2
1968	41.3	45.7
1969	43.8	49.6
1970	54.4	58.5
1971	40.1	41.2
1972	37.0	38.2
1973	43.1	45.2
1974	43.8	47.5
1975	43.5	51.1
1976	42.3	50.3
1977	51.1	62.8

Sources: Author's calculations based on *Anuario 1972*, p. 46; *Anuario 1975*, p. 68; *Anuario 1976*, p. 62; and *Anuario 1977*, p. 66.

produced 82 percent of the crop in 1976. This performance is particularly important in view of the limitation imposed on private farms by the state, including the prohibition to sell the land except to the state, restrictions and penalties to sell their surplus in the market, obligation to sell a significant percentage of their crops to the state, social pressure to become integrated into cooperatives or into the state sector, and dependency on the state to get credit, seed, fertilizer and tools. The private farmer, in spite of these restrictions and poor economic incentives, has overcome most of the productivity problems that plague the state sector. Castro explained the difference in attitude of private versus state farmers using as an example the treatment of tractors: "the former owner of a private farm had a tractor and it lasted twenty years, but later, when the ownership of that farm passed to the state, a tractor lasted only two, three, or maybe four years."[69] Another example of decline of productivity resulting from collectivization of private business involves 30,000 small groceries and shops mostly seized by the state in 1968. In an unconscious paraphrasing of Nobel-Laureate economist Friedrich A. von Hayek's argument published in the 1930s, Castro said that under the market system most of these groceries and shops were operated with either primitive accounting methods or no accounting at all, but with high efficiency because the owner knew all details of supply, demand, and distribution. When these small businesses were nationalized, the state was unable to gather, aggregate, and use all the necessary information, while new managers did not have adequate knowledge of local conditions and, hence, inefficiencies rapidly appeared in the distribution system.[70]

7
Equality in Distribution

According to Marxist theory, with the socialist Revolution, the state collectivizes most means of production, transforming the surplus value (for example, profits made by the capitalists) into a surplus product controlled by the state. Part of that surplus goes to pay the monetary wage of the workers (wage fund) and part goes to support the social wage, that is, the social services provided free by the state. The distribution of monetary wages in the transitional, socialist stage (between capitalism and full communism) is done according to labor effort, while distribution according to needs is postponed to the "society of abundance" when full communism is ultimately achieved. The distribution of social services, however, should in the socialist stage attenuate wage inequalities and take care of some of the workers' needs. Since no country, not even the USSR, claims to be in the full communist stage, it is obvious both by theory and praxis that inequalities exist in socialist countries, particularly in terms of wages. In fact some comparisons made by Western economists indicate that income distribution in a socialist economy may be more unequal than that of a market economy at a similar level of development.[1]

Among socialist countries, Cuba has one of the highest percentages of state ownership of the means of production and, during the Mao-Guevarist stage, claimed to have the most egalitarian system of distribution in the socialist camp—if not the world. Indeed the information available largely supports that claim, although in the 1970s there was a return to what a sympathic sociologist has paradoxically called "stratified equality." It is disappointing, therefore, that Cuba has not produced the statistics to support her claims. In this chapter I delve into all available information to offer an analysis of distribution under the Revolution, trying to evaluate the impact of divergent policies (for example, under the Mao-Guevarist and the current stage) on topics such as overall income distribution, wage differentials, and the role of rationing, prices, and social services in distribution. A special analysis is done, whenever possible, of the potential impact of revolutionary policies in location (urban versus rural) and racial inequalities related to income and services.

INCOME DISTRIBUTION

It is impossible to do an accurate comparison of income distribution prior to and after the Revolution because of the lack of data in both periods. The only prerevolutionary series on broad income distribution, published by the National Bank, referred to the percentage of national income paid out to labor in wages, fringe benefits, and pensions as opposed to that paid to capital in dividends, rent, interest, and so forth. According to this series, the labor share steadily increased from 55 percent in 1947 to 68 percent in 1952 but then declined to 62 percent in 1958. Still, on the eve of the Revolution, Cuba's labor share of the national income was the fourth highest in the Western Hemisphere.[2] But this series on functional income distribution did not throw any light in terms of personal distribution of income or within economic activities of the labor force or between rural and urban areas. Based on data from the 1953 census, a foreign scholar estimated that the national average per capita income for that year was about 430 pesos, but the per capita income of the nonagricultural labor force amounted to 1,600 pesos. According to a private survey undertaken in 1957 in selected rural areas, more than 50 percent of rural families in those areas had annual incomes below 500 pesos a year and only 7 percent earned more than 1,000 pesos a year. The average family of six had an annual income of 549 pesos, a little more than 91 pesos per capita.[3] Although an accurate comparison between the 1953 study and the 1957 survey is not possible, their figures suggest that the ratio between urban and rural average incomes was about 17 to 1. Finally the labor survey conducted by Cuba's National Economic Council throughout the island in 1956–57 divided the labor force only into two income categories: 62 percent earned 75 pesos or more monthly (900 pesos annually) and the remaining 38 percent earned less than 75 pesos. The same survey estimated the agricultural labor force at 39 percent and the nonagricultural labor force at 61 percent.[4] Again, a true comparison among all these figures is not possible, but they suggest extreme inequalities in income in Cuba, particularly between the urban and rural sectors. Scattered data also denote that blacks were more affected by unemployment than whites and overrepresented in low paying occupations. As a result, blacks were concentrated in the lower income brackets.

In the early years of the Revolution, income distribution shifted dramatically by sharply reducing the income of the wealthy and increasing that of the poor. The agrarian reforms of 1959 and 1963 eliminated both the latifundia owner and the middle-sized farmer, while the collectivization waves of 1960 also took away the income received by real estate owners, industrialists, bankers, and other businessmen. On the other hand, minimum wages and pensions were increased, overall wages raised significantly (as much as 25 to 30 percent), agricultural rents were eliminated while urban rents were reduced by one-half, mortgages were abolished, and the cost of public utilities cut. Rough estimates made by both Cuban and foreign economists indicate that probably about 15 percent of the national income was transferred in 1959–62 from the top to the bottom income brackets of the population.[5] The policies of expansion of free social services (education, health, and social security) and achievement of full employment also resulted in increases of income or disposable income of the poorest strata.

In light of the obvious elimination by the Revolution of extreme income inequalities, it is surprising that no hard data are available to substantiate it. Income data published under the Revolution are limited to the total wage bill and average wages paid to state-civilian employees, excluding the military, the private sector, pensioners, and other income categories. There have been a few income studies conducted by JUCEPLAN, but they have not circulated outside Cuba and the 1970 census did not include questions on income. Because of these reasons, there were no attempts, until the late 1970s, to estimate income distribution in Cuba.

Presented in Table 37 are the results of two ingenuous but highly speculative estimates by Western economists—Arthur MacEwan and Claes Brundenius—to fill the existing vacuum.[6]

TABLE 37. Crude Estimates of Income Distribution, 1958 and 1962, and 1953, 1962 and 1973

Quintiles	Family Income		Personal Income		
	1958	1962	1953	1962	1973
0– 20	5.7	9.5	2.1	7.7	7.8
21– 40	8.9	12.2	4.1	12.3	12.5
41– 60	12.5	13.5	11.0	18.3	19.2
61– 80	18.3	18.3	22.8	23.9	25.5
81–100	54.6	46.5	60.0	37.8	35.0
	100.0	100.0	100.0	100.0	100.0

Sources: Family income from Arthur MacEwan, "The Distribution of Income in Cuba," An Essay Prepared for the ILO, September 1978, Table 12.A.1. Personal income from Claes Brundenius, "Measuring Income Distribution in Pre- and Post-Revolutionary Cuba," *Cuban Studies* 9:2 (July 1979):43, Table 12.

Although these estimates are afflicted by deficiencies in data and methodology that result in an overestimation of the degree of equality achieved under the Revolution, Table 37 still has value to indicate the trend toward a much more egalitarian income distribution in Cuba. In MacEwan's estimates of family income distribution, the change between 1958 and 1962 was less marked with a transfer of 8 percent of income from the wealthier quintile to the poorest two quintiles. According to Brundenius' estimates of personal income, there was an income transfer, between 1953 and 1962, of 22 percent from the wealthier quintile, but the bulk of such transfer (16.6 percent) went to the middle two quintiles, not to the poorest quintile. Furthermore, between 1962 and 1973, the poorest two quintiles had not practically accrued any gains, but the middle two quintiles benefitted from an additional 1.1 percent transfer from the wealthier quintile. In 1973, the wealthier quintile was making almost five times the income of the poorest quintile; and in Brundenius' original data disaggregated in deciles, the wealthier decile made almost seven times what the poorest decile made. (If the distributional biases in Brundenius' estimates were taken into account, such differences would be enlarged.) Therefore, the poorest groups improved their income mostly in the early years of the Revolution, thereafter the middle income groups were the greater beneficiaries; the wealthier groups have been the main losers although still moderate income differences persist. And yet Cuba's distribution is probably the most egalitarian in Latin America. In another study, Brundenius compares income distribution in Brazil, Cuba, and Peru showing that the income ratio between the wealthier and poorest quintiles was about 24 to 1 in Brazil and Peru but it was only 4.5 to 1 in Cuba with even more marked differences in the ratios between the wealthier 5 percent and the poorest 20 percent.[7]

Scanty data exist on Cuba's income distribution between urban and rural areas. A national survey on family income (including salaries, wages, pensions, and state payments) compared the family income distribution between Havana province and the rest of the country in 1953 and 1972. According to the survey, in 1953, families in Havana were 14.7 percent above the national average while families in the rest of the country were 10.6 percent below, for a gap of 25.3 percentage points between the two. In 1972, Havana was 13.2 percent above the national average and the rest of the country was 6 percent below, for a gap of 19.2 percentage points.[8] These results are not too impressive, only a reduction of 6 percentage points in the income gap between Havana and the rest of the nation after fourteen years of Revolution. Furthermore data released by Castro in 1968, pertaining to total population income not just to family, suggest that in 1967 the gap might have actually expanded: Havana's income per capita was 49.3 percent above the national average, while the rest of the country was 17.8 percent below, for a gap of 67 percentage points.[9] This happened in the midst of the campaign against bureaucracy prior to the Revolutionary Offensive and the subsequent increase in labor transfers to the countryside, and before wage egalitarianism was pushed, which increased agricultural wages and reduced or froze industrial and other urban wages (more on this later). Hence distribution apparently was more equal in 1972 than in 1967 but not necessarily more equal than in 1953.

WAGE POLICIES AND DIFFERENTIALS

Because the Cuban state has collectivized all means of production—except for one-fifth of agriculture and pockets in services—practically all income earned in Cuba is paid by the government in the form of wages and salaries. Even the private farmers receive state payments for the acopio or as rent. For several years, expropriated owners (basically of real estate) who stayed in Cuba received indemnization payments from the state. Most of these should have ended by now—for example, payments to middle-sized farmers expropriated in 1963 ended in 1973, though some of them received pensions thereafter. Those who had deposited old currency in banks before or immediately after the change in currency in 1961 were not affected by collectivization. These depositors have been allowed to withdraw funds, although usually not in excess of 10,000 pesos and in small amounts. Since eighteen years have passed, surely few of those people or funds are left. Finally, although money can be inherited either in a lump sum or in monthly payments, land cannot be inherited. It must be sold to the state as must homes unless the heir is living in it and does not have another. Therefore an analysis of income distribution in Cuba is basically limited to wage differentials.

The substantial and uncontrolled wage increases that took place in the first two years of the Revolution accentuated, according to the official view, the "capitalist wage anarchy" of 25,000 divergent classifications and 90,000 types of wages. This variety resulted from the market oriented policy of paying different wages to workers performing the same task, though employed in enterprises of varying productivity and profitability. Change was apparent by the end of 1960 when the majority of enterprises were collectivized, the Ministry of Labor assumed the power to fix wages and salaries, and the trade unions began a movement, first, to freeze wages and, second, to yield "privileges" such as higher wages and fringe benefits enjoyed by the labor aristocracy. Then the government announced that the benefits of productivity and profitability should not be shared by a few privileged workers but shared collectively by all the working class. Following the socialist principle, payment would be according to work regardless of enterprise profit, and hence all workers performing the same job would receive an equal wage.[10]

Preliminary studies to establish centrally fixed wage scales in Cuba were conducted in 1962, a pilot plan was tested in mid-1963, and the system was established throughout the country by the end of 1965. Success varied according to economic activities; for example, it was good in industry, fair in services, and poor in agriculture. Workers in the state civilian employment sector are clustered in five major occupational groups: (a) productive workers (obreros), that is, blue collar workers in agriculture or nonagricultural activities such as fishing, industry, construction, whether unskilled, semiskilled, or skilled (for example, a cane cutter, a tractor driver, a ditchdigger, a factory operator, or a bricklayer); (b) white collar employees in services, possible both in productive services (for example, transportation, communications, and commerce) and social "nonproductive" services (like education and health); (c) administrative employees such as typists, stenographers, bookkeepers, and other clerical workers; (d) technicians, that is, those who have finished a university education or training in a technological school or have creative abilities applied to the arts, such as physicians, engineers, agronomists, scientists, economists, university professors, experts on electricity, refrigeration or mechanics, writers, musicians, actors, dancers; and (e) executives (dirigentes), that is, anyone who plans, organizes, coordinates or directs the activities of government agencies (for example, state committees and ministries), the party, enterprises (such as factories and farms), or mass organizations (like unions, or women, student, and peasant associations). Workers from some of the five groups may coincide within an economic activity, such as agriculture, or an economic branch, such as sugar. It should be noted that private farmers and the self-employed are excluded from the wage scale system, while those in the armed forces probably have their own wage scales.

The distribution of state civilian employment by the five groups, available only for 1969–76, shows that the greatest increase was for executives (144 percent) followed by technicians (85 percent). Administrative employees and productive workers increased somewhat (46 and 41 percent) above the overall increase of state civilian employment (30 percent), and employees in services sharply declined (by 34 percent).[11] These changes, unless they result from definitional differences, suggest that those in services have moved up in the occupational ladder into executive and technical positions.

Two sets of wage scales are presented in Table 38, one from 1965 reconstructed mostly from published data and another from 1979 given to me in Cuba. In both sets, scales 1 and 2 apply to the group of productive workers (scale 1 to agricultural workers and scale 2 to nonagricultural workers); scale 3 to administrative

TABLE 38. Wage Scales and Grades, c. 1965 and 1979 (in pesos per month)

| | Workers (Obreros)[a] | | | | Administrative Employees[b] (Scale 3) | | Technicians and Executives (Scale 4) | |
| | Agriculture (Scale 1) | | Non-agriculture (Scale 2) | | | | | |
Grades	1965	1979	1965	1979	1965	1979	1965	1979[c]
1	70	63	91	82	85	75	285	118
2	80	70	107	95	98	86	314	138
3	91	82	124	110	114	100	344	163
4	107	95	145	128	134	118	392	192
5	124	110	170	150	157	138	450	211
6	145	128	200	177	185	163	523	231
7	170	150	234	208	218	192	606	250
8	—	—	284	250	263	250	700	275
9	—	—	—	—	—	—	—	300

[a]Wages in scales 1 and 2 were only given—in 1965—in hourly and daily rates and I converted them into monthly rates (for comparative purposes) multiplying the daily rate by the average number of work days in the month. The 1979 scales showed the conversion into monthly rates.

[b]Probably includes service workers.

[c]Actually two scales, the one shown in the table for technicians, and a lower one for executives starting with 100 pesos in grade one, then 118 pesos for grade two, with subsequent increments similar, and ending with grade 10 equal to 300 pesos.

Sources: 1965: Scale 1, from Israel Talavera and Juan Herrera, "La organización del trabajo y el salario en la agricultura," *Cuba Socialista*, 5 (May-June 1965): 70. Scales 2 and 3, from "Bases para la organización de los salarios y sueldos de los trabajadores," *Suplemento de la Revista Trabajo* (10 June 1963): 10. Scale 4, was not officially released and figures in the table are crude estimates based on the methodology explained in Carmelo Mesa-Lago, *The Labor Sector and Socialist Distribution in Cuba* (New York, 1968), pp. 100–102, adjusted with more recent data. 1979: All from Comisión Estatal de Trabajo y Seguridad Social, Havana, July 1979.

employees probably including those in services; and scale 4 applies both to technicians and executives. Within each scale are from seven to nine grades; these grades are determined by the degree of complexity and precision of the job and, therefore, the skill required by the worker: the higher the grade, the more skill required by the job and the higher the wage to be paid. Incomplete information on the distribution of workers among scales and grades, released in 1963, showed that 42 percent of all workers fell under scale 1 (agriculture) and almost 43 percent under scale 2 (nonagriculture). Within the agricultural scale, 74 percent of the workers fell into the two lowest grades (the worst paid) and only one percent in the best paid grade. Within the industrial scale, 83 percent fell into the four lowest grades and less than one percent in the best paid grade. Commenting on this distribution, Guevara stated: "The skills of our workers run so low, and, in general, such broad experience is necessary to reach the last levels or higher grades, that we can assume that it will take many years . . . before this situation is improved."[12]

The introduction of the wage scales in the early 1960s together with other distributive measures discusssed above, was a great stride toward reducing income differentials in Cuba, although an official publication has acknowledged that, to begin with, wage differentials prior to the Revolution were not as large in Cuba as in most of Latin America.[13] The raising of the minimum wage in agriculture to 70 pesos per month (840 pesos per year) was a great improvement over the average 549 pesos per year for a family of six in 1956. Even if we assume that the majority of agricultural workers were concentrated in the lowest four wage grades of scale 1 in 1965, it meant that most of the agricultural labor force was close to the 1,000 pesos mark per year, a privilege enjoyed by probably only 7 percent of rural *families* ten years before. A Cuban specialist claims that prior to the introduction of the wage scales, 74 percent of agricultural workers still received less than 65 pesos monthly, and the lowest wage grade became about 70 pesos in the mid-1960s.[14] Concerning extreme wage differentials, the ratio between the highest-paid grade in scale 4 (700 pesos to a cabinet minister) and the lowest paid grade in scale 1 (70 pesos to an unskilled peon in a state farm) was 10 to 1, while in 1958 the ratio between the President's salary (not to say the income of a wealthy industrialist, banker, or sugar plantation owner) and the *average* income of a rural *family* was about 1,000 to 1. But this dramatic cut in inequality does not mean that either wage differentials were eliminated or, as a sympathetic sociologist wrongly argues, that simply no gap existed between the income of production workers and administrative and technical personnel.[15]

As seen in Table 38, in 1965 the scale of agricultural workers was the lowest of all, and it had two grades lower than the lowest grade of the scale of nonagricultural workers besides lacking the three top grades of the latter. The scales of nonagricultural workers and administrative employees were quite similar, grades in the latter being about 8 percent lower than in the former, but grades in these two scales were 25 to 35 percent higher than the corresponding grades in scale 1. Finally scale 4 began with a grade similar to the top grade of scales 2 and 3, and a technician or executive earned close to three times what an administrative employee or nonagricultural worker in the same grade received. A comparison of *industrial* average wages between Cuban and other Latin American countries done by JUCEPLAN in 1966 showed that Cuba's extreme wage differentials were significantly narrower than those in Venezuela and Colombia, slightly smaller than those in Chile and Peru, similar to those in Mexico, and greater than those in Brazil.[16] In all fairness, however, it should be noted that if the overall wage structure instead of the industrial average wages had been used in the comparison, Cuba would have been well ahead of all these countries in the matter of wage egalitarianism.

During my visit to Cuba in mid-1979, the vice-president of the State Committee on Labor and Social Security gave me a new set of wage scales not published before, which are reproduced in Table 38. Wage rates for scales 1 through 3, in the 1979 set, appear to be about 13 percent lower than the corresponding rates of 1965, but this may be the result of differences in the conversion of daily rates into monthly rates. What is really significant is the difference in the technical-executive scale: wage rates in 1979 appear to be less than half of those in 1965. And yet in an interview, held also in mid-1979, with the director of the Cuban Institute of Domestic Demand, I was told that the highest official wage rate was 700 pesos. This and other information to be discussed later cast a doubt on the accuracy of the technical-executive scale for 1979 shown in Table 38.[17]

The above discussion is limited to basic wage rates, but other factors exist that introduce variations to the wages of workers falling under the same scale and grade. Some of these factors are directly related to workers' effort: those who work overtime (after workday hours or on holidays) are bound to receive an unknown percentage increase over their wage rate; workers performing their jobs under harmful or extremely arduous or dangerous conditions are supposed to be paid respectively 20 and 35 percent over their wage rate; and workers who fulfill their work quotas receive their full wage rate, those who do not fulfill the quota a reduction in the wage rate proportionate to the nonfulfillment, and those who overfulfill the quota receive a bonus proportionate to the wage and the overfulfillment. For example, a worker who has a wage rate of 100 pesos and underfulfills his quota by 10 percent receives 90 pesos, but if the quota is overfulfilled by 10 percent the wage is increased to 110 pesos.

The most important factor introducing variation in basic wage rates is not related to the worker's effort but rather to past productivity or profitability in his job. This is the so-called historical wage, or the difference resulting between the wage a worker received before the wage scale system was established and the new wage rate assigned to the same worker by the corresponding scale and grade. The government's initial attempt to extirpate this appendage, which impeded the eradication of the connection between wages and profits and the full implementation of equal wage for equal work, was unsuccessful. Hope was then placed in the gradual elimination of the historical wage by the natural process of retirement, promotion, and transfers; for instance, when a job was left vacant, the new worker hired was supposed to receive just the wage established by the scale, without the addition of the historical wage.

Finally, apart from wages and other types of payments connected to the job, there are important "fringe benefits" received by only a small part of the labor force. These benefits have an enormous importance in the frugal economy of Cuba. Involved are advantages in obtaining extremely scarce housing, access to purchasing scarce goods such as automobiles or to assignment of a car and chauffeur as part of a job, possibility to travel abroad and receive additional clothing and travel funds, priorities in hospital treatment and vacation resorts, and access to goods outside of the rationing system.[18] Counteracting these privileges are equalizing factors such as the rationing system, price controls, free or low-cost housing, and provision of gratuitous social services, all to be discussed later in this chapter.

During the Mao-Guevarist stage a big push was made toward further equalization in Cuba. Material incentives were deemphasized and largely substituted by moral incentives. Workers were asked to waive overtime pay, bonuses for the fulfillment of work quotas, and historical wages while the implementation of extra payments for work done under extremely arduous conditions was postponed. At the same time, social services conferred gratuitously by the state were expanded including public phone calls, burials, day-care centers, and sports events, and it was promised that housing, recreation, transportation, and public utilities would soon be free. Wage differentials were to be reduced in a gradual manner by raising the lowest wages and pensions and freezing the higher wages; eventually every worker would earn the same wage whether a cane cutter or an engineer, and even food and clothing would be free, thus making wages and money virtually unnecessary. Cuba aspired in this stage to implement fully the utopian full-communist principle of distribution according to need instead of the more realistic socialist principle of distribution according to work.[19]

The failure of the Mao-Guevarist experiment led to a drastic reversal of the wage and distribution policies in the 1970s.[20] The trend toward wage equality and distribution according to need was criticized as an idealistic error (or "petty bourgeois egalitarianism") that did not take into account the worker's productive effort; hence wage differentials were defended as a means of motivating those with labor skills, heavy responsibilities, and tough or dangerous jobs. In 1973 the CTC officially proclaimed the return to the principle of distribution according to work instead of need. Wage scales were reestablished and the rates for technicians and executives raised by 132 million pesos annually, for an average increase of 280 pesos per capita, higher in itself than the top monthly wage grade of the other groups except nonagricultural workers. On the other hand, the increase in wages in the agricultural sector, endorsed by the CTC in 1973, was postponed in 1978 to avoid rapid inflation. Wages were also linked again with work quotas, while bonuses for overfulfillment of production were reintroduced at a higher rate than in the mid-1960s. In addition, a new system of *primas,* or bonuses, for fulfillment and overfulfillment of quality and saving indices was put into effect. The renunciation of overtime was also considered a mistake because unpaid overtime turned out to be more costly than regular paid hours. Workers performed poorly while operating costs were fixed, reducing real production and labor productivity; therefore paid overtime was also reinstated. An attempt was made to use wages as incentives for allocation of labor where it was most needed, not always with good results, thus salaries of university professors were increased so much that now "many people do not want to work anywhere else" and important agencies like JUCEPLAN face problems keeping their employees.[21] Author's royalties, abolished in the early 1960s, were reinstated in the late 1970s. The government pays from 5 to 12 pesos per page according to the quality and relevance of the work and the author's prestige, and it seems that, in addition, there will be in the future a percentage of the sales paid to the author.[22] To reinforce the connection between productivity-profit and reward, the new economic system (SDPE) gradually introduced in the late 1970s sets part of the enterprise profits into an economic incentive fund distributed among the enterprise employees either as individual bonuses (*premios*) related to their productivity or through enterprise services such as cafeterias or day-care centers. In 1979 two-thirds of the fund was given in bonuses and one-third in services. In the Ariguanabo Textile Factory in Havana, 300,000 pesos of the incentive fund were distributed as bonuses among workers; some of the individual bonuses were as high as 2,000 pesos but 16 percent of the workers did not receive any bonuses because of their low productivity.[23] The new emphasis on material incentives has also reached the allocation of durable consumer goods, many of which are now distributed by a mixed criteria in which productivity is a major factor (more on this later).

A new attempt was made in the 1970s to curb the historical wage, which is now seen as a disincentive to new workers who joined the labor force after the introduction of the wage scales because they are paid less than workers doing the same job who were hired earlier. In 1973, during its thirteenth congress, the CTC decided to eradicate the historical wage through a joint review of each case by the administration and the union. If a worker was found to have the proper skills, he would be offered a better job. If he did not have such skills, he would have the option of retraining; workers who refused the transfer or retraining would be devoid of their historical wages. In spite of these measures, the total sum paid in historical wages in 1973–78 did not decline because new historical wages were introduced in this period through special regulations. New historical wage—a contradiction in terms—is a euphemism created to refer to higher wages than those in the corresponding wage grade to attract badly needed personnel. Apparently two situations are common. In one, a worker who enjoys a historical wage is wanted in a top priority job, but if he were to transfer he would lose as much as half of his salary; hence he is allowed to take the historical wage into the new job. In another situation, an agency or enterprise wants a worker to perform the same job that he performs elsewhere; the worker does not have a historical wage, but he is offered an extra payment, disguised as such, in order to get him. In spite of a law enacted by the National Assembly in 1977 to prohibit the creation of new historical wages, in the fourteenth congress of the CTC held at the end of 1978 it was publicly acknowledged that the situation continued.[24] Unfortunately no data are available on the impact of historical wages in wage differentials.

All the measures discussed above are widening cracks in the initial philosophy behind the introduction of wage scales in Cuba—wages should be determined according to work regardless of the enterprise's profitability and productivity. An official report on Cuba's industry published in 1966 proudly asserted that the wage policy was not based on partial criteria of efficiency in specific enterprises, in fact the opposite was true: "the higher or lower productivity of an industry conveys—in general terms—an inversed relationship concerning the wage share of the value added."[25] Data on labor productivity shown in Table 34 and wage data discussed in this chapter suggest indeed an inverse relationship between the two in 1966–71: agriculture had the second worst productivity decline in the economy but received the highest wage increase, while industry had the second highest increase in productivity but got the worst wage cut. Productivity and wages show—with few exceptions—a positive correlation in 1971–76: increases in productivity in commerce, industry, transportation, and communication (in that order) were rewarded with almost proportional wage increases; however agriculture had the second worst productivity performance and still got the highest wage raise while construction had the second best productivity gain and received the lowest wage raise.[26]

Accurate measurement of the impact of wage policies on wage differentials in the 1960s and 1970s is impossible because the available data are limited to state civilian employment basic wage rates (excluding historical wages) and are divided into two unconnected series: one for 1962–66 and the other for 1971–76.[27] Both series provide averages by economic activity and, since in each activity there are workers belonging to all wage scales, these averages hide extreme wage differentials intra and inter scales. For instance, the average wage in agriculture in 1965 was 87 pesos, but in that economic activity there were actual wages ranging from 70 pesos earned by a peon to 700 pesos earned by the Minister of INRA. In any event, the 1962–66 series showed average-wage increases in low-paid occupations such as agriculture and fishing and sharp declines in high-paid occupations such as electric power, petroleum, and communications.[28] A comparison between 1966 and 1971 indicates another sharp increase of average wages in agriculture and to a lesser extent construction, and sharp declines in industry, transportation, and communication.[29] Although comparisons between 1962–66 and 1971–76 are not accurate, the extreme differential between the highest and lowest wage *means* declined from 4.1 to 1.0 in 1962 to 3.6 to 1.0 in 1966. It then fell sharply during the Mao-Guevarist stage to 2.6 to 1.0 in 1971 and declined further to 1.79 to 1.0 in 1973. The latter was the year in which the CTC endorsed the change in wage policy and distribution, and as a result the differential slightly rose to 1.81 to 1.0 in 1974 and 2.02 to 1.0 in 1975.

In trying to avoid somewhat the "average trap" and provide a better picture of current wage differentials, I have contrasted in Table 39 selected official wage averages both of overall economic activities and specific branches with scattered data on actual wages (which may include the historical appendage) collected by recent visitors to Cuba, including myself. The national minimum wage in 1978 was 81.96 pesos, but during the first six months of work—prior to evaluation—a lower wage was paid.[30] In agriculture, the overall average monthly wage was 128 pesos, which was above the reported wage of most state farm workers. This suggests farm workers are still concentrated in the lowest three or four grades of the wage scales. Cane cutters during the sugar harvest made at least eight times what most state farmers were paid, and private tobacco growers earned seven times that amount during the three-month crop. A successful fisherman in a private cooperative made almost four times the average wage for that branch. In industry, only two branches were below the overall average, with the most productive branches (chemistry, metallurgy, and electricity) having an average wage close to twice the average of the least productive branch (tobacco). Notice also that well-paid cement-plant workers made 75 percent more than the average in their industry; engineers earned as much as three times the industrial average, and some high-skilled technicians got as much as seven times that average. In transportation, top priority branches like the merchant marine and airlines still had higher averages than the sector average. In commerce, the best-paid branch—foreign trade, whose average wage in the mid-1960s was 60 percent higher than retail domestic trade—was deleted

TABLE 39. Average Wages in State Civilian Sector (1975) and Actual Wages/Income in Selected Occupations (1977–79)
(monthly wages in current pesos)

Economic Activities	Wage	Economic Activities	Wage
Agriculture	**128**	**Commerce**	**122**
State farm worker	80–100[a]	Tourism	117
Private farm tobacco grower	630[a]	Domestic trade	126
Cane cutter	800[a]	**Services**	**121**
Fishing	151[a]	**Personal**	
Fisherman in private coop	500–600[a]	Cleaning woman	75–80[a]
Industry	**136**	Day-care centers	98
Tobacco	109	Chef in small hotel	140[a]
Light	132	**Education**	**136**
Food	138	Schoolteacher	100–190[a]
Construction materials	143	School principal	230–300[a]
Sugar	152	University professor	325–500[a]
Mining	153	**Culture**	**167**
Oil	166	Well-known musician	700[a]
Electricity	188	**Health**	**127**
Metallurgy	190	Laboratory worker	150[a]
Chemistry	198	Dentist	300–450[a]
Electricians	120–220[a]	Physicians	300–600[a]
Cement plant workers	100–250[a]	Director of hospital	600–750[a]
Engineer	300–400[a]	**Bureaucracy**	
High-skilled technicians	700–1,000[a]	Middle-level employee	200–300[a]
Transportation	**162**	Cabinet Minister	700[a]
Merchant Marine	177		
Airlines	180		

[a]Actual wage (or income); rest are wage averages.

Sources: Average wages from *Anuario 1976*, p. 52. Actual wages/income from Joe Nicholson, Jr. *Inside Cuba* (New York: Sheed and Ward, 1974), pp. 85, 144; Fred Ward, *Inside Cuba Today* (New York: Crown Publishers, 1978), pp. 18, 123; Marcel Niedergang, "Cuba: le point de non-retour," *Le Monde*, 10 May, 1978, p. 6; Jon Nordheimer, "20 Years with Fidel," *The New York Times Magazine*, 31 December, 1978, p. 29; Howard and Nancy Handelman, "Cuba Today: Impressions of the Revolution in its Twentieth Year," *American Universities Field Staff Reports*, no. 8 (1979), p. 6; and my own observations and interviews in December 1978 and July 1979.

from the official list. The lowest wages in services were paid to women working in cleaning jobs or in day-care centers; a well-paid university professor made much more than a school principal and 3.3 times what most schoolteachers got; a well-paid physician made 3.5 times the branch average; and a cabinet minister earned about 3 times what a middle-level bureaucrat earned. The table suggests that in the late 1970s the extreme wage differential was about 10 to 1.0, going even higher in some cases probably due to historical wages. This is similar to the extreme differential computed from the 1965 wage scale and much higher than both the differential from the doubtful 1979 wage scale (4.8 to 1.0) and the often quoted ratio 3.5 to 1.0 by visitors to Cuba.[31]

What about wages and incomes outside state-civilian employment? This question is the most difficult to answer due to the total lack of data on the military—not even average wages for the Ministry of the Armed Forces are included in Cuba's statistical yearbook—and only occasional gross figures available for the private farmers. Crude estimates to fill the statistical vacuum on those two sectors, in Table 40, show that the average wage for the military steadily increased in 1971–73. In the later year it equaled the average wage of the civilians and thereafter surpassed that group. By 1977 the average military wage was 17 percent above the civilian one. This was a result of the process of professionalization of the armed forces, the reorganizations of military ranks at the end of 1972 and again at the end of 1976 (which had their full impact on wages in 1974 and 1977), and the military involvement of Cuba in Africa since 1975.[32]

In 1965, a government survey conducted among 92,000 private farmers showed that the average annual payment for state purchases (acopio) was 1,500 pesos, with the highest payment— 2,450 pesos—going to tobacco growers.[33] If this information is correct, then state payments declined dramatically during the Mao-Guevarist stage so that by 1970 they were 60 percent below the 1965 level. This may have been caused by low state prices paid to the farmers, which probably forced them into selling most of their crop to the black market. The latter so boomed in the late 1960s that the government had to mount a frontal attack in 1968. It is possible that facing state penalties or low prices the private farmers deliberately cut their production in 1969–70, which contributed to the economic debacle of those years. Since 1970, however, average state payments to private farmers seem to have risen due to increased production and acopio sales to the state, possibly helped by higher prices since 1976, as well as increasing rent paid by the state. By 1977 those payments almost recuperated the 1965 level.

But to estimate the total income of the private farmers, one must take into account the value of their own family consumption plus cash sales to consumers and barter among farmers. The

TABLE 40. Annual Income Per Capita of Population, State Civilian and Military
Employees, and Private Farmers, 1962–77 (in current pesos)

Years	State Civilian	State Military	Private Farmers[a]	Population
1962	1547			400
1963	1562			450
1964	1587			536
1965	1593		1500	509
1966	1601			484
1967	1517			457
1968	1531			
1969	1440			
1970	1379	1315	609	468
1971	1395	1366	647	470
1972	1456	1437	763	485
1973	1514	1513	857	521
1974	1563	1675	934	543
1975	1638	1738	1181	589
1976	1688	1750	1300	608
1977	1676	1889	1484	627

[a]State payments to private farmers through acopio, rent, and other arrangements;
excludes the value of private barter and sales as well as own consumption.

Sources: State Civilian per capita based on *Boletín 1970*, pp. 35–36; *Anuario 1972*,
pp. 36–37; *Anuario 1976*, p. 52; and *La economía cubana 1977*, p. 21. Income per
capita of the population in 1962–66 from UN *Monthly Bulletin of Statistics*, 22 (June
1968): 176, checked against *Compendio 1968*, p. 8. Population (1967 and 1970–77),
military and private farmers' per capita are crude estimates based on the labor
force composition (Table 26) and my reconstruction of the distribution of the total
population income by groups based on the same sources as Table 9 plus *Economía
y Desarrollo, 34* (March-April 1976): 188; *ibid.*, 35 (May-June 1976): 12; and *ibid.*,
38 (November-December 1976): 222.

abovementioned survey estimated the average annual private
revenue of the farmers at only 500 pesos, but at the same time
the American Marxist economists Leo Huberman and Paul Sweezy
reported that some farmers made as much as 10,000 and 20,000
pesos a year, obviously from their private sales.[34] A visitor to
Cuba in 1978 reported that private tobacco growers could make
a profit of 2,000 pesos in the three months of the crop and then
plant other crops during the rest of the year. Another visitor
reported that peasants' daily sales in open markets were 200
pesos,[35] certainly more than 20,000 pesos annually. In 1977, a
resolution was passed in the fifth congress of the National
Association of Small Farmers (ANAP) establishing taxes on
private agricultural cooperatives to reduce income differences
between private and state farm workers.[36]

The population's income per capita (at current prices) stood at
300 pesos in 1953 and rose to 350 pesos in 1957–58.[37] There are

no figures for 1959–61, but it is safe to assume that income per capita increased in those years—possibly reaching 500 pesos in 1961. The last column of Table 40, although affected by comparability problems,[38] suggests (together with the first column of the table) that the population income per capita peaked in the mid-1960s, declined in the frugal Mao-Guevarist period, and rose again in the 1970s helped by the new policy in favor of economic incentives. Income per capita in 1977 may have been 80 percent higher than in 1957–58, for an average annual increase of 4 percent. A good part of this increase was due to inflation but, on the other hand, income was more equally distributed in 1978 than in 1958. Moreover, disposable income was larger in 1978 because of the significant expansion of social services provided free by the state. But what was the purchasing power of the population income in 1978? I will attempt to answer that question in the next section.

THE ROLE OF RATIONING AND PRICES

The monetary income of the population rose in 1959–61 much more than the supply of consumer goods, forcing the Cuban government in early 1962 to make a decision either to allow the market forces to set the allocation of goods or to establish rationing. In the first alternative, prices would have skyrocketted allowing those with higher incomes to buy the available goods but reducing consumption among the low-income groups; this solution was politically unfeasible. The second alternative would both hurt incentives because those with higher incomes would not have much to buy and introduce the danger of a black market sustained by the high-income groups, many of whom were—still in 1962—remnants of the old elite. Offsetting these effects was the assurance of minimum consumption for those who supported the Revolution. Rationing was introduced in March 1962 and has gradually expanded thereafter, becoming an important tool of equalization.

Presented in Table 41 are the rationing quotas at four points in time: at its inception (1962); in the midst of the frugal Mao-Guevarist stage (1969); in the years of economic recuperation and return to material incentives (1971–72); and after the recession induced by the decline in sugar prices (1978–79). Moral incentives and scarcity of consumer goods hurt all Cubans in 1969, and they endured a reduction in the quotas of eleven basic goods, while quotas of five other goods remained unchanged and only three quotas increased. The new policy of the 1970s resulted in an improvement in supply, with increases in the quotas of nine consumer goods and reduction only in sugar (to take advantage

TABLE 41. Monthly Per Capita Quotas of Selected Rationed Consumer Goods in Havana, 1962–79 (in pounds)

	1962	1969	1971–72	1978–79[a]
Meat[b]	3	3	3	2.5
Fish	1	2	4	free[c]
Rice	6	4	3–6	5
Beans	1.5	1.5	1.5–3	1.25
Tubers	14	9	n.a.	n.a.
Fats	2	1	2	1.5
Eggs (units)	5	15	15–24	free
Butter	0.125	0.125	free	free
Coffee	1	0.375	0.375	0.125
Milk (canned)[d]	6	2	3	3
Sugar	free	6	6–4	4
Bread	free	15	n.a.	15
Cigarettes (package)	free	4	4	4
Gasoline (gallon)	free	n.a.	n.a.	10
Detergent (medium package)	1	1	n.a.	0.5
Soap (cake)	2	2.5	n.a.	1.5
Toilet paper (roll)	free	1	n.a.	1
Toothpaste (small tube)	1	1	n.a.	0.33
Cigars (units)	free	2	4	4
Beer (bottle)	free	1	free	free

[a]Also free in 1978–79 were macaroni, spaghetti, butter and yogurt; cakes and vegetables (according to season); and bread (after 4 P.M.).

[b]Beef; if not available, chicken is provided—only through this way.

[c]Small fish. Seafood has not been available for more than a decade.

[d]Children under 7 have a daily ration of half a liter of fresh milk; and adults over 65 receive six cans of condensed or evaporated milk monthly.

Sources: *1962:* Law 1015 of 12 March 1962; *Revolución,* 13 March 1962, pp. 1, 9. *1969:* René Dumont, *Cuba est-il socialiste?* (Paris: Seuil, 1970), p. 241, app. 1. *1971–1972:* Frank McDonald, "Report from a Cuban Prison VI," Institute of Current World Affairs, 6 February 1973, pp. 4, 23; and Joe Nicholson Jr., *Inside Cuba* (New York: Sheed and Ward, 1974), p. 33. *1978–1979:* Nelson Valdés, "Food Rations and Prices in Havana" Mimeographed, December 1978; and my own observations in Havana, December 1978 and July 1979.

of rising prices abroad) and the rest remaining unchanged. Improvement stagnated, however, because of the recession. Thus by 1978–79 only the quotas of two more goods increased while four declined and the majority remained unchanged. In spite of the significant improvement in the 1970s, rationing in 1978–79 was tougher than in 1962: quotas on fourteen goods were lower, two were the same, and only three were higher. Actually these three—fish, eggs, and butter—had been removed from rationing. The serious economic recession of 1979–80, combined with import cuts in poultry and grains, affected the supply of meat and beans.

Cuban planners do not expect a significant improvement in rationing until 1986–90.[39]

Another analysis of supply conducted by Susan Eckstein and based on official data of consumption per capita of some 70 items (including food, beverages, tobacco, textiles, clothes, shoes, and household appliances) in 1966–74 confirms my conclusions. In 1970, at the end of Mao-Guevarism, consumption per capita of two-thirds of those goods had declined in relation to 1966 and only one-third increased. By 1974, in the midst of the sugar boom, consumption per capita of 56 percent of the goods had increased in relation to 1970, 36 percent had declined, and eight remained equal.[40]

Due to increasing concern for internal demand, in 1971 the government created, with the aid of Soviet experts, an Institute for Research and Orientation of Domestic Demand. Two of the Institute's objectives are to balance production and consumption and to forecast population income and expenditures. The Institute conducts periodic surveys (a stratified national sample of 10,000 families in 1979) about consumer behavior, tastes, and complaints on the availability and quality of goods.[41] According to the Institute, less than one-third (measured in value) of all goods are still rationed, but the list in Table 41 indicates that this one-third includes the most important foodstuffs, beverages, and tobacco. These have a low price and account for the low one-third while most nonrationed goods are very high priced and hence account for the remaining two-thirds. There are other items not included in the table for lack of information, for instance, few fruits are available except those in season for which there is not a large external market. Rationed articles are often sold out before the turn of a customer thus provoking the long lines in front of state shops. According to various official estimates, rationing assured a minimum of 2,100 to 2,846 calories per day in 1977–78, but Dudley Seers reported that rationing in 1962—when quotas were higher—allowed only 1,307 calories for those older than seven and 2,155 for those younger than seven. In any event, figures from the late 1970s are below the average national per capita availability for 1951–58, which were reported at 2,740 to 2,870; however, distribution then was less egalitarian than now.[42] Some people in Cuba claim that the current rationing food quota is used up in two weeks, while others argue that though sufficient it is fattening and provides little variety.[43] Those who have enough income supplement their diet by often eating in cafeterias and restaurants. Workers and students benefit from free or subsidized meals in work places and schools, although these are being gradually eliminated to fight inflation.[44] The rationing of foodstuffs is apparently better in Havana than in other cities, but food availability is probably better in rural areas where private farmers produce their own food and barter or sell the surplus.[45]

State farmers used to have family plots they could harvest for their own consumption, but these were taken away in 1967 and apparently have not been restored. In summary, although the national average per capita caloric intake has probably declined since 1962, rationing has been instrumental in making food distribution more egalitarian. As a consequence, low income groups and rural areas probably have increased their caloric intake while urban middle-income groups have experienced a decline.

Since 1973 some manufactured goods such as cameras, cosmetics, and stationery have been freed from rationing. Others have been put on limited distribution allowing the consumer to choose one or two items from a given list, including underwear, socks, pajamas, rubber shoes, and pots and pans. But most essential clothing and shoe items remain rationed—for example, one each annually of a pair of pants, a skirt, a shirt, a blouse, a dress, a pair of leather shoes, and just four meters of fabric.[46] Once again, one's quota or option to buy does not guarantee that either the item is in stock or available in the consumer's size; hence queues for manufactured good are often worse than for foodstuffs. In December of 1978 I saw lines in front of state stores that had begun the night before and were one and two blocks long early in the morning; the people were waiting to buy Japanese electric fans. Also in 1973 a new plan began to distribute certain consumer durables that are no longer available in stores. The Ministry of Domestic Trade allocates a quota of such goods to state enterprises, farms, and agencies that in turn advertise the goods available and provide forms to be filled out by prospective buyers (loans without interest are available through the National Bank). A committee of workers ranks the applicants mainly by their work effort, productivity, and, to a lesser extent, by their need. According to the CTC, in 1973–78 the following durables were distributed through this plan: 268,000 refrigerators (all domestic production), 317,500 television sets, 254,200 washing machines, 153,400 sewing machines, and 130,600 bicycles.[47] An average of one out of every three state workers bought one of these items in that five-year period. Finally, automobiles can be bought only by high officials and professionals through quotas to government enterprises and agencies. The buyer has to make a down payment of 10 percent of the car's cost, and pays the rest in monthly installments (without interest) for a period of three years.

There are several tiers of prices of consumer goods in Cuba. The lowest is the rationing system in which most prices, particularly of foodstuffs, beverages, and tobacco, have been unchanged since 1962. Rising production costs make the real price of those goods much higher today than it was seventeen years ago; consequently, the state subsidizes the price of rationed goods. For instance the real price of a pound of beef is at least 0.80 pesos, but it is sold from 0.44 to 0.55 pesos depending upon the quality of cut; the price of beans is 0.25 pesos per pound but is sold for from 0.18 to 0.20 pesos.[48] A few foodstuff and beverage prices have increased for such items as coffee, eggs, and ham, and prices for these are close to ones for those goods in the United States. But, in general, Cubans paid at least one-third less for their basket of foodstuffs in 1978 than if real prices were charged.

The scarcity of consumer goods and the underpricing in the rationing system generated a black market that the government tried unsuccessfully to curtail in 1968. There are several sources of "supply" to the black market, but most important is private farmers' sales. Owners of taxis, one of the few private sectors in existence, often operate as intermediaries, buying from the farmers and selling in urban areas at a profit. In the late 1970s the government became more tolerant and private-farmers' markets began to spread in small towns and farmers went to Havana and other towns to sell their products.[49] In 1980 this practice was generalized with the authorization of "free peasant markets" (more on this later). Home-made manufacturing of consumer goods, quite important in the 1960s until it was almost suppressed in 1968, seems to be booming again. People who do not consume such rationed goods as cigarettes sell them in the black market for a much higher price or barter them for other goods. Moreover, there are always some who do not use up their quota, and they dispose of the extra in various ways. The head of a grocery store who sometimes increases the surplus by weight cheating sells these goods to well-trusted customers at black market prices. Drivers of state vehicles may deliberately overestimate their fuel needs to receive more coupons than actually used; those extra coupons are sold to gasoline station operators who, in turn, resell them to regular black-market customers. Officials in state enterprises may also overestimate their needs or even steal enterprise goods for sales in the black market.[50] A so-called red market is fed by foreign technicians (mostly from the USSR and Eastern Europe) as well as diplomats who have access to diplostores and resell goods at five or six times the official price. The servants, chauffeurs, gardeners, and others who work for diplomats also receive part of their salary in consumer goods only available in diplostores; of course, some of those goods also end up in the black market. Minor sources of supply are also foreign tourists who either bring or buy goods in tourist shops, then sell them to eager natives in pesos. And Cuban diplomats and government officials who travel abroad import goods in high demand, most of which are for their own consumption but some are sold to friends for a profit. The existence of the black market has been acknowledged by top Cuban officials including Castro. The director of the Institute of Domestic Demand has euphemistically called it "additional market" and "barter system."[51] Prices in the black market are from five to fifteen times higher than the rationing price (see Table 42).

To combat the black market and create legal incentives to high income groups, the government inaugurated an official parallel market in 1973. Cuban economists consider it a transitional step between rationing and the open market. The head of JUCEPLAN has ardently defended it as a material incentive for those who earn more because, through it, labor effort, skills, and productivity are rewarded.[52] In the parallel market, goods are sold from three to eight times the rationing price but substantially below the black market price(see Table 42). The latter has not been eliminated, however, because only certain goods are sold in the parallel market and even these are not always available or are of inferior quality to those in the black market. In 1980, "free peasant markets" were legalized, allowing private farmers to sell in them any agricultural surplus—except beef, tobacco, and coffee—once the farmer has fulfilled his acopio obligations with the state. Prices, set by supply and demand, are much higher than the rationing price but lower than the black market price.[53] As the parallel and peasant markets grow both in number and quality of goods available, the black market should decline. In the late 1970s, with the increasing flow of tourists, special shops were opened in the major hotels. Here goods not available elsewhere can be bought in hard currency. Both in tourist shops and diplostores one can buy the high quality Cuban rum (Havana Club) and export cigars (like H. Upmann) that simply cannot be bought in regular stores.

Although the cost of rationed goods in Cuba is quite low, most wage earners average monthly income was 140 pesos in 1978. With this meager income they could hardly afford to buy goods in the parallel, red, or black markets, or through the CTC plan. The cheapest refrigerator or television cost the equivalent of five months average wages and a car almost three years average wages. Even clothing and some foodstuffs are unaffordable at black market prices for the average citizen. An entire monthly wage could be spent on one pound of coffee, a pair of shoes, a meter of fabric, and a couple of pounds of beef. Fancy restaurants in Havana also have prices prohibitive for the average wage earner: 5 to 10 pesos for lunch or 10 to 20 pesos for dinner. A single room in a good hotel in Havana costs 30 pesos a day. But there are cheaper restaurants in which a meal costs about 2 pesos; the government offers inexpensive vacations for honeymooners and highly productive workers at subsidized prices; and the CTC grants, as material rewards for top workers, a night at the famous Tropicana night club, dinner and drinks included for two, for only 15 pesos. This may be a once-in-a-lifetime chance, but for many in this income group that opportunity would have never been possible before the Revolution.

TABLE 42. Prices of Selected Goods in Cuba, 1977–78 (in pesos)

Goods	Rationing	Official Parallel Market	Black Market
Food (pounds)			
Beef	0.44−0.55		8
Ham	1.30−2.70	6.00	10
Rice	0.21		2
Beans	0.18−0.20	1.25	2−3
Coffee	2		10−20
Fats	0.22−0.30		3
Manufactures			
Bottle of rum		7.50−12	25[b]
Cigarettes (package)	0.20	1.60−2.00	1[b]
Cigars (one)	0.12	1.50	2[b]
Pair of shoes	3.50−10.5		70
Fabric (meter)	0.40−2.50	1.50−10.5	30
Gasoline (gallon)	0.60	2	1
Consumer Durables[a]			
TV (B & W) 17"		650−900	
Refrigerator (small-medium)		650−850	
Record player		350−1,200	
Car (Soviet FIAT)		4,500	
Car (U.S. 1950s)			5,000−15,000

[a]Most available only through quotas to state enterprises; a few through the parallel market.

[b]Goods of higher quality than those available through rationing or the parallel market.

Sources: According to reports of visitors to Cuba by Francois Raitberger, "Cuban Diplostores for Foreigners Only," Miami Herald, 14 February 1977; Jerry Flint, "Cubans Admit their Economy is in Serious Trouble," New York Times, 25 April 1977; John Virtue, "Foreigners are a Privileged Class in Cuba," Miami Herald, 28 April 1977; Robert Keatley, "Island Incentive," Wall Street Journal, 5 May 1977; Marcel Niedergang, "Cuba: Le point de non retour," Le Monde, 12 May 1978, p. 5; Harold Sims, personal notes, summer 1978; Nelson Valdés, "Food Rations and Prices in Havana," Mimeographed December 1978; and my own observations, December 1978.

THE DISTRIBUTION OF SOCIAL SERVICES: EDUCATION, HEALTH, SOCIAL SECURITY, AND HOUSING

Throughout the first two decades of the Revolution, but especially in the 1960s, there was an impressive expansion of social services provided free or at a very low cost by the state. In the Marxist terminology these services are part of the social wage that a worker receives in addition to the monetary wage. In 1962, 35.7 percent of the state budget was spent on social services—education, public health, social security, housing, and sports and recreation. But the financial crunch and shift in priorities gradually reduced it to 32.7 percent in 1965. Data are not available for the period 1967–77 since the budget was discontinued in these years, but it is safe to assume that, proportionally, expenditures to social services gradually declined during the frugality of the second half of the 1960s and recuperated with the economic boom of the first half of the 1970s. In 1978, the social service share of the budget was 32.8 percent, identical to that of 1965, and it rose to 35.3 percent in 1979.[54] In pesos per capita, state expenditure to social services was as follows: 91 in 1962, 105 in 1965, 308 in 1978, and 337 in 1979. Although part of the 1970s' increase was due to inflation, there has been a remarkable jump in the late 1970s. In addition, the distribution of these services—particularly in the 1960s—has been much more equal than prior to the Revolution. This more equitable distribution is apparent from a discussion of the four most important social services in terms of costs and benefits—education, health, social security, and housing.[55]

Fundamental to a consideration of educational services are the topics of illiteracy, enrollment rates at various educational levels, and distribution of educational opportunity between rural and urban areas.[56] The illiteracy rate in 1943 was 28.7 percent and declined to 23.6 percent in 1953; if the 1943–53 trend is projected into 1958, it can be assumed that the rate in the later year was 21 percent. At the end of the massive literacy campaign conducted mostly in rural areas in 1961, the Cuban government reported that illiteracy had been reduced to 3.9 percent, a figure considered too low by some experts.[57] In fact, the 1970 population census registered a much higher illiteracy rate of 12.9 percent. Thus the annual average rate of illiteracy reduction in 1958–70 was 0.68 percent as compared to 0.51 percent in 1943–58, an important improvement indeed but not as remarkable as originally thought. More impressive than the cut in the national rate was the reduction in the gap between urban and rural illiteracy rates. The urban-rural illiteracy gap was cut for 12 and 42 percent respectively in 1953 to 7 and 22 percent in 1970. Yet the relative positions remained almost unchanged for a rural/urban ratio of

3.5 to 1.0 in 1953 and 3.1 to 1.0 in 1970. The urban areas in Havana province stood ahead of the nation in 1970 with the lowest illiteracy rate—2.9 percent. The 1970 illiteracy rate among those in the ten to thirty-four age bracket was only 7 percent while it rose to 21 percent among those thirty-five and older, showing the impact of the Revolution's educational effort among the youth. Illiteracy was slightly higher among males (13.5 percent) than among females (12.4 percent), and no information was released for race although data was collected on this variable.[58]

Figures on educational enrollment presented in Table 43 summarize one of the most significant revolutionary achievements: the expansion of elementary education from about half of the school-age population in 1953 to practically all that population in 1970–76. We have to assume, therefore, that by 1978 the illiteracy rate had been reduced even more, possibly to 7 or 8 percent. The expansion of secondary school coverage was almost stagnant in the 1960s, but in the 1970s, once full elementary school coverage was achieved, the emphasis was put into secondary education, thus coverage rapidly expanded to almost half of the school-age population in 1976. Enrollment in universities declined from 1958 to 1961, increased slowly thereafter, but still in 1970 was below the prerevolutionary level. By 1972 the prerevolutionary coverage had been recuperated, and it rapidly expanded thereafter reaching 10.8 percent in 1976. Most of the expansion of elementary school facilities and enrollment took

TABLE 43. Percentage of School Attendance by Educational Level, 1953, 1970, and 1976

Educational Level[a]	1953[b]		1970		1976	
	Enrollment (thousands)	Percent[c]	Enrollment (thousands)	Percent[c]	Enrollment (thousands)	Percent[c]
Elementary	656	58.0	1,665	98.6	1,922	99.9
Secondary	156	19.2	239	22.3	579	47.0
University	29	5.5	35	4.9	82	10.8

[a]Excludes teacher and vocational schools, adult, and special education.

[b]Only public schools, exclude private education.

[c]Total enrollment in K-6 grades as percent of population in the five to twelve age bracket; total enrollment in 7-13 grades as percent of population in the thirteen to nineteen age bracket; and total enrollment in universities as percent of population in twenty to twenty-four age bracket.

Sources: 1953 Oficina Nacional de los Censos Demográfico y Electoral, *Censos de Población, Vivienda y Electoral, Enero 28 de 1953: Informe General* (La Habana: P. Fernández y Cía., 1955), p. 99, Table 34. Enrollment in 1970–71 and 1975–76 from *Boletín 1971*, pp. 270–77 and *Boletín 1975*, p. 207; population from Table 6 infra disaggregated by age using distribution of the 1970 population census.

place in rural areas, which suffered serious educational deficiencies prior to the Revolution. Thus in 1958–59, although 47 percent of the population lived in the countryside, it only had 30 percent of elementary school teachers and student enrollment. In 1970 the percentage of the rural population declined to less than 40 percent but teaching personnel and student enrollment in rural schools increased respectively to 42 and 40 percent.[59] On the other hand the expansion of secondary school facilities to the countryside did not take place until the 1970s and still by 1975 only 25 percent of the schools and students were in rural areas.[60] All Cuban universities are also in major cities, but there is a special program for peasants at some of the universities. Besides the provision of free education, the state grants scholarships which cover costs of housing, food, clothing, shoes, and transportation. In 1975–76, 14 percent of all Cuban students had these scholarships with higher proportions in secondary education (50 percent) and universities (33 percent); reportedly most fellowships in secondary schools are granted to students from rural areas. The head of JUCEPLAN stated in 1978 that if education were not free, it would monthly cost the breadwinner the following sums in pesos per child: 25 for elementary school, 52 for secondary school, 70 for technical school, and 100 for university.[61]

Cuba's overall advances in health care are not as impressive as those in education because of the relatively high health standards that the nation already enjoyed prior to the Revolution and the deterioration suffered in those standards in the 1960s.[62] Cuba's statistical yearbook figures for 1958 on general and infant mortality rates, when compared with similar data from Latin America, demonstrate that, at the eve of the Revolution, Cuba had the lowest rates. But as seen in Table 6, both general and infant mortality rates increased in 1959–69, with an interval of decline in 1963–67. Thereafter, they declined steadily so that in 1976 they were, again, the lowest in Latin America. Throughout the 1960s, then, health standards deteriorated, and they did not recuperate or improve until the 1970s.

Morbidity rates for contagious diseases in 1958–77, shown in Table 44, are consistent with mortality rates. With the exception of polio, which was controlled through massive vaccination and disappeared in 1963, morbidity rates steadily increased in the early years of the Revolution. A few peaked in 1962 and declined thereafter due to vaccination, but most continued increasing and peaked between 1965 and 1969 declining thereafter with a few increasing again in 1975–77. Although accurate comparisons of 1976 over 1958 (or early 1960s) are not always possible, Table 44

TABLE 44. Rate of Contagious Diseases in Cuba, 1958–77 (per 100,000 inhabitants)

Year	Acute Diarrhea	Chicken Pox	Diptheria	Hepatitis	Malaria	Measles	Polio	Syphilis	Tetanus	Tuberculosis	Typhoid
1958	—[a]	—	2.4	—	2.0	2.9	1.6	0.7	—	18.0	5.1
1959	—	—	4.7	—	2.1	10.3	4.3	0.7	4.1	27.6	13.0
1960	—	—	8.1	—	19.0	10.7	4.8	8.3	4.6	27.2	17.5
1961	—	—	19.1	5.0	46.6	0.4	4.9	6.9	—	37.8	13.7
1962	—	—	19.4	51.1	49.8	22.5	0.7	11.4	9.0	38.6	14.2
1963	—	—	12.8	64.4	11.5	94.0	...	23.4	6.0	38.3	5.8
1964	—	—	8.6	70.6	8.4	28.9	...	25.1	5.5	52.6	15.6
1965	5,707	118.6	8.2	115.8	1.7	121.6	...	30.4	6.7	65.0	3.1
1966	5,876	138.3	4.6	115.1	0.5	136.4	...	26.3	6.1	36.5	2.2
1967	6,165	209.2	5.5	139.6	0.6	165.9	...	13.1	5.4	37.2	2.4
1968	6,319	—	1.6	208.6	...	145.5	...	6.7	3.9	41.0	12.0
1969	6,417	104.6	0.6	85.3	...	132.2	...	7.1	3.5	43.3	5.5
1970	7,694	150.1	0.1	102.6	...	105.2	...	7.8	2.6	30.8	5.0
1971	7,879	76.3	...[a]	151.9	0.1	129.7	...	11.1	2.0	17.9	4.8
1972	8,038	65.4	...	114.5	0.4	59.9	...	24.3	1.7	14.3	5.1
1973	8,286	93.0	...	133.6	0.1	78.3	...	48.9	1.1	15.4	3.5
1974	7,317	178.4	...	205.9	0.4	150.9	...	50.6	1.0	15.4	3.7
1975	6,876	161.7	...	217.0	0.9	113.4	...	47.6	0.7	14.2	4.0
1976	6,346	261.4	...	145.8	1.9	157.2	...	41.1	0.6	13.5	4.3
1977	7,358	144.3	...	123.2	1.8	263.3	...	39.2	0.6	13.1	4.7

[a]Dashes indicate figures are not available. Ellipses indicate figures are minimal or null.

Sources: See Mesa-Lago, "Availability and Reliability of Statistics in Socialist Cuba," Table 7; *Boletín 1968*, pp. 192–94; *Boletín 1971*, p. 205; *Anuario 1975*, pp. 236–37; *Anuario 1976*, p. 237; *Guía Estadística de Cuba 1977*, p. 18; Ministerio de Salud Pública, *Informe Anual 1978* (La Habana, 1979), p. 145; and *Anuario 1977*, p. 251.

shows a mixed performance: two diseases have been eradicated, and rates of four other diseases have declined although most of them slightly, while rates of five diseases have increased, most of them significantly.

Explanations for changes in health standards are found in vaccination policies, the pool of medical personnel, state budgetary allocations to health, and the supply of medical equipment and medicines. There has been an increase in preventive medicine under the Revolution, and diseases easy to control through cheap vaccination have been eliminated—for example polio and diphtheria. On the other hand, measles vaccination was not massively applied until 1972 while other contagious diseases—such as of the digestive tract and venereal—proved more difficult to control and have increased. There were 920 inhabitants per physician in 1958, but about one-third of the physicians left the country in the early 1960s while the number and quality of graduates from medical schools declined. The lowest point was reached between 1962 and 1964 in which the ratio probably rose to 1,200–1,500 inhabitants per physician; thereafter the number of graduates increased with an acceleration since 1973 (the prerevolutionary ratio was recuperated in 1976) and by 1978 Cuba had 675 inhabitants per physician—the lowest ratio in all Latin America. The ratio of inhabitants per dentist showed a similar trend, but here the improvement has been less marked than with physicians due to less urgency and a lower priority: 3,120 in 1958 and 2,982 in 1978.[63] There were 184 inhabitants per hospital bed in 1958 (taking into account both public and private hospitals and clinics), but in 1967 the ratio had deteriorated to 203. It rapidly improved in the late 1960s, however, and in 1975 was back to 185 inhabitants per bed.[64] The state budget in public health increased an astonishing eighteenfold in the first two decades of the Revolution, but most of the increase was concentrated in the first decade. Thus the health budget increased ten times in 1958–68 but less than twofold in 1968–78.[65] Finally the hemispheric embargo against Cuba and the poor supply from socialist countries seriously affected in the 1960s the availability of medical equipment, spare parts, and medicines thus contributing to the deterioration in health. In summary, overall health standards deteriorated badly in 1962–69 because of the confluence of all the negative factors explained above; the Cuban government had to make an enormous investment of resources in the 1960s to recuperate the prerevolutionary standards and that investment began to pay off in the 1970s when progress was made beyond the 1958 mark.

But if it took Cuba one decade to recuperate overall health standards, the 1960s made the distribution of health care much more equal than before. In 1961 all major private hospitals were nationalized (medical cooperatives survived until 1969), and by

1963 health care became state administered and free for all the population. The government made a special effort to reduce the gap between health standards in urban and rural areas: in 1958 there was only one rural hospital while in 1978 there were 57; and while in 1968, 60 percent of the physicians and 62 percent of hospital beds were in Havana, in 1978 the proportions had declined to 36 and 29 percent while the city had 21 percent of the population. Still the inhabitant/hospital bed ratio of Havana was almost twice as good as in the rest of the provinces. The comparison was even worse with poor provinces, thus in 1976 the city of Havana had 94 inhabitants per hospital bed but in Tunas province the ratio was 410 per hospital bed.[66] The number of beds in rural hospitals increased steadily from 10 in 1959 to a peak of 1,607 in 1968 and thereafter declined to 1,234 in 1975. The share of rural hospital beds in relation to urban hospital beds peaked at 9.6 percent in 1968 and declined to 5.5 percent in 1975,[67] thus there seems to be a reversal in the 1970s in favor of urban areas. Information on other types of inequalities in access to health care is not available, but money does not make any difference because the few physicians who have a private practice are seriously handicapped due to lack of equipment and diagnostic facilities. On the other hand, power can make a difference; thus a sociologist sympathetic to the Revolution visited Cuba in the early 1970s and reported that top officials did not have to wait in long queues to receive service and enjoyed better attention.[68] In 1958 blacks had worse medical attention than whites because the former were concentrated in the lowest income brackets and did not have the same access to the better private hospitals and physicians; thus the nationalization of medicine must have benefitted them. And yet Domínguez has studied surveys of the late 1960s and early 1970s that suggest that some inequality persists as blacks were overrepresented in reports of all types of diseases as well as of those typical of poor people.[69]

Social security has improved significantly under the Revolution, both in terms of overall coverage and distribution. In 1958 about 63 percent of the labor force was covered for old age, disability, and survivors insurance, while all the labor force was covered against occupational accidents and diseases, and female employees had maternity insurance. At the eve of the Revolution, Cuba had the second highest social security coverage in Latin America. Protection, though, was rather unequal because there were fifty-two autonomous social security funds—each with its own insured group, legislation, financing sources, and benefits. High status occupations normally had the best funds and conditions, while low status occupations had the worst; for instance, minimum pensions fluctuated from 30 to 200 pesos a month and maximum pensions from 60 to 400 pesos a month. There was neither national health insurance nor unemployment compensation.[70] In

1959 all pensions were raised to a monthly minimum of 40 pesos, which benefitted thousands of insured who, in spite of the legislation in force, received pensions as low as five pesos per month. The fifty-two social insurance funds were gradually seized by the state, and in 1963 all the administration was unified, the legal system made uniform, and coverage extended to all the labor force (for old age, disability, and survivors) and all the population (for health and maternity). The new system embraced all state employees (including state farmers) as well as the few employees in the private sector—mostly in private farms. Special regulations were enacted for the armed forces, private farmers, members of fishing cooperatives, self-employed (for example, private taxi drivers and cargo porters), and professionals. Only excluded is the small number of domestic servants. The insured does not pay any contribution, and costs are paid by a social security tax charged to all state enterprises, farms and agencies. Pensions are fixed proportionally to salary and time of service, but extreme pension differentials are reduced by minimum and maximum pensions (60 and 250 pesos as compared to 30 and 400 pesos before) and by establishing a decreasing percentage over the salary above a ceiling for calculating the pension. Social welfare payments are limited to the elderly without income or relatives, the totally disabled, and single mothers.[71] A new social security law was enacted in July 1979.[72]

As seen in Table 45, social security total expenditures increased more than fivefold in 1959–78, with pensions being the major component. In the 1960s three big waves of pensions were granted: 56,000 in 1959–61 as a result of administrative changes and nationalization; 85,000 in 1963–65 as those newly covered by the law, former farmers affected by the second agrarian reform, and *excedentes* released due to the introduction of work quotas received pensions; and 35,000 in 1968 as an outcome of the nationalization of small business and the incorporation of other groups. Still the annual average number of new pensioners in 1959–70 was 19,000 as compared to 36,000 in the 1970s when no dramatic reforms or incorporations took place. The reason was that in 1965–67, facing a labor deficit and economic constraints, the number of pensioners stagnated due to a government campaign to avoid retirement. Thus 60,000 who had applied for pensions in 1964 withdrew their applications and thousands of pensioners returned to work.[73] Conversely in the 1970s with the pressure of unemployment, the government reversed its previous policy and more than 200,000 retired thus opening new jobs in the tight labor market. Expenditures for subsidies rose in the 1960s because of payments to vanguard workers of 100 percent of their salaries while sick or incapacitated, as well as the addition of free burials and other subsidies. These expenditures declined after 1974 when the vanguard workers' privilege was eliminated as inflationary.

TABLE 45. Social Security Expenditures and Pension Per Capita, 1959−78
(in current pesos)

Years	Total[a] (In Million	Subsidies and Welfare[b] Million	Pension[c] Pesos)	Number of Pensioners[d] (In Thousands)	Pension Per Capita[d] (In Pesos)
1959	114.3		114.3	154	740
1960	124.3		124.5	170	732
1961	150.5		150.5	210	727
1962	151.9		151.9	213	713
1963	177.0		177.0	250	708
1964	235.7	39.1	196.6	280	702
1965	249.8	41.5	208.3	298	699
1966	247.0	41.7	205.3	298	689
1967	245.3	38.0	207.3	301	688
1968	308.9	85.0	223.9	334	670
1969	393.9	118.2	275.7	342	806
1970	440.7	154.2	286.5	363	790
1971	486.5	175.4	311.1	394	790
1972	514.5	170.5	342.9	432	796
1973	554.4	171.1	383.3	470	816
1974	553.4	136.2	417.2	507	823
1975	585.4	137.2	448.2	544	824
1976	609.4	136.2	473.2	581	814
1977	626.0	134.5	491.5	629	781
1978	647.6	140.1	507.5	652	778

[a]Only monetary payments; excludes costs of health care provided by the Ministry of Health.

[b]Includes payments to the partially disabled; subsidies to those suffering illness and accidents both common and occupational, maternity leave, former landowners; workers who are studying, relatives of military recruits, and to those who cannot afford the cost of meals in workers' cafeterias.

[c]Includes pensions for old age, disability, and survivors.

[d]1960−67 are author's estimates checked with the State Committee on Labor and Social Security.

Sources: Comité Estatal de Trabajo y Seguridad Social (CETSS), La Seguridad Social en Cuba (La Habana: Agosto de 1977), pp. 33, 50; and data provided by the CETSS, Havana, July 1979.

The average annual pension per capita steadily declined in 1959−68 due to the large number who retired under the new law with a lower maximum and because of low pensions granted to special groups. The average pension increased in 1969 surpassing for the first time the 1959 level. This reflected the raising of the minimum pension to sixty pesos following the Mao-Guevarist goal of income equalization. It stagnated until 1971 and then increased slowly with the economic recuperation but declined since 1976 probably as a result of the recession. Welfare recipients seem to be receiving a declining annual per capita subsidy in the 1970s—for example 57 pesos in 1973 versus 47 pesos in 1975. The average pension measured in current pesos in 1978 was only 5 percent above that of 1959, hardly a gain if inflation is taken into account. But prior to the Revolution, the extreme differential ratio among pensions was 13 to 1.0 by law but more if actual low pensions were taken into account, while now it is 4 to 1.0. Today not only 40 percent more of the labor force qualify for pensions, but these are more equal than before.

Of all social services, housing is the worst in terms of revolutionary performance. Significant improvements have been made in terms of cost and to a lesser extent in distribution, but the housing deficit is expanding. In 1959 house rent was reduced as much as 50 percent and in 1960 lessees were entitled to buy the house in which they lived by paying the rent to the state for a period ranging from five to twenty years. In 1969, 268,089 families had become owners of homes under that plan,[74] but it was suspended in 1970 because of its inflationary effects. The government also built low-cost housing in the first years of the Revolution, practically eliminating the slums. Rent on new housing was set at 6 percent of the monthly family income, although in practice only the head of household income is taken into account. Later on, rent was increased to 10 percent of income, but with two exceptions: the retired or sick pay only 8 pesos monthly, and families with a per capita income below 25 pesos monthly do not pay any rent.[75] In 1972, 75 percent of all families owned their own home (67 percent in urban areas and 89 percent in rural areas), 10 percent were still buying, 8 percent paid rent, and 6 percent were exempted of paying any rent (4 percent in urban areas and 10 percent in rural areas.)[76]

Since 1962 the government has faced a construction material shortage, which resulted in a very low priority to housing in relation to industry, agriculture, roads, dams, schools, and hospitals. In 1970 housing represented only 5 percent of total construction; although it increased to 16 percent in 1972, it declined to 10 percent in 1976. Furthermore throughout this period, housing received a lower share of the construction allocation than other activities listed above.[77] The annual construction of dwellings—both state and private—in the first two decades of the Revolution is given in Table 46. In 1946–53 an annual average of 26,827 homes were built and the number probably increased in 1953–58, although Cuban officials have grossly underestimated it. New demand for that period, estimated at 28,000 homes, was probably fulfilled.[78] In 1959–70 annual housing construction steadily declined to a trough of 4,004 in 1970.[79] In 1972–79 the annual average increased to 17,700 units, recuperating the level of 1959–63. And yet, in 1979, dwelling construction stood at 1.5 per

TABLE 46. Housing Construction in Cuba, 1959−80

Years	Dwelling Units[a]
1959−63	17,089[b]
1964−67	15,209[b]
1968	6,458
1969	4,817
1970	4,004
1971	5,104
1972	16,807
1973	20,710
1974	18,552
1975	18,602
1976	15,400
1977	20,024
1978	17,012
1979	14,498[c]
1980 GOAL	15,000

[a]Includes all state and private housing construction.

[b]Annual average.

[c]Preliminary.

Sources: Alberto Arrinda, "El problema de la vivienda en Cuba," *Cuba Socialista,* 4 (December 1964): 16, Table 4; *Boletín 1968,* pp. 127−28; *Anuario 1975,* p. 119; *La economía cubana 1976,* p. 3, ibid., 1977, p. 24, and ibid., 1978, p. 13; *Guía Estadística 1978,* p. 9; Fidel Castro, "Speech in Closing the 14th Congress of the CTC," *Granma Weekly Review,* 17 December 1978, p. 8; Humberto Pérez, *Sobre las dificultades objetivas de la Revolución* (La Habana: Editora Política, 1979), pp. 92−93; *Granma Weekly Review,* 6 January 1980, pp. 2−3; *Anuario 1978,* p. 103; and *Cuba en cifras 1979,* p. 23.

1,000 inhabitants, substantially below the rate of 2.3 per 1,000 inhabitants in 1959−63.

In 1964 Fidel Castro estimated the housing deficit at 655,000 units and raised the figure to one million in 1966.[80] These estimates probably took into account the real and latent housing deficit at the beginning of the Revolution, which according to various revolutionary sources fluctuated from 250,000 to 700,000. My own estimate of the deficit created *under* the Revolution is 700,000.[81] Contrasted with the dismal reality shown in Table 46, government goals for housing construction have been overly optimistic. In 1973, for instance, a goal of 100,000 dwellings was set for 1980, then it was reduced to 50,000 and the 100,000 target postponed for 1985, later it was reduced to 30,000 and, finally, the 1980 plan cut if further to 15,000.[82] The housing shortage has become a matter of national concern: in 1970, 90 percent of the people who approached top officials had a housing claim and, in 1978, there was a public appeal for "the strict enforcement of the legal regulations in force aimed at impeding the occupation of houses."[83] Trying to cope with the housing problem, Fidel Castro launched a plan of construction minibrigades in 1971. The government would supply construction materials while surplus labor released from enterprises would provide the manpower. Targets were set at 70,000 to 80,000 homes annually; however, in 1978 when actual construction was only 17,012 units, Castro called back the minibrigades. He said that the plan was not efficient enough, was too costly, and would take forty years to pay off the cost of materials. As a result, it is being changed into state brigades using mechanized equipment. Rent of the homes built under the new plan will not be based on a percentage of income, but by square meter, in order to pay back the state investment faster. Also since 1978, 70 percent of funds allocated to municipal agencies or construction are being used for repairs to avoid a further deterioration of the existing housing stock, and new housing units are smaller than before 1978.[84]

Distribution of housing between urban and rural areas does not seem to have improved significantly. In the years 1959–63 when most housing was built, 47 percent was allocated to rural areas, a big improvement in relation to 1958 when half of the houses were built in Havana, but not enough to reduce the gap. In 1953, 44 percent of the population, who lived in rural areas, occupied 37 percent of the housing. In 1972, the situation had slightly deteriorated since the rural population declined to 38 percent but their share of houses shrank further to 30 percent.[85] In 1970, 1.2 million rural inhabitants (36 percent of the total) still lived in *bohíos* (palm-thatched homes). A comparison of living facilities in rural homes between 1953 and 1970, although showing improvement in running water and electricity, revealed a deterioration in water toilets.[86] The situation could not have improved in the 1970s because housing construction has been shifted to Havana, to correct neglect of construction there in the 1960s. In 1945–53, 46 percent of new housing was built in Havana, but the proportion steadily declined to 7 percent in 1970. In 1973, however, it had increased again to 41 percent, thus coming in a full circle back to the prerevolutionary allocation.[87] Data on housing allocation by race, although collected in the 1970 census, have not been published. Prior to the Revolution, blacks had the worst housing and things have improved only slightly since 1959. Even if it is assumed that blacks benefitted more than whites from the allocation of both newly built homes and those left by exiles, this accounted for less than one-fifth of the housing stock and it would have done little to correct significantly the previous racial imbalance in housing. Since the majority of the population probably occupies the same housing that it had in 1960, blacks still live in the worst homes. Perhaps that is why the 1970 population census did not release data on housing distribution by race.

8

Evaluation of Socioeconomic

Performance

Summarized in this chapter are the major findings of this book by evaluating the Cuban Revolution's performance, in its first two decades, on the five goals selected for study. In the discussion of each goal, significant shifts in goal priorities in the various historical stages and the reasons behind those shifts are summarized, but the analysis concentrates on the key issue of whether Cuba has succeeded in achieving growth, diversification, economic independence, full employment, and equality in distribution. The summary of each goal ends with a brief exploration of possible trends in the third decade of the Revolution.

SUSTAINED ECONOMIC GROWTH

Economic growth was sacrificed through most of the 1960s, to consumption in the first stage of the Revolution, to diversification in the second, and to egalitarian distribution in the fourth. In the current pragmatist stage, economic growth rose from bottom to top priority, and such predominance may continue in the 1980s. This dramatic shift in priorities has been associated with a positive transformation in the Revolution's attitudes toward market mechanisms, cost analysis, training of economists and managers, material incentives, capital efficiency, and labor productivity. While in the first decade the revolutionaries did not know or ignored economic laws and reality, in the second decade they seemed to have learned about the latter and the limitations and compromises that they impose on policy makers.

There are no data on economic growth for 1959–61, although these probably were years of steady growth. The 1962–63 attempt to apply the Soviet pre-economic reform model in Cuba resulted in a loss of at least 7 percent in total growth or 12 percent per capita. But economic recuperation in 1964–65 generated average annual growth rates of 5.2 percent and 2.7 percent per capita. During the Mao-Guevarist stage (1966–70), the annual growth rate stagnated at 0.4 percent and in per capita terms declined at -1.3 percent, for a total per capita loss of 6.5 percent. The economic recuperation in 1971–75 was impressive, with record average annual rates of 16.3 percent and a per capita of 14.5 percent. However, in 1976–80 two recessions occurred and average growth rates sharply declined to 4.1 and 3.1 percent, the former equal to two-thirds of the modest target of 6 percent annually set by the 1976–80 five-year plan.

Physical output of most products—mostly in traditional agriculture and industry—either increased in the first half of the 1960s, declined in the Mao-Guevarist stage and recuperated in the 1970s, or declined throughout the 1960s and recuperated in the 1970s. The FAO index of agricultural output shows that total output reached its lowest point in 1963 and in 1976 was only slightly above the 1959 output level, while output per capita in 1976 was two-thirds that of 1959. Cuba's own index of industrial product indicates that output was almost stagnant in the 1960s but grew impressively in the 1970s: in 1977 total output was almost twice that of 1959 and in per capita terms was about 70 percent higher. The better performance in industry over agriculture can be partly explained by natural factors that affected the latter, but mainly because industry is more modern and capital intensive than agriculture.

The dismal economic performance of the 1960s, and particularly the second half of that decade, was caused by numerous factors: too rapid and wide collectivization of the means of production; several short-lived changes in economic organization and development strategy; predominance of politics over economics and loss of technical personnel; poor sugar harvests combined with low sugar prices; the early emphasis on consumption that depleted investment and the later emphasis in investment which was hampered by poor capital efficiency; the cost of the hemispheric economic embargo and the dramatic shift of international economic relations towards the USSR; and the heavy burden of military expenditures.

The vigorous economic recuperation of the first half of the 1970s was a result of the following: a more efficient economic organization and rational development strategy steadily applied; the payoff of previous investment and the more efficient allocation and use of capital; the predominance of economics over politics; the emphasis in training of managerial personnel; the booming sugar prices in the international market; the postponement of the Cuban debt to the USSR and provision of new Soviet credits; and the relaxation of the hemispheric embargo combined with a substantial flow of credit from market economies. The slowdown of 1976–80 was caused by the decline of sugar prices in the international market, plagues that affected the major two industrial crops, a sharp reduction in the flow of credit from market economies, complications in the implementation of the System of Economic Management and Planning (SDPE), and the cost of the military involvement in Africa.

The decline in population growth rates throughout the Revolution had a positive impact in economic growth. Through most of the 1960s, high birth rates were offset both by increases in mortality rates and by emigration resulting in lower population growth rates. In the 1970s, birth rates declined sharply, more than offsetting declines in mortality rates and emigration with the net effect of even smaller population growth rates. The exodus of qualified personnel, especially in the early 1960s, negatively affected production and productivity, but tighter controls later reduced the brain drain; emigrants also left significant assets that were seized by the state and helped to alleviate the housing and unemployment problems. The baby boom of the 1960s increased the dependency ratio and the burden of state-provided services such as education; furthermore, the population bulge began to enter the labor market in the second half of the 1970s when efficiency measures made it difficult to find jobs for all of them. Because of these problems, a state population policy is now considered a necessary component of development, while before, socialist development was supposed to take care of population growth.

Economic growth was hindered either by decline or poor use of investment in the 1960s, but through most of the 1970s it was helped by an increase of both investment and capital productivity. Because of the priority given consumption in 1959–61, investment probably declined from 18 percent of GNP in the 1950s to 14 percent of GMP. Since 1962, restrictions on consumption induced an increase in investment, which reached 25 percent in 1967. In that year, investment was 47 percent above the 1962 level, while consumption was 4 percent below. In 1962–67 the percentage of state investment going to production increased while that going to social services declined by nine percentage points. Investment data for 1968–70 are contradictory, but consumption either stagnanted or declined. If the investment ratio continued to rise in this stage, it then failed to boost economic growth due to the inefficiency in the allocation and use of capital. But if the investment ratio declined, then it is a proof of the failure of the Mao-Guevarist policy to increase capital accumulation in spite of the curtailment of consumption. Scattered data available for the first half of the 1970s suggest that both investment and consumption incresed aided both by external factors and the improvement in capital and labor productivity. In the second half of the 1970s, however, stagnation or decline may have occurred in investment and consumption due to the economic recessions. In spite of the improvement in capital efficiency in the 1970s, the prerevolutionary levels probably have not been recuperated.

Since 1967 all Cuban figures on economic growth, investment, and consumption are given in current prices; hence, they do not take inflation into account. Although Cuba does not publish data on cost of living, the index of the monetary surplus—that is, excess money in circulation with which nothing can be bought—can be used as a rough surrogate for inflation. As a percentage of total population income, the monetary surplus probably rose throughout the 1960s and in 1970 stood at 86 percent. In that year the total income of the population exceeded by almost two-fold the value of available supply; hence, money was almost useless and, without an incentive to work, one-fifth of the labor force stayed at home. As a result of a better use of prices and curtailment of inflationary free social services, since 1972 money was gradually extracted from circulation and by 1975 the monetary surplus had declined to 36 percent of the population income. A new burst in inflation took place in 1976–77, induced by declining sugar prices and increasing prices of imports in the international market. In 1978 the monetary surplus stood at 38 percent; if in that year all rationed products, which are sold at prices below the market price, would have been set free, prices would have gone up by a similar percent.

A significant portion of capital and human resources that could have gone into Cuba's development has been used in national defense and military involvement abroad. In 1962 when the external threat of U.S. invasion peaked, Cuba had some 350,000 men in arms and military expenditures took 6.7 percent of GMP and 13.3 percent of the state budget. After the missile crisis that threat declined and so did military expenditures, which by 1965 represented 5.2 percent of GMP and 8.4 percent of the budget. In the 1970s the need for defense dwindled further, and the professional armed forces were cut by more than one-half. This trend seemed to be consolidated with the lessening of tensions between the United States and Cuba in 1975. But the trend was reversed in the second half of the 1970s by Cuba's military involvement in Africa: by 1978 the armed forces were increased by 25 percent, Cuba sent approximately 38,650 men abroad (75 percent of the total communist countries' military personnel stationed in the Third World), and military expenditures rose to a historical record of 7.8 percent of GMP. The African adventures also took their toll in terms of the depletion of qualified personnel from the economy, the use of part of the fishing and merchant marine fleet to transport the troops, and a slowdown in the implementation of the SDPE. All this probably contributed to the decline in output and economic growth in the second half of the 1970s.

In the third decade of the Revolution, unless another sugar boom like in the "Dance of the Millions" of the 1920s and the 1970s occurs, it will be impossible to replicate the growth rates of 1971–75. Economic growth, then, will be modest. In 1986, the Cubans will also have to start repaying the Soviet debt—unless it is postponed again—and this will put an extra burden on the economy. It is expected that in 1981–85, the growth rate will be stagnant, investment will rise at a slower pace than in the 1970s, social consumption will freeze, and frugality for consumers will continue. In view of all this, it is difficult to conceive that the Cubans will maintain their costly military involvement abroad.

DIVERSIFICATION OF PRODUCTION

Diversification was an idealistic goal in the first two stages of the Revolution, promoted vigorously but irrationally in 1961–63 with poor results. Since 1964, economic reality pushed diversification down to the bottom of Cuba's priorities. In spite of great expectations, sugar continues to be the dominant sector in the economy, and only modest advances have been made in the diversification of the nonsugar sector.

In 1962–78, the industrial share of GSP declined by 12 percentage points, that of agriculture by 6 points, while that of communications was virtually stagnant. The decline in industry would actually be larger and the decrease in agriculture smaller if distortions created by centrally-fixed prices and double counting were corrected. The basic expanding economic activity was commerce, which increased by 14 percentage points, and to a lesser extent construction and transportation (about 2 percentage points each). The value of commerce and transportation is somewhat overestimated because of inflation. Probably the most important increase in the period was that of social services—education, health, and social security—and defense, but these are not taken into account in the system of material production used by Cuba. The shrinkage of the agricultural share and increase in the commerce/service share in Cuba goes along with the trend of most Latin American countries in that period, while the sharp reduction in the industrial share goes against the regional trend. It is surprising, and a proof of the failure of the diversification program, that in Cuba, a socialist economy, the most dynamic sector is not industry but commerce and services.

When the agricultural and industrial sides of sugar production are combined, it is clear that sugar continues to be the most important single line of production. Within the agricultural sector, the share of sugar in 1976 was almost 8 percentage points higher than in 1962, while that of nonsugar agriculture was almost 6 points lower and that of livestock 3 points lower. Only the share of forestry slightly increased. Within the industrial product, food had in 1976 as in 1962 the largest share, while sugar fell from second to third place, below chemistry; the largest increase, however, was in metallurgy (almost 5 percentage points). The shares of all other industrial lines declined or were stagnant in this period.

The antisugar-prodiversification strategy of the early stages of the Revolution, combined with other factors, provoked a sharp decline in sugar output in 1962–63, which in turn rapidly expanded the balance of trade deficit and made unfeasible the ambitious program of industrialization. As a result, sugar was restored to its traditional predominance in 1964. The "new" development strategy, based on the theory of intentional disequilibrium, centered all the nation's resources and efforts on the sugar sector with the ultimate goal of a more balanced development. Sugar output would increase from 6 million tons in 1965 to 10 million tons in 1970, and to 11 and 12 million tons in the 1970s. This increase would transform the balance of trade deficit into a surplus, which would be used to repay the Soviet debt, resume the industrialization effort, and enhance the standards of living of the population. The sugar plan, however, was not preceded by a technical study of feasibility and opportunity cost. Most of its premises regarding investment, extension of sugar land, irrigation, and mechanization were not well-founded. It was seriously handicapped by lack of technical and managerial personnel, low productivity of the army of volunteer nonprofessional cane cutters, and transportation difficulties. The actual sugar output of 1965–70 was 25 percent the planned output; although the 1970 harvest broke the prerevolutionary output record, it fell 15 percent below the target and provoked a serious decline in the rest of the economy making evident the failure of the second development strategy. In the 1970s, although sugar continued to be the engine of the Cuban economy, a more rational policy was implemented which gave control to the technicians, set feasible output targets to be accomplished only with the resources allocated to the sugar sector, and tried to solve the manpower deficit with two technological alternatives—the Australian system of burning the cane, which failed, and mechanization, which seemed to have succeeded although lagging behind planned schedule. The new plan appears to have worked: sugar output declined by almost one-half in 1971–72, it increased steadily since 1973 (with the exception of one year), and in 1979 the second largest sugar harvest in history was completed—all this without creating any serious economic dislocation but with declining industrial yields since 1976. A sugarcane plague, however, rapidly spread to as much as one-third of all planted cane and sharply reduced sugar output in 1980.

The return to sugar since 1964 has worsened sugar monoculture. In 1975 sugarcane took nine percentage points more of major cultives than in 1960. Production of tobacco, coffee, and most tubers has significantly declined while rice production—after a significant dip—recuperated the prerevolutionary level in 1975–76. Tobacco plantations were practically wiped out in 1979–80 by blue mold. The only truly successful agricultural ventures of the Revolution are eggs and, to a lesser extent, citrus, and for both, important capital investments have been made. The number of head of cattle per capita slightly increased from 0.83 in 1958 to 0.87 in 1967 but then sharply declined to 0.58 in 1975; complications with breeding, fodder, artificial insemination, illnesses, and administration have been responsible for the decline. Performance in pig raising, though better than that for cattle, has also been poor, while that of poultry shows moderate success. In sharp contrast with agriculture, fishing is the success story of the Revolution. The total catch of fish increased almost tenfold in 1958–78, as a result of a capital-intensive program to expand the fishing fleet with the most modern of vessels.

Within mining, nickel is the mineral with best possibilities. Cuba's nickel plants were actually built prior to the Revolution (the largest one was not fully operational in 1958), and their output was affected by the exodus of technicians and lack of spare parts. Once the plants were put in operation, however, output increased by twofold over the prerevolutionary level, but it has been practically stagnant since 1968 and 25 percent below installed capacity. Production of nickel in Cuba is technologically obsolete due to its high fuel consumption and hence it is not profitable to sell nickel outside of the USSR. Plans to triple output capacity with two or three new plants supplied by the USSR and COMECON, the first initially scheduled to enter production in 1980, have been postponed until 1986–90. Most industrial lines increasing their share of GSP are connected with agriculture, including food (dairy and wheat products, canned fruits and vegetables, frozen fish and seafood) and chemistry (fertilizers). The largest increase in industrial output is in metallurgy and metallic products, mainly steel, steel derivatives, machinery (for example, harvesters), electronics, and a few domestic appliances. Within the construction materials sector, cement is the most important product; its output has increased almost fourfold through the Revolution.

Oil output has increased almost six times, but current production is small and satisfies only about 3 percent of the nation's needs. Output of electricity has increased threefold, but maintenance of the old equipment has been neglected and population growth and economic expansion have created electricity shortages. Since Cuba does not have energy sources, it is heavily dependent on oil imports, and has exhausted all conservation possibilities;

the alternative for the future seems to be nuclear energy. Construction of a Soviet nuclear power plant with four reactors was scheduled to begin in 1979 but has been delayed by the discovery of the seismic nature of its location. Consequently, operations will not start until the late 1980s or the early 1990s.

In 1958, some 300,000 tourists visited the island and were a significant source of foreign exchange, but the flow of tourists had declined by 99 percent ten years later. In the 1970s, however, a change in the political climate and economic considerations induced an increase of investment in the tourist industry. Hence the number of foreign tourists gradually rose to more than 130,000 in 1979, mostly Cuban emigres. This raised the hope that in the 1980s Cuba would get back to the prerevolutionary figure of 300,000 tourists, most of them coming from the United States, including a large number of Cuban emigres. But the massive exodus of Cuban exiles in 1980 and subsequent reversal in the political climate cast a doubt on such expectations.

If the mechanization of the sugar harvest and plague control are finally solved in the early 1980s, Cuba should be able to push moderately forward diversification in the third decade of the Revolution. To expand nonsugar agricultural output, particularly in crops such as coffee, tobacco, and some tubers that are difficult to mechanize, it would be highly advisable in view of the poor performance of the state sector to continue strengthening incentives to the private farms. The two economic lines with the highest potential for rapid and significant expansion seem to be nickel and tourism, with fishing and steel in a second rank. If in the 1980s Cuba were able to increase threefold both nickel output and the number of tourists, these two combined could generate about half of the current value of the whole sugar sector, significantly diversify output, and reduce the impact of international price fluctuations on the Cuban economy. Plans for the expansion of both the nickel and tourist industry could greatly benefit from U.S. technology, cooperation, and markets, but friction over Cuba's involvement in Africa, Soviet troops in Cuba, the new wave of exiles, and the change in the U.S. administration has worsened relations between the two countries. In spite of the impressive investment and expansion of the fishing industry in the first twenty years of the Revolution, it only generated about 0.5 percent of GSP in 1976 and was affected by difficulties in 1979. Even a doubling of the fishing catch in the 1980s, which would require even more resources than the tenfold increase of the first two decades, would not significantly reduce Cuba's monoculture. Metallurgy and metallic products contributed to GSP about eight times what fishing did in 1976. If the planned Soviet steel plant becomes operative in the 1980s, steel output should increase about threefold—giving a significant boost to this sector. In closing it should be noted that all these are plans for the current decade, and that actual work on some of them has not even begun. One should temper excessively optimistic forecasts for the current decade by carefully looking at the diversification record of the past twenty years, the many unfulfilled dreams, and the current capacity of the Cuban economy.

EXTERNAL ECONOMIC INDEPENDENCE

Cuba's external economic dependency on the United States was eliminated in the first stage of the Revolution, but a new dependency was established with the USSR and the socialist camp in the second stage. In general, dependency did not change significantly in the 1960s and worsened in the 1970s. Although it could be argued that there has been some positive changes in Cuba's economic relationship with the USSR as compared with the relationship Cuba had with the United States, these have not reduced the vulnerability of the island.

Cuba's overall trade dependency improved in the 1960s in relation to the prerevolutionary period, but it worsened in the first half of the 1970s and by 1975 surpassed the dependency levels of 1958. The improvement in the 1960s was actually more apparent than real, due to distortions created by the pivotal role of sugar. Dependency measured by the proportion of exports in relation to GMP declined in the 1960s because of the drop in value of sugar exports, while it increased in the 1970s boosted by the rising value of sugar exports.

Export concentration has not changed during the Revolution. Sugar exports as a percentage of total exports fluctuated from 74 to 90 percent in 1959–76, due to changes in sugar output and export prices. The revolutionary average was 82 percent, slightly higher than the 81 percent average of 1920–50. Nickel exports have risen and replaced tobacco as Cuba's second major export, and there have also been small increases of the export shares of fish and citrus fruits. Still, all nonsugar exports combined stood at 18 percent, confirming that little diversification has taken place in the composition of Cuban exports. A very high correlation exists between the value of sugar exports and both GMP and GSP, additional proof of the continued predominance of sugar in the Cuban economy.

The composition of imports did not change significantly in 1963–75 in relation to 1959 except for a decline in imports of manufactures; however, this may have been in part the result of definitional differences and the abnormally high proportion on nonspecified imports (one-fourth of the total). Foodstuffs continued to take the highest share of imports, although with a significant decline (together with the share of manufactures) during the Mao-Guevarist stage when preference was given to capital accumulation over consumption. The remaining imports in order of importance were machinery and transportation (mostly linked with the sugar sector), manufactures, fuel, chemicals (mainly linked with agriculture), and raw materials.

In 1960–78 Cuba's terms of trade with the USSR were better than with other socialist countries because of the substantial Soviet subsidies granted to the bulk of Cuban exports and oil imports, subsidies that are not paid by other COMECON countries. Cuba also gained in her exports to the USSR vis-à-vis market economies. The USSR paid on the average a higher price for Cuba's sugar and nickel (which combined are equal to 90 percent of Cuba's exports) than the prevailing world price. But the situation is not as clear concerning imports. In 1973–77 Cuba bought oil from the USSR at a price below the world price, but this gain may have been offset by prices higher than those on the world market charged by the USSR for capital, intermediate, and manufactured goods imported by Cuba. Available statistical analyses of Cuba's terms of trade done in the United States indicate worse terms with the USSR and socialist countries than with market economies, but these studies suffer from methodological flaws in the indexing of exports—if not in that of imports. Since 1976 the price of Cuba's fundamental export has been tied up with the price of Soviet oil and other "basic" imports, resulting in an improvement in Cuba-Soviet terms of trade.

Throughout the prerevolutionary Republic (1902–58), the Cubans had a trade deficit for only three years, and the cumulative surplus in this period stood at two billion pesos. In 1959–78, Cuba's balance of trade ended in deficit except for two years, and the cumulative trade deficit stood at 5.5 billion pesos. The USSR was responsible for 48 percent of Cuba's cumulative deficit, other socialist countries for 3 percent, and market economies for the remaining 49 percent. More than 78 percent of the deficit with market economies occurred in 1975–78 due to decline in world sugar prices, while at the same time Cuban-Soviet trade generated for the first time a substantial surplus for Cuba due to concessionary prices paid by the USSR.

Cuba's trade-partner concentration has improved under the Revolution from an average of 69 percent of total trade with the United States in 1946–58 to 50 percent with the USSR in 1961–78. But in 1978, Cuba's total trade with the USSR alone reached a record of 69 percent, and an additional 10 percent of trade was with other COMECON countries that are under the Soviet sphere of influence. The lowest percentage of Cuban-Soviet trade has occurred when sugar prices in the world market were at a high, thus providing Cuba with sufficient foreign exchange to expand its capacity to choose her trade partners. When sugar prices in the international market were at low points, though, Cuban-Soviet trade was at its highest.

In 1961–76 Cuba sold an average of 45 percent of her sugar exports to the USSR; while this was ten percentage points less than the average she had sold to the United States before 1959, an additional 15 percent was exported to other COMECON countries—mainly to those having the closest relations with the USSR. Cuba also exported most of her nickel and practically all of her citrus and rum to COMECON; for cigars and fish, however, the island enjoyed the most diversified trade partners.

The USSR supplied Cuba with practically all her oil needs as well as most foodstuffs and raw materials; other socialist countries also supply a significant proportion of foodstuffs. In the 1960s and early 1970s, socialist countries also supplied most of Cuba's imports of manufactures, machinery, and transportation. But in 1974–75, when Cuba had a considerable inflow of hard currency due to the international sugar boom, the percentage supplied by the USSR and other socialist countries of the island's imports of manufactures, transportation, and machinery declined sharply as Cuba chose to buy most of these products from market economies. In the second half of the 1970s, however, due to low world prices of sugar and Soviet subsidies, Cuba became more dependent on Soviet imports.

Cuba is not well endowed with energy sources and has to import from the USSR an average of 98 percent of the oil it consumes. Oil imports have steadily increased in spite of the introduction of drastic conservation measures. Nuclear energy seems to be the solution in the long run (and through the USSR), but in the meantime the island fully relies on the USSR for oil supplies and pays high freight costs.

The island's heavy trade dependency and the long distance of her major trade partners—the USSR, Eastern Europe, and Japan—are responsible for high freight costs. To reduce them somewhat, Cuba expanded the tonnage of her merchant marine fleet by tenfold in 1958–75. In spite of this considerable investment, the island's own ships carried only one-tenth of her foreign trade in 1975. Even if the 1980 goal of doubling the 1975 tonnage is achieved, the percentage of trade carried will increase from only 13 to 15 percent. Another 9 to 15 percent of trade is carried by ships rented by Cuba, mostly from socialist countries.

The USSR has replaced the United States as Cuba's major source of foreign capital. Half of the Soviet aid has been in the form of nonrepayable military equipment as well as subsidies to Cuban exports and imports; the other half—about $4.9 billion in 1976—is in repayable loans. An additional $260 million has come from other socialist countries and probably had been repaid by Cuba in 1976. Finally, western international banks and market economies have supplied $1.3 billion in hard currency loans with shorter maturity and higher interests than the loan terms of the socialist countries. Cuba's total foreign debt in 1976 was approximately $6.2 billion, 136 times the amount of the foreign debt in 1959. In 1972 the USSR postponed until 1986 both capital amortization and interest of her loans. And yet it seems that repayment of the debt was the expenditure in the Cuban budget, except for "reserves," that increased the most in 1979 over 1963: 639 percent as compared to an average of 310 percent for other budget categories. Cuba's foreign debt per capita and the proportion of the debt in relation to GMP was the highest in Latin America in 1975, while Cuba's hard currency debt in relation to GSP was the highest within COMECON. Cuba's capacity to start servicing the bulk of her debt with the USSR in 1986 is quite low, and hence the island will desperately seek a renegotiation of that debt.

In summary, the analysis of the mechanisms of external economic dependency shows little change between the prerevolutionary and the revolutionary situation with a tendency to worsen in the 1970s.[1] Overall trade dependency apparently improved in the 1960s but deteriorated in the 1970s to become worse in 1975 than in 1958. Export concentration has slightly deteriorated while import composition has slightly improved. Overall terms of trade are difficult to estimate: a prerevolutionary cumulative trade surplus has been transformed into a colossal cumulative trade deficit; Cuba has received favorable prices from the USSR on sugar, nickel, and oil but may have paid higher prices for other Soviet imports; in the late 1970s terms of trade with the USSR seemed to improve. Trade partner concentration declined until the end of the 1970s and then became similar to the prerevolutionary situation. Energy dependency has not changed and worsened concerning freight costs. Cuba has become slightly more independent in its capacity to handle its own foreign trade. Last but not least, Cuba's foreign debt has increased 136 times in relation to the debt at the eve of the Revolution.

If the dependencia criteria is applied to Cuba some situations appeared unchanged but some differences are evident under the Revolution. On the one hand, the Cuban economy is still heavily determined by outside forces over which national leaders do not have significant control. The USSR has basically the power to set prices, grant subsidies, and extend credit to the island. Part of Cuba's trade is still with market economies and hence the island is not totally removed from the international market in terms of price fluctuations, need of credit, and so forth.[2] Cuba basically remains a monoculture economy which exports a few raw materials to the USSR and buys from the latter most of the needed intermediate and capital goods. The island has been unable to accumulate enough capital from domestic resources, has shown little progress in the expansion of the capital-good sector, and has been incapable of self-sustained economic growth. To keep its economy running, Cuba has had to borrow heavily from the

USSR—but also from other socialist and market economies—thus increasing her foreign debt dramatically. On the other hand, the USSR does not have direct investment in Cuba and hence cannot expatriate profits. In addition, it has provided loans and credits under favorable conditions, postponed part of the Cuban debt, supplied most military aid free, and subsidized the price of Cuba's two major exports and one key import. It is difficult, therefore, to see the USSR as extracting an economic surplus from Cuba; even if prices of most Soviet imports were indeed unfavorable, this would not offset other favorable terms granted to the island. Thus Cuba remains heavily dependent on the USSR by most criteria, but the Soviets do not seem to exploit the island economically.

Political scientists may argue, however, that the USSR extracts significant political and military benefits from Cuba. Furthermore, the island is highly vulnerable to Soviet pivotal economic power and political influence. The USSR has the capacity to cut the supply to the island of virtually all oil, most capital, foodstuffs, and raw materials, about one-third of basic capital and intermediate goods, and probably all weaponry. Additionally, loss of Soviet markets would mean an end to their buying about half of Cuban sugar at three times the price of the market as well as purchase of substantial amounts of nickel also at a subsidized price. The USSR could also exert powerful influence over such COMECON countries as the GDR, Czechoslovakia, and Bulgaria, which are particularly the key ones in trade with Cuba, to stop economic relations with Cuba. Finally the USSR could stick to the 1972 agreements and ask Cuba to start repaying in 1986 the debt owed the Soviets. These are not hypothetical scenarios because in 1968 the USSR used the oil stick and in the 1970s the economic-aid carrot to influence crucial shifts in Cuban foreign and domestic policies just as it had tried before, unsuccessfully, in Yugoslavia and China. Both those countries, though, had certain options— Yugoslavia, Western aid, and China an enormous and well-endowed country—to resist Soviet pressure. The possibility for Cuba to find alternatives for Soviet aid are very slim. The United States could play that role, but with Cuba's African ventures and the change in U.S. administration in January 1981, relations between the two nations have deteriorated. Strong animosity against China rules out any help from that country. Other world powers or blocks either lack the resources or the motivation to come to the rescue of the Cubans. Unless an unforeseen dramatic change occurs in the 1980s, Cuba's dependency on the USSR will continue and probably increase.

FULL EMPLOYMENT

Open unemployment grew worse in the first stage of the Revolution, but by the end of the second stage it had been cut to one-half of the prerevolutionary rate, and by 1970 further reduced to a small percentage—mainly a frictional phenomenon. This significant feat, however, was in large measure achieved by transforming open unemployment into underemployment at the expense of a sharp decrease in labor productivity. In the 1970s the priorities were reversed, and labor productivity rose from bottom to top priority while full employment deteriorated. Although open unemployment has been temporarily cut back again, its definite eradication is linked to structural problems not easy to solve.

The labor force participation rate—in relation to the total population—declined in the 1960s because an increasing number of youngsters went to school rather than to work, a significant segment of the labor force went into exile, and retirement laws were liberalized. These trends offset intensive labor mobilization campaigns and the incorporation of females into the labor force. In the 1970s, the rate of labor force participation increased due to reduction of emigration, acceleration of female incorporation and, since 1976, the entrance into the labor force of those born in the baby boom of the 1960s.

State employment represented about one-tenth of the labor force prior to the Revolution but rapidly rose, due to collectivization of private businesses, farms and other activities, reaching almost 95 percent of total employment by 1978. Private employment has been mostly confined to agriculture, with tiny pockets in fishing, transportation, and in commerce and personal services.

More than half of the labor force in 1970 was concentrated in the 20–39 age bracket, and only a combined 17 percent was either less than 20 or older than 60. Female incorporation into the labor force did not happen all of a sudden but has been the result of a long process that accelerated under the Revolution, particularly in the late 1960s and early 1970s. In 1978 females made up 24 percent of the labor force as compared to 13 percent in 1958. They are still concentrated in conventional women's jobs such as services, commerce, and the garment industry; however, a significant decline occurred in domestic service, which provided most female employment prior to the Revolution. Although no data are available on the race composition of the labor force, scattered information suggests that blacks have benefitted from the virtual elimination of open unemployment. Still they are underrepresented in the most-skilled occupations and overrepresented in the least-skilled occupations.

Within the labor force and among economic activities, services expanded the most in the 1960s. Moderate increases occurred in industry—with a temporary jump in 1970 associated with the 10 million ton sugar harvest—construction, and transportation-communication. Small increases were recorded in commerce, while agriculture contracted. Although no data exist on the distribution of the labor force since 1970, an analysis of the distribution of employment in the state civilian sector—when proper adjustments are done for job transfers from the private to the state sector—suggests a continuation of the employment decline in agriculture and of the increases in services and to a lesser extent construction and transportation-communication. Contrary to the 1960s trend, though, industry and commerce declined or stagnated.

Open unemployment stood at about 12 percent of the labor force in 1958, increased in 1959, and reached a peak of 20 percent early in 1960; thereafter it declined to reach a low of 1.3 percent in 1970. Unemployment increased in the early 1970s, peaked in 1974, declined again possibly until 1978, and increased in 1979–80. The typical unemployed person under the Revolution is a male, between 17 and 24 years old, searching for a job for the first time, and an urbanite possibly living in Havana.

Open unemployment was eliminated in the 1960s through planned and unplanned measures: the exportation of part of the labor force abroad; the depletion from the labor market of the labor force tails through education and social security; rural-to-urban migration combined with annual guaranteed jobs and overstaffing of state farms, which eliminated seasonal unemployment in agriculture; and the phenomenal expansion of jobs in the social services, armed forces, and the administrative bureaucracy combined with overstaffing in industry and subsidies to redundant workers, which avoided open unemployment in the cities. Contrary to the Revolution's expectations, the labor surplus coming from the countryside did not find productive jobs in industry during the first half of the 1960s; instead, they were employed mostly in the tertiary sector. In the second half of the 1960s, when the development strategy shifted in favor of agriculture, the urban labor surplus had to be pushed back to the countryside to alleviate the artificial manpower deficit. To correct the imbalance, rural-to-urban migration was curtailed, the labor surplus in industry and services was detected through work quotas, a campaign was launched to reduce bureaucracy, and part of the surplus was mobilized to work in agriculture through the military draft, voluntary labor, and labor brigades made up of youngsters.

In the first half of the 1970s, open unemployment rose again because of the emphasis on productivity—which released the labor surplus—the reduction in the size of the armed forces and social services—two major absorbers of unemployment in the 1960s—the entering into the labor market of an increasing number of females, and the sharp decline in emigration. To cope with the problem, several measures were taken: opening to males jobs that were previously reserved for females and closing for the latter jobs that they could perform before; concentration of new industrial plants and new construction in Havana and urban locations that have a labor surplus; slowdown of the application of work quotas, particularly in agriculture, and continuation of the underemployment practice in the industrial sugar sector; payment of subsidies to those laid off until they got a new job; legalization of the private practice of trades and professions in the service sector; and the increase of the armed forces for Cuba's involvement in Africa.

In the 1960s, Cuba transformed most open unemployment into various types of underemployment, which provoked sharp declines in labor productivity and in turn adversely affected the standard of living of most of the population. Overall productivity rates probably declined in 1961–62, slightly recuperated in 1964–65, declined catastrophically in the Mao-Guevarist years of 1967–70, vigorously recuperated from 1971 to 1975, and declined again in 1976–80. The last decline occurred with the introduction of the new economic system, the slowdown in the application of work quotas, and problems of labor discipline.

The sharpest declines of productivity in the second half of the 1960s occurred in the major economic activities: agriculture, industry, and construction and communications, while apparently slight increases were recorded in commerce and transportation—both probably an illusion caused by inflationary distortions. In the 1970s, commerce and construction registered the highest increases in productivity followed by industry and transportation; agriculture declined until 1973 and recuperated thereafter. There are various reasons for the divergent productivity performance of the different sectors besides inflation and enforcement of work quotas. The industrial lines with the most advanced technology—chemicals, oil, power, and nickel—recorded the highest productivity gains, while labor-intensive lines showed the lowest gains. Agriculture and probably services, being mostly labor intensive, has also shown low gains in productivity. Additional labor-related reasons are overstaffing, use of low-productive volunteers, subsidies to redundant workers, and slackened labor effort. There are also other reasons such as shutdowns and slowdowns of factories, breakdowns of equipment, administrative flaws, and natural phenomena that affect mainly agriculture. Finally, productivity in the small private sector—basically agriculture—has been higher than in the state sector. Since the late 1960s, sugarcane and tobacco yields of private farms have been consistently higher than yields in the state farms.

If current trends continue into the 1980s (that is, if the emphasis on productivity is maintained) unemployment pressures will increase because of the full entry into the labor force of the baby boom of the 1960s, the female push to enter the labor force (although the possibilities of a rapid increase in the female participation are small), and the tendency to release labor surplus from inefficient enterprises and to create a few new productive jobs in capital-intensive lines. Alternatives to this problem may be the further expansion of productive but labor-intensive service activities such as tourism, as well as private activities such as repairs and other personal services, and agriculture (which seem to be happening since 1980); the increased involvement in military ventures abroad (which is difficult due to economic limitations); and the exportation of the labor surplus abroad (which was obviously done in the spring and summer of 1980). If these avenues are not enough to solve the problem, then the leadership may decide to expand underemployment again at the cost of neglecting labor productivity.

EQUALITY IN DISTRIBUTION

Throughout the 1960s equality in distribution had first priority, with a slowdown in 1964–65 and a big push during the Mao-Guevarist stage. This policy achieved success in greatly reducing prerevolutionary inequalities but seriously affected economic stimuli and productivity and became a heavy burden for the economy. In the 1970s, the previous egalitarian policies were criticized as idealistic mistakes and more realistic distributive policies, which take into account skills and productivity rather than needs, were implemented.

In the early years of the Revolution income distribution shifted dramatically. On the one hand, latifundia owners, industrialists, bankers, real estate owners, middle-sized farmers, and renters were dispossessed of their property and virtually all of their income through collectivization. On the other hand, the unemployed got jobs and income, minimum wages and pensions were raised, house and land rent and utility rates were reduced, and free social services provided by the state were significantly expanded. Crude estimates of income distribution suggest that in the early years of the Revolution, 20 percent of income was transferred from the wealthier to the poorest segment of the population; however, in 1962–73, the process of income distribution significantly slowed down, and the 3 percent of income transferred from the wealthier benefitted the middle-income group rather than the poorest group. Although the wealthier group suffered a sharp decline in income, still, the wealthiest 10 percent of the population earned almost seven times what the poorest 10 percent made in 1973.

Since 1963, practically all income earned in Cuba comes from the government in the form of wages, except for the small private sector in agriculture. Through Soviet-style wage scales, first introduced in 1963-65, the government attempted to standardize all wages throughout the nation to implement equal wage to equal work regardless of enterprise productivity and profitability. The state labor force was divided into four categories, each one falling under a different wage scale: (1) blue-collar workers in agriculture; (2) blue-collar workers outside of agriculture; (3) white-collar workers in services and government administration; and (4) technical and executive personnel. Wage rates in scale (1) were substantially lower than in scales (2) and (3), which were almost identical, and these two, in turn, had wage rates lower than in scale (4). The extreme differential wage ratio, between the lowest wage rate (paid to an agricultural peon) and the highest wage rate (paid to a cabinet minister), was 1 to 10. In spite of wage differentials, the wage-scale system dramatically reduced prerevolutionary wage and income inequalities, when the differential wage ratio was probably one hundred times larger; however, the basic wage in the mid-1960s could be increased by overtime, extra payments for work performed under abnormal conditions, bonuses for overfulfilling work quotas, and the historical wage—in other words, the difference between the old wage and the new wage introduced by the scales. Furthermore, top officials enjoyed privileges such as easier access to scarce housing, and exclusive access to cars, travel abroad, and goods outside rationing. In spite of all these additives, however, Cuba probably had the most egalitarian distribution system in Latin America by 1965.

During the Mao-Guevarist stage, income equalization was pushed forward by the substitution of moral for material incentives, the reduction in wage differentials, the disconnection between wages and work quotas, the elimination of overtime and production bonuses, the postponement of extra payments for work performed under abnormal conditions, and the expansion of social services provided free by the state. In this stage the connection between work and remuneration was almost severed and distribution done according to need. The catastrophic failure of this idealistic experiment forced, in the 1970s, a reversal of the previous policies: material incentives substituted for moral incentives; wage differentials expanded; wage scales were reintroduced and connected with work quotas; overtime and production bonuses were reinstalled; expansion of free social services was frozen and in some cases reversed; durable consumer goods became distributed mainly based on work performance; author's royalties were paid for the first time under the Revolution; and incentive funds were created in enterprises with part of their profits. Although the historical wage was under attack both in the second half of the 1960s and throughout the 1970s, it has survived as an indication of the power of the labor market. It is used to get the best workers and technicians into priority jobs, and managers circumvent the limitations of the wage scale by offering them an extra payment disguised as a historical wage. In the current stage, not only has there been a return to the principle of distribution according to work, but also an attempt to reestablish the connection between labor reward and enterprise productivity and profitability.

Extreme wage differentials declined in 1966–70 and continued to shrink until 1973 when the new wage policy was officially proclaimed; thereafter they began to increase. An analysis of average wages by economic activities and their branches, on the one hand, and actual wages paid in specific jobs, on the other, suggests that the extreme wage differential ratio in the state civilian sector in 1977–78 was 10 to 1, equal to that of 1965. In the 1970s a substantial number of workers—mostly service employees—moved up into the best-paid wage scale, while most agricultural workers remained concentrated in the lowest grades of the worst paid wage scale.

The average income of the population, as well as the average wage of state-civilian and military employees and state payment to private farmers, increased in the first half of the 1960s, deteriorated in the second half of the 1960s, reached a trough in 1970, and recuperated in the 1970s surpassing—or at least equalling—the mid-1960s peak. But some groups did worse than others in the frugal Mao-Guevarist stage, and some groups got a bigger piece than others of the expanding pie in the boom of the 1970s. Overall income per capita in 1977 rose 34 percent above the 1970 trough, but only 17 percent above the 1964 peak, certainly not a significant gain and probably a loss if inflation is taken into account. Private farmers were the most squeezed group in the Mao-Guevarist stage with a loss of 60 percent of their state income and, in spite of their improvement, in the 1970s they only managed to approximate their 1965 peak; however, they had an additional private income that still seemed to be quite sizable. The military probably got the best deal in the 1970s boom: an increase of 44 percent over their average wage in 1970, which placed them as the best paid group. State civilian employees came up in the middle, with an increase of 22 percent of their average wage over 1970 although only a 5 percent increase over their 1966 peak.

An analysis of revolutionary distribution cannot be limited to monetary income but should take into account the role of rationing, prices, and social services. Taxes did not play an important role in distribution in most of the 1960s and 1970s since they were eliminated in the mid-1960s and not reintroduced until the end of the 1970s. In the new economic policy, however, a sales tax is to be imposed that should play a regressive role in income distribution, while new taxes already in force for farm cooperatives and the self-employed possibly should play a progressive role.

The decision to introduce rationing in 1962 was an egalitarian one, otherwise the excess of demand over supply of consumer goods would have resulted in a price spiral and a sharp reduction of the purchasing power of the low income groups. But rationing could not suppress altogether the powerful forces of supply and demand, and for those able to pay, the black market was available. In the Mao-Guevarist stage, rationing quotas became meager but increased in the 1970s and yet rationing in 1978 was still tougher than in 1962 and extended to at least one-third of consumer goods, including the most essential foodstuffs and manufactures. Data on consumption per capita denote a similar trend. According to official estimates, rationing assured from 2,100 to 2,846 daily calories in 1977–78, a questionable figure in view of a substantially lower estimate for 1962 when rationing quotas were higher. Even if the 1977–78 figures were accurate, they were below the average of 2740–2870 calories reported for 1951–58. It is important to remember that rationing, with some exceptions, assures a minimum and equal caloric intake for all the population while the prerevolutionary average hid significant inequalities in nutrition. Still those who have higher incomes can supplement their diets eating in restaurants; many workers and students benefit from subsidized meals in enterprises and schools, but such subsidies are gradually being eliminated. Some consumer durables and manufactures have been taken out of the rationing list and are increasingly allocated according to job importance and labor effort.

Prices of most rationed foodstuffs have remained unchanged since 1962, which protects the purchasing power of low income groups. But an increasing number of manufactured, beverage, tobacco and foodstuff products, as well as gasoline, are being sold since 1973 in an official parallel market at prices three to eight times the rationing price of the same products. There is also a "red market," fed by foreign technicians and diplomats who have access to exclusive diplostores in which goods are sold at five or six times the buying price. Diplostores and tourist shops carry numerous goods either not available elsewhere or of a much better quality, but one has to buy those goods with hard currency, which effectively prohibits access to almost all the native population. Finally in the black market, goods are sold from five to fifteen times the rationing price. The majority of the labor force with an average wage of 140 pesos in 1978 could not afford to buy goods in the parallel, red, or black markets, or even to eat in good restaurants. The government has tried to attenuate this inequality by providing credit without interest for installment payments of consumer durables, and by offering as awards to the best workers vacations in resorts, honeymoons in hotels, and nights at top cabarets.

The four most important social services, both in terms of their cost and need, are education, health care, social security, and housing; the first three are provided free to all, the fourth is either free or at a very low rent. The Revolution has performed best in education, where significant improvements have been achieved both in expansion of coverage and raising overall standards—at least in relation to public education in 1958. The illiteracy rate was reduced from an estimated 21 percent in 1958 to 13 percent in 1970 and possibly to 7 or 8 percent in 1978 (but not to the allegedly 3.9 percent officially reported at the end of 1961.) Elementary education was expanded from 58 percent of the school-age population in 1953 to practically all that population in 1976. Secondary education grew from 19 to 47 percent, and university education expanded from 5.5 to 10.8 percent.

The expansion of social security equals that of education: coverage of the labor force for old age, disability, and survivor insurance increased from 63 percent in 1958 (the second highest in Latin America) to practically 100 percent in the late 1960s. No health insurance was offered in 1958 and maternity insurance was limited to employed females, while today coverage is universal thus placing Cuba first in Latin America. Prior to the Revolution, fifty-two social security funds existed and were stratified along occupational lines, with significant and largely unjustified differences that favored top occupations in terms of coverage, financing, and benefits. All these funds were unified and standardized in 1963 and inequalities eliminated. The average pension declined steadily in the 1960s, due to economic difficulties and coverage of low income groups, but it slowly increased after 1969. By 1976 the average pension was 11 percent higher than in 1959, probably a loss if inflation is taken into account. But current pensions are more equally distributed than before, for example, the extreme differential ratio was 4 to 1 in 1978 as compared to 13 to 1 in 1958.

Performance in health is less impressive than in education and social security because of the very high standards Cuba enjoyed in 1958 and the significant deterioration suffered in the 1960s due to the exodus of medical personnel, decline in the number and quality of graduates, and reduction in the supply of medical equipment and medicines. General mortality and infant mortality rates increased through most of the 1960s, as much as 13 and 40 percent above the prerevolutionary levels; however, they declined in the 1970s and by 1976 were 13 and 32 percent below the 1958 rates. With a few exceptions, morbidity rates also increased in the 1960s and declined in the 1970s. By 1976, half of the reported contagious diseases were either eliminated or with rates below the prerevolutionary level, but the other half showed substantially higher rates than in 1958. The ratio of inhabitants per physician rose from 920 in 1958 to 1,500 in 1964, but by 1978 it had declined to 675. The ratio of inhabitants per hospital bed increased from 184 in 1958 to 203 in 1967 but in 1975 was back to the 1958 level. In order to recuperate and in some cases surpass the prerevolutionary health levels lost in the 1960s, it was necessary to increase by eighteenfold the state budget allocation to health, to develop massive vaccinations, and to launch crash program to graduate medical personnel.

Revolutionary performance in housing is disappointing. In the early years, house rent was cut by at least 50 percent, a plan was introduced to make lessees owners of the houses in which they lived, and state-subsidized housing was built to eliminate the slums and improve rural housing. Later on rent on new housing was fixed at 6 to 10 percent of family income, and those with very low income were exempt. In the early 1970s housing dropped to the bottom in construction priorities, thus dwelling construction per 1,000 inhabitants declined from 2.3 in 1959–63 to 0.5 in 1970 and then increased to 1.5 in 1979, still below the 1959–63 level. The estimated housing deficit created under the Revolution stood at 700,000 units in 1977. Government goals for housing construction have been overly optimistic, ranging from as high as 70,000 to 100,000 per year, while the actual highest number ever built under the Revolution has been about 21,000. Even if 100,000 homes were built annually in 1981–2000, the housing deficit still will not be eliminated by the end of the century.

Prerevolutionary inequalities between urban and rural areas have been significantly reduced under the Revolution, particularly in the early years; however, propaganda claims seem to overrun reality. Available data on income distribution suggest that the gap between Havana and the rest of the country significantly expanded in 1953–68, and it was finally reduced by only 6 percentage points in 1972 over 1953. In spite of the introduction and rise of the minimum wage and the increase of average wages in agriculture throughout most of the 1960s and 1970s, the state agricultural labor force (with the exception of canecutters) is still the worst paid in the country. In 1978 a delayed wage increase to agricultural workers was postponed again as inflationary while significant increases had been granted before to technical and executive personnel. Private farmers, however, do much better than state farmers and are considerably less affected by rationing. The gap in the illiteracy rates between urban and rural areas has been dramatically reduced by a half, from 30 percentage points in 1953 to 15 points in 1970. Still in 1970 the illiteracy rate in the city of Havana stood at 2.9 percent while the *average* rural rate was 22 percent. In 1970, rural needs for elementary schools and teachers were fully satisfied, but in 1975 only 25 percent of secondary schools and students were in rural areas—in contrast with 39 percent of the population living there. In 1958 there was only one rural hospital in contrast with 57 in 1978; and while in 1958, 60 percent of the physicians and 62 percent of the hospital beds were in Havana, by 1978 the proportions had declined to 36 and 39 percent. Still in 1976, the capital city had about one-half of the inhabitants/hospital bed ratio of most provinces and less than one-fourth of the ratio of the poorest province. In 1970 a higher proportion of rural than urban families owned their home or were exempted from paying rent, but 36 percent were still living in *bohíos*. Provision of rural housing seemed to have proportionally shrunk in 1972 over 1953, and the situation could hardly improve in the 1970s since Havana was absorbing again the prerevolutionary lion's share of housing: 41 percent in 1973 compared to 7 percent in 1970.

There is no doubt that the Revolution has significantly reduced race inequalities in income, education, health, social security and, to a lesser extent, housing. Although the 1970 census presented the golden opportunity to statistically prove these accomplishments, the racial data collected by the census have not been published. This increases the suspicion, raised by some black militants and white scholars, that some significant racial inequalities persist. An analysis of reported diseases, for instance, suggests that blacks are overrepresented in all diseases and in those that particularly affect the poor. Blacks are apparently underrepresented in the best paid, most prestigious, and highly-skilled occupations and overrepresented in the worst paid, least prestigious, low-skilled occupations, hence income differences between whites and blacks are still noticeable. Finally, since blacks had the worst housing in 1958 and moves into new housing or that left by exiles represented only one-fifth of total housing stock, one has to conclude that the majority of the population probably lives today in the same housing it occupied at the beginning of the Revolution. Consequently, blacks have improved somewhat their housing standards, but they still inhabit the worst of the existing stock.

If the current pragmatist trend perseveres in the 1980s, then wage differentials will continue to expand and a closer connection made between wages and labor productivity. The incentive fund should be implemented throughout the nation, reinforcing the association between labor reward and enterprise profits. Prices should gradually substitute for rationing as allocators of consumer goods, although many scarce goods should remain rationed at subsidized prices. The distribution of key social services such as education, health, and social security will remain free and fairly equal, but privileged consideration for the elite and their children will grow through special schools, separate treatment in hospitals, and higher ceilings in pensions. Housing rent will be tied to space rather than to income, and the rates of public utilities will be according to consumption. These changes, although leading to stratification, should not reintroduce the gross inequalities existing prior to the Revolution.

The best picture of what the third decade of the Revolution will be like was melancholically drawn by Fidel Castro as the year of the twentieth anniversary of the Revolution opened and closed:

There is a story in the Bible about seven very good years, the years of fat cows, and seven very bad years, the years of the lean cows. . . . We must maintain a lean cow mentality for several years. [They] will be marked by effort and hard work. It would be demagogic to say that coming years which face this generation are going to be easy ones. . . . I firmly believe that we actually should not think of increasing our consumption . . . we should not speak of improving living conditions. . . . It is more important for us [to concentrate on development], to put our economy on a sound footing, [to maintain the levels of production] and change the structure of our economy. . . . We should aim our efforts mainly in this direction in the next seven or eight years. . . . There is always a generation whose lot is to do the hardest work . . . to create other conditions for the coming generation. . . . The most sacred duty of this generation is to devote their efforts to the development of the country. . . . This generation must make sacrifices. . . . Other generations will live better.[3]

Appendix 1

Problems in Dealing with Cuba's Macroeconomic Indicators

Socialist countries including Cuba do not use the Western concept of the *gross national product* (GNP) and the corresponding system of national accounts but rather the Soviet-developed concepts of the *global social product* (GSP), *total material product* (TMP), and *gross material product* (GMP) and the corresponding *system of material product balances*.[1] The Marxist doctrine distinguishes between: (1) "material production sphere," which is the "productive" one and includes the output of "material goods" (for example, in agriculture, fishing, mining, industry, and construction) and the delivery of "material services" or those directly connected with the production of material goods (such as transportation, "commodity circulation" or trade, and communication); and (2) "nonmaterial sphere" which is "nonproductive"—that is, it does not increase the total quantity of material goods—and embraces all services that satisfy personal and social needs of the population (such as finance, public administration, defense, health care, education and culture, housing, sports and recreation, and household services). GSP is the annual value resulting from all the material-production sphere, both material goods and material services, hence it excludes the value of nonmaterial services. TMP is the value of material goods alone hence it leaves out material services. In summary TMP embraces the agricultural, fishing, mining, industrial, and construction sectors, while GSP comprises these three plus the transportation, communication, and trade sectors, and both exclude other services.[2]

A second methodological difference pertains to the process of aggregation in calculating GSP and TMP. The Western concept of value added, where only the additional value contributed in each stage of production and distribution of a given good is taken into account, is not used in Cuba; instead they have the "system of complete circulation," which results in considerable double counting. If production is done by units of the same enterprise (for example, leather and shoes), then the value of leather is summed only with the value *added* of shoes hence avoiding double counting, but if these were two independent enterprises, the *total* value of shoes will be counted by each firm hence duplicating the value of leather therein.[3] As enterprises have proliferated in the 1970s, from 300 to 3,000, the amount of double counting may have increased, thus inflating GSP. Some Cuban publications argue that "to permit international comparisons, GMP measures the net output of products thus avoiding double counting of intermediate products."[4] In other words, GMP results from subtracting the value of intermediate inputs ("insumos") from TMP. This seemed confirmed by comparing annual TMP and GMP, in current prices in 1967–74, which resulted in TMP being above the GMP by an annual average of 16.6 percent.[5] And yet, one of the top officials of the State Committee on Statistics was skeptical in 1979 that GMP "actually cleaned duplications and made possible the comparison with national accounts."[6] Cuban statisticians are now working in a double accounting system to eliminate both duplication and add the value of nonmaterial services to GSP making it truly comparable with GNP.[7]

An additional complication is that there have been three changes in methodology since the system of material production balances began to be used—in 1967, 1970, and 1976. We do not know the exact nature of those changes, but they have produced four series that cannot be properly connected.[8] In addition, data for 1959–61, which were years of steady economic growth, have not been published, and the first series based on the Soviet methodology begins in 1962, the economic nadir of the Revolution; hence growth rates are related to a trough instead of to a normal starting year.

There is also considerable confusion on whether GSP, TMP, and GMP are given in constant prices (measuring real growth through correction of inflation) or in current prices (affected by inflation). For the period 1962–66, Cuba has published GMP data both in constant and current prices but since 1967 only in current prices. Cuban statisticians argue that state-fixed prices in agriculture, industry, construction, and communication have not changed since 1965, thus TMP and GMP figures in current prices are actually in constant prices. This assertion, however, is questionable as discussed elsewhere in this book. On the other hand, Cubans say that foreign trade has been affected by inflation. Domestic trade prices have increased somewhat in the 1970s and international transportation prices have also changed; therefore, GSP is given at current prices.[9]

Unless specified, all monetary figures in this book are given in the Cuban currency, the peso which, as the U.S. dollar, is divided into 100 cents. From 1914 to 1971 the Cuban peso was exchanged par with the dollar, but since the early 1960s it has not been freely exchanged in the international market. Exchange rates are artificially set by the Cuban government and the peso has been tied with the ruble whose exchange rate, in turn, is arbitrarily fixed by the Soviet government. Parallel with the gradual devaluation of the dollar (particularly in 1971 and 1973) the value of the ruble and the peso has been raised. In 1978 the official exchange rate was set at $1.31 U.S. dollars for one Cuban peso.[10]

The above discussion suggests that Cuban macroeconomic indicators are not too reliable and hence should be used with caution and in combination with microeconomic indicators— mainly physical output. In the analysis of macroeconomic indicators, we should consider that GSP is smaller than GNP because the former excludes the value of nonmaterial services, while TMP and GMP are even smaller than GNP because both leave out all services both material and nonmaterial. This is important because of the Revolution's significant expansion of social services as well as defense and the public bureaucracy. On the other hand, GSP is probably a less reliable indicator than GMP because the former is more distorted both by the double counting process of aggregation and inflation in commerce and transportation. In terms of growth *rates,* the smaller size of GMP is a lesser problem than the more inflated nature of GSP, hence I consider the former the most reliable indicator.

Notes

1. See United Nations, *Yearbook of National Account Statistics 1973,* vol. 1 (New York, 1975), pp. xxix–xxxiii. To the best of my knowledge, the only attempt to calculate Cuban GNP using Western methodologies has been done by the CIA (for 1970–75) but the calculations are besieged by innumerable problems. See Central Intelligence Agency, Research Aid, *The Cuban Economy: A Statistical Review, 1968–1976* (Washington, D.C.: ER 76-10708, December 1976), p. 2.

2. Banco Nacional de Cuba, *Desarrollo y perspectivas de la economía cubana* (La Habana: XXV Aniversario del BNC, 1975), p. 23.

3. Interview with Felino Quesada Pérez and Francisco Martínez Soler, JUCE-PLAN, Havana, 12 July 1979.

4. *Anuario* 1975, p. 38; and Banco Nacional de Cuba, La Habana, 1977, p. 9.

5. The overvalue of TMP over GMP oscillated from a high of 34.7 percent in 1970 to a low of 6.5 percent in 1974. I am greatly in debt to Claes Brundenius for clarifying the difference between TMP and GMP. See his ground breaking study "Measuring Economic Growth and Income Distribution in Revolutionary Cuba," Lund University Research Policy Studies, Discussion Paper Series, April 1979. The aggregation process in Cuba's national accounts was shown in *Anuario 1972,* p. 30.

6. Miguel González Lincheta, head of Information and International Relations of the State Committee on Statistics, interview with the author, Havana, 13 July 1979.

7. As reported by Miguel Dotres, JUCEPLAN, discussion in New York, 2 November 1979.

8. See my article "Cuban Statistics Revisited," *Cuban Studies/Estudios Cubanos* 9: 2 (July 1979): 59–62.

9. *Ibid.,* and Banco Nacional de Cuba, *Desarrollo y perspectivas de la economía cubana,* p. 23.

10. Pick's Currency Yearbook (New York, several years). It is interesting to note that in Eastern Europe there are different exchange rates for the ruble and the peso. In the USSR, in 1978, the exchange was about par, but in Poland and the GDR the exchange rate for the peso was lower. This suggests that the USSR subsidizes the peso while other socialist countries take market reality more into account.

Appendix 2A

Percentage Distribution of Agricultural Product, 1962–76

Years	Sugar	Livestock	Other Agriculture	Forestry	Total[a]
1962	29.5	34.2	34.9	1.4	100.0
1963	27.2	37.8	34.3	0.7	100.0
1964	29.1	39.7	30.5	0.7	100.0
1965	36.0	38.0	25.3	0.7	100.0
1966	27.7	40.6	30.7	1.0	100.0
1967	34.8	35.6	28.7	0.9	100.0
1968	39.8	29.5	27.3	3.4	100.0
1969	43.9	29.1	24.7	2.3	100.0
1970	47.3	29.2	22.0	1.5	100.0
1971	43.2	30.0	24.5	2.3	100.0
1972	39.7	31.5	26.3	2.5	100.0
1973	40.0	31.0	26.1	2.9	100.0
1974	38.1	29.9	29.0	3.0	100.0
1975	38.5	30.6	28.2	2.7	100.0
1976	37.3	31.0	29.2	2.5	100.0

[a]In the years 1962–67, agricultural services were provided as a disaggregated fifth category; its value was proportionally assigned to the four categories in this table.

Sources: 1962–65 *Boletín 1966*, p. 22; 1966–67 *Boletín 1971*, p. 45; 1968–69 *Anuario 1974*, p. 46; 1970–74 *Anuario 1975*, p. 53; 1975–76 *Anuario 1976*, p. 59.

Appendix 2B

Percentage Distribution of Industrial Product, 1963–76 (1963–66 constant prices/1967–76 current Prices)

	1963	1964	1965	1966	1967	1968	1969	1970	1971	1972	1973	1974	1975	1976
Mining	2.0	2.5	2.4	2.1	2.0	2.3	2.1	1.7	1.7	1.7	1.5	1.4	1.4	1.3
Metallurgy and metallic	5.7	4.5	3.5	4.1	4.1	5.1	4.6	5.6	6.4	7.0	8.4	9.7	10.5	10.3
Construction materials	5.0	3.9	5.3	5.8	5.8	4.3	3.6	2.5	3.6	4.9	5.4	5.6	6.0	5.9
Oil and derivatives	7.8	9.4	9.8	10.3	9.5	8.9	9.2	8.0	7.9	8.1	8.2	7.3	7.0	6.7
Chemistry	9.2	9.6	8.3	8.8	9.8	11.0	11.3	11.5	12.3	12.1	11.8	11.7	11.9	11.6
Leather	11.4	11.4	9.7	9.6	9.2	8.5	7.9	8.1	9.1	9.5	9.4	9.4	9.5	9.9
Sugar	15.3	15.8	20.1	15.6	18.2	15.3	16.4	17.6	15.6	11.6	11.5	11.5	10.9	10.5
Food	21.1	20.5	20.2	22.4	19.4	25.7	26.5	25.8	25.8	26.0	24.5	24.2	23.1	23.0
Beverages and tobacco	10.3	11.2	10.4	10.9	10.4	10.0	9.3	9.9	7.9	8.5	8.3	8.6	8.7	9.5
Electricity	3.7	3.5	3.4	3.7	3.2	3.5	3.7	3.0	3.0	3.0	2.9	2.8	1.7	2.9
Others[a]	8.5	7.7	6.9	6.7	8.4	5.4	5.4	6.3	6.7	7.6	8.1	7.8	8.3	8.3
Total	100.0	100.0	100.0	100.0	100.0	100.0	100.0	100.0	100.0	100.0	100.0	100.0	100.0	100.0

[a]Printing, wood, paper, etc.

Sources: 1963–66 Boletín 1966, p. 79; 1967–68 Boletín 1971, p. 45; 1969 Anuario 1972, p. 31; 1970–73 Anuario 1974, p. 35; 1974–75 Anuario 1975, p. 39; 1976 Compendio 1976, p. 17.

Appendix 3

Summary of Major Statistical Compendia 1964–79

Socialist Cuba began to regularly publish annual statistical compilations in 1965 when the Statistics Directory of the Central Planning Board (Junta Central de Planificación—JUCEPLAN) centralized the statistical process. In 1976, the State Committee on Statistics (Comité Estatal de Estadísticas—CEE) was established as a separate entity from JUCEPLAN and took over the publication of statistical compilations. A summary of major statistical compendia is presented in the following table.[1]

Publisher	Year	Boletín	Anuario	Compendio	La economía cubana
JUCEPLAN	1964	X			
	1965	X		X	
	1966	X		X	
	1967	X			X
	1968	X		X	
	1969				
	1970	X			
	1971	X			
	1972		X		X
	1973		X		X
	1974		X	X	X
CEE	1975		X	X	X
	1976		X	X	X
	1977		X	X	
	1978		X	X	X
	1979		X	X	X[a]

[a]Available only for the first half of 1979.

Source: C. Mesa-Lago, "Cuban Statistics Revisted," *Cuban Studies/Estudio Cubanos,* 9.2 (July 1979):61; and Ibid., 10 no. 1 (January 1980):99, updated with information gathered in Cuba in August 1980.

From 1964 to 1971 (with the exception of 1969), Cuba published an annual statistical bulletin *(Boletín Estadístico de Cuba* abbreviated in this book as *Boletín)*. In 1972 the bulletin changed its name to Yearbook *(Anuario Estadístico de Cuba* abbreviated in this book as *Anuario)* although its content continued to be basically the same. This is the most complete compilation of Cuban statistics, contains some 250 pages, and is available only in Spanish. It is usually ready six months after the year ends but printing difficulties normally delay its publication about two years. Nevertheless the publication of the *Anuario* was speeded up in 1980 with the release of the 1978 issue and plans to release the 1979 issue before the end of the year.

A summary of the *Boletín/Anuario* has been irregularly published since 1965 *(Compendio Estadístico de la República de Cuba* abbreviated in this book as *Compendio)*. It runs some 70 pages, since 1974 is available both in Spanish and English, and is usually released shortly before the full yearbook. Starting in 1979, the *Compendio* was reduced in size and changed its title to *Cuba en cifras*. Since 1975, Cuba has regularly published a brief evaluation of its yearly economic performance *(La economía cubana)*. It runs some 22 pages, is available in Spanish (and occasionally in English) and is normally released three months after the year ends.[2]

Notes

1. Since 1970 I have regularly reviewed Cuban statistical compendia first in *Cuban Studies Newsletter:* 2:1 (November 1971):22–23; and 4:1 (December 1972):36; and later in *Cuban Studies/Estudios Cubanos:* 5:1 (January 1975): 39–41; 6:1 (January 1976):96–98; 6:2 (July 1976): 79–80; 7:2 (July 1977):226–227; 8:1 (January 1978):65; and 9:2 (July 1979):108–9.

2. The most complete collection of Cuban statistics from the revolutionary period, outside of Cuba, is at the University of Pittsburgh. Chadwyck-Healey Ltd. (Cambridge, England) is reproducing in microfilm most of the Cuban statistical compendia.

Notes

Chapter 1

1. At this point the reader may want to know about my background and biases. I was born in Cuba, from a middle class, Catholic family, and completed there all my education, including a degree in law, shortly before the revolutionary takeover. Initially I was a sympathizer of the Revolution and worked two years in important government posts, but became increasingly alienated by revolutionary attitudes on religion, ideology and civil freedoms, hence I left the country in mid-1961. After one year in Spain, I came to the United States in 1962, completed graduate work in economics, and became a citizen in 1968. I do not consider myself either an adversary or an activist sympathizer of the Revolution. In my writings, I have tried to assume a relatively detached, balanced, and objective attitude. And yet my value framework and legal training favors political pluralism and civil freedoms as well as social justice, while my economic training emphasizes efficiency and economic rationality. As a result, my previous works have been critical of Cuba's economic and political performance but favorable to her social performance, particularly in education, public health, and improved equality.

2. I first analyzed Cuba's performance on these five goals in my chapter "Economic Policies and Growth," in *Revolutionary Change in Cuba,* Carmelo Mesa-Lago, ed. (Pittsburgh: University of Pittsburgh Press, 1971), pp. 277–338. Later on, Sergio Roca and Roberto E. Hernández followed a similar approach in "Structural Economic Problems," in *Cuba, Castro and Revolution,* Jaime Suchlicki, ed. (Coral Gables: University of Miami Press, 1972), pp. 67–93. Archibald R. M. Ritter significantly expanded all previous works in terms of analytical framework, sophistication of analysis, systematization and provision of data in *The Economic Development of Revolutionary Cuba: Strategy and Performance* (New York: Praeger Publishers, 1974).

3. I have further developed these ideas in my paper "A Scheme to Compare Alternative Strategies of Socio-Economic Development in Latin America," University of Pittsburgh, Fall of 1978.

4. The opposite can also be said of developmental strategies that sacrifice social goals in the rigid pursuit of economic growth. In this case the cost paid is often sociopolitical instability (upheavals, uprising, revolution), which ultimately jeopardizes the survival of the status quo and the pursuit of growth.

Chapter 2

1. This section is taken from my chapter "Economic Policies and Growth," *Revolutionary Change in Cuba* (Pittsburgh: University of Pittsburgh Press, 1971), pp. 277–80. See also Archibald R. M. Ritter, *The Economic Development of Revolutionary Cuba: Strategy and Performance* (New York: Praeger, 1974), pp. 9–62.

2. The discussion of policies in the first four stages is mostly a summarized integration of scattered materials from several chapters of *Revolutionary Change in Cuba:* "Central Planning" by Mesa-Lago and Luc Zephirin, pp. 145–84; "Managing and Financing the Firm" by Roberto M. Bernardo, pp. 185–208; "Labor Organization and Wages" by Roberto E. Hernández and Mesa-Lago, pp. 209–49; "International Economic Relations" by Eric N. Baklanoff, pp. 251–76; "Economic Policies and Growth" by Mesa-Lago, pp. 281–338; and "Inequality and Classes" by Nelson Amaro and Mesa-Lago, pp. 341–74. For these four stages see also Ritter,

*The Economic Development of Revolutionary Cuba,*pp. 63–345. The discussion of the fifth stage (and part of stage four) is based mainly on the second edition of my book *Cuba in the 1970s: Pragmatism and Institutionalization,* 2nd ed. (Albuquerque: University of New Mexico Press, 1978), pp. 25–58; and on *Cuba in the World,* Cole Blasier and Mesa-Lago, eds. (Pittsburgh: University of Pittsburgh Press, 1979), pp. 169–98. For the process of policy making through Cuban history in the twentieth century, see Jorge I. Domínguez, *Cuba: Order and Revolution* (Cambridge: Harvard University Press, 1978).

3. This is a summary of major statements made by Fidel Castro in the following speeches all published in *Granma Weekly Review:* "Speech at the Rally Celebrating the 10th Anniversary of the FMC," 30 August 1970, pp. 4–5; "Speech at the Closing Session of the National Plenary Meeting of Basic Industry," 20 December 1970, pp. 2–3; "Speech in the Rally to Celebrate May Day," 16 May 1971, pp. 7–8; "Speech to the Workers in Chuquicamata," 28 November 1971, p. 6; "Press Interview," 19 December 1971, pp. 12–13; "Speech in the Closing Session of the 13th Congress of the CTC," 16 November 1973, p. 2–11; "Main Report Presented to the 1st Congress of the Communist Party of Cuba," 4 January 1976, p. 2; and "Speech in the Closing Session of the 14th Congress of the CTC," 17 December 1978, p. 9. Also Raul Castro, "Speech at the Inauguration of Three Courses at the National School of Management," *Granma Weekly Review,* 14 March 1976, p. 2. A recent attempt has been made to reconcile Guevara's ideas to current Cuban practice, by Humberto Pérez, "Speech at the Ceremony Closing the Constituent Congress of the National Association of Economists of Cuba," *Granma Weekly Review,* 8 July 1979, supplement.

Chapter 3

1. For estimates of Cuba's foreign advisors see my article "Availability and Reliability of Statistics in Socialist Cuba," *Latin American Research Review,* part one, 4:2 (Summer 69):49–50. My own estimate is from *Cuba in the World,* Cole Blasier and Mesa-Lago, eds.(Pittsburgh: University of Pittsburgh Press, 1979), p. 170, Table 9.1.

2. Author's computations based on Tables 3 and 6 infra.

3. The brunt of the U.S. embargo ("blockade" for the Cubans) was felt in Cuba in the first half of the 1960s. However in the 1970s, the island was able to trade with most countries in the world including the Western Hemisphere (e.g., Canada, Argentina, Mexico, Colombia, Venezuela); U.S. multinationals abroad sold goods to Cuba; more than 100,000 U.S. tourists visited the island in 1979; and substantial credits were provided by market economies from the Western Hemisphere, Europe and Asia. Cuba remains affected by minor consequences of the embargo, e.g., higher freight, more expensive U.S.-made spare parts, and lengthier time to get goods previously imported from the United States. In contrast with the old rhetoric, Cubans have recently accepted that the embargo is often used as a scapegoat. Raul Castro in his "Speech at the Main Event to Commemorate the 23rd Anniversary of the November 30 Uprising," published in *Granma Weekly Review,* 9 December 1979, p. 2, candidly observed that "On more than one occasion, the negative consequences of the economic blockade . . . have been used as pretexts to hide our deficiencies and inefficiencies. . . ."

4. See Domínguez, *Cuba: Order and Revolution* (Cambridge: Harvard University Press, 1978), pp. 175, 178. Domínguez observes that declines in the 1970s may be hidden by omitting reports of those products in Cuba's statistical yearbook.

5. FAO, *Production Yearbook 1976* (Rome, 1977), pp. 74–75.

6. See *Revolutionary Change in Cuba,* pp. 328–30.

7. Some U.S. specialists have often hypothesized but not proved that better reporting of deaths under the Revolution created for a while an illusion of rising mortality rates. This may be a plausible hypothesis concerning infant deaths, but adult deaths could hardly go unreported prior to the Revolution. Furthermore, although this argument might partly explain rising mortality rates in the early years of the Revolution, it could not as easily account for increasing rates in 1968–1969 after a decade of supposedly better reporting. Finally, morbidity rates follow a similar pattern as mortality rates, and there have been increases in several contagious diseases in the 1970s, which would be even more difficult to explain by better reporting.

8. See Lisandro Pérez, "The Demographic Dimensions of the Educational Problem in Socialist Cuba," *Cuban Studies/Estudios Cubanos,* 7:1 (January 1977): 33–57; José Moreno, "From Traditional to Modern Values," in *Revolutionary Change in Cuba,* pp. 482–83; "On the Use of Contraceptives," *Granma Weekly Review,* 9 July 1967, p. 1; Fidel Castro, "Speech on the 11th Anniversary of the Events of March 13, 1957," *ibid.,* 24 March 1968, p. 5; Havana Radio, 20 February 1969; and Enrique González Manet, "Cuba y su población: Perspectivas para 1980," *Granma,* 5 February 1970, p. 2.

9. Centro de Estudios Demográficos, *La población de Cuba* (La Habana: Editorial de Ciencias Sociales, 1976), pp. 206–9.

10. See Jesús Montané Oropesa, "Ante los economistas cubanos se abre hoy un inmenso horizonte en el terreno de la investigación," *Economía y Desarrollo,* 43 (September-October 1977): 162.

11. Banco Nacional de Cuba, 1977, pp. 8–9.

12. Silvio Baro Herrera, "Población, subdesarrollo y desarrollo económico," *Economía y Desarrollo,* 41 (May-June 1977): 63–83. A more traditional position arguing that the population structure is shaped by the economic structure is defended by Raúl Hernández Castellón and Pedro Valdés Suárez, "La población en América Latina," *ibid.,* 44 (November-December 1977): 89–121.

13. Interview with Blanca Morejón, Professor of Demography at the University of Havana, 5 July 1979.

14. The monetary loss of the Cuban exodus has been estimated at $457 million by Evelio Pentón, *Educación y economía: El capital humano* (Madrid: Editorial Playor, 1979), p. 189.

15. See Rafael J. Prohías and Lourdes Casal, *The Cuban Minority in the United States* (Boca Raton: Florida Atlantic University, 1973), pp. 26–31.

16. The estimate for 1959–60 is from Charles Bettelheim, "Cuba en 1965, resultados y perspectivas económicas," *Nuestra Industria Revista Económica,* 4:18 (1966):13. See also my article "Availability and Reliability of Statistics in Socialist Cuba," pp. 49, 51.

17. Castro, "Speech on the 11th Anniversary," p. 5.

18. *Anuario* 1972, p. 30; and Banco Nacional de Cuba, *Desarrollo y perspectivas de la economía cubana* (La Habana: XXV Aniversario del Banco Nacional, 1975), p. 24.

19. This conflict may be explained by the shift in methodology introduced by the Cubans in 1967 or the deterioration in the collection and reliability of statistics at the end of the 1960s. It is intriguing that a statistical series on investment and consumption has not been published since the 1972 statistical yearbook.

20. Castro, "Speech at Rio Verde Sheep Farm, Magallanes," *Granma Weekly Review,* 5 December 1971, p. 8.

21. See footnote 17.

22. Banco Nacional de Cuba, 1977, pp. 10–12.

23. In 1970–77, Cuba's top economic journal published eighteen articles dealing with evaluation and efficiency of investment, in general and in specific sectors such as sugar, construction, transportation, electricity. See index in *Economía y Desarrollo,* 44 (November-December 1977): 158–59.

24. I have roughly estimated gross investment in 1977–78 at 27 percent of GMP, higher than in 1962–67 but lower than in 1975, based on Humberto Pérez, *Plan de la Economía Nacional para 1979* (La Habana: CICT-JUCEPLAN, 28 December 1978), p. 4.

25. Interview with Eugenio R. Balarí, Director of Institute of Domestic Demand, Havana, 14 July 1979.

26. Castro, "Discurso en la Clausura del II Período de Sesiones de 1979 de la Asamblea National del Poder Popular, Palacio de las Convenciones, 27 de diciembre de 1979, Departamento de Versiones Taquigráficas."

27. SDPE, *Plenaria Nacional de Chequeo sobre el Sistema de Dirección y Planificación de la Economía* (La Habana: JUCEPLAN 16 February 1979).

28. Castro, "Speech in the Closing Session of the 14th Congress of the CTC," *Granma Weekly Review,* 17 December 1978, p. 6–9.

29. Part of this section is based on my book *Cuba in the 1970s: Pragmatism and Institutionalization,* 2nd ed. (Albuquerque: University of New Mexico Press, 1978), pp. 40–44.

30. Castro, "Speech at the Closing Session of the National Plenary Meeting of Basic Industry," *Granma Weekly Review,* 20 December 1970, p. 6, and "Speech at the Closing Session of the 13th Congress of the CTC," *ibid.,* 25 November 1973, pp. 6–10.

31. *Ibid.*

32. Roberto Veiga, "Informe Central en la Apertura del XIV Congreso de la CTC," *Granma,* 30 November 1978, p. 3.

33. Banco Nacional de Cuba, "Statement of Condition," Havana, 31 December 1976 and 31 December 1977.

34. A comparison of Cuban series of GSP and GMP, given both in constant and current prices for 1962–66, gave different results either because of methodological differences or faulty statistics. Surprisingly the estimated average annual rate of inflation for GSP (4.7 percent) was lower than that of GMP (5.5 percent), although the Cubans argue that the former is more affected by inflation due to increasing prices in foreign trade and transportation. Since 1967 all Cuban figures are given in current prices and hence it is not possible to do the same calculation. GSP and GMP at constant prices were published in *Boletín 1966,* p. 20, and *Anuario 1972,* p. 30. GSP in current prices in *Compendio 1968,* p. 8; and GMP in current prices in U.N. *Monthly Bulletin of Statistics,* 22 (June 1968), pp. 176, 182, 188.

35. *Desarrollo y perspectivas de la economía cubana,* p. 27.

36. One of the anonymous referees of my manuscript argued that black market prices do not truly reflect supply and demand: since the black market is illegal there is not free interaction of supply and demand nor free flow of information hence transactions are highly personalized by needs of the seller and the buyer's ability to pay. Nevertheless in my three visits to Cuba I found relative uniformity in black market prices particularly for goods which are sold by established (not ambulant) vendors such as butchers, grocery employees and gasoline dispatchers. These people steal quantities of the merchandise they sell—by cheating in the weight—have regular customers, and set the price of the goods according to demand. The referee also underestimated the magnitude of the phenomenon, the flow of information about black market prices, and the accessibility to black marketeers. Although technically illegal, probably a majority of Cubans—including

militant revolutionaries—have at one time or another resorted to the black market.

37. Jorge Domínguez has argued that the official military budget is understated and a considerable portion of the allocation of the Cuban budget (e.g., under the categories of "others" and "reserve") remains at the discretion of the top leadership. See "Political and Military Limitations and Consequences of Cuban Policies in Africa," *Cuban Studies/Estudios Cubanos,* 10:2 (July 1980): 22–24.

38. Castro, "Speech in the Meeting with Leaders of the Central Organization of Workers of Santiago de Chile," *Granma Weekly Review,* 5 December 1971, p. 12.

39. Central Intelligence Agency, *Communist Aid Activities in Non-Communist Less Developed Countries, 1978* (Washington, D.C.: National Foreign Assessment Center, ER 79-10412U, September 1979), pp. 3–4, 13–15.

40. This issue was obliquely referred to by Castro in his "Speech Closing the 14th Congress of the CTC," p. 8. Responding to President Carter's televised speech on the presence of Soviet troops in Cuba (1 October 1979), Castro rejected Carter's statement that the USSR supplied free weapons to Cuba.

41. For extensive discussions of the economic cost of Cuban military involvement in Africa, see Sergio Roca, "Economic Aspects of Cuban Involvement in Africa," and Jorge Domínguez, "Political and Military Limitations and Consequences of Cuban Policies in Africa," as well as the commentaries in "Cuba in Africa," *Cuban Studies/Estudios Cubanos,* 10:2 (July 1980): 1–90.

42. The first official Cuban explanation for the declines in fish output was the poor showing of some species, as well as malfunctions of ships and refrigeration equipment; most of the latter, however, are new. A Cuban-American scholar has argued that the declines may have been caused by the closing off of fishing zones frequented by Cuban fishermen (the North Atlantic since 1975, and the North Sea and the Gulf of Mexico since 1976) as a result of claims by nations to 200-mile fishing limits. [See Jorge F. Pérez-López, "Comment: Economic Costs and Benefits of African Involvement," *Cuban Studies/Estudios Cubanos,* 10:2 (July 1980): 80–81.] But the sharp increase in the fish caught in 1978 cast a doubt on that explanation. Castro also blamed fishing zone restrictions (and the cancellation of a profitable fishing contract with Peru) as culprits for a sharp decline in fishing output in 1979. See "Discurso en la Clausura del II Período de Sesiones. . ."

43. *Anuario 1975,* pp. 130–33; *Anuario 1976,* pp. 108–11.

44. Cited by Domínguez, *Cuba: Order and Revolution,* p. 355. This book is the best treatment of Cuban military costs; see particularly pp. 345–56.

45. SDPE, *Plenaria Nacional de Chequeo sobre el Sistema de Dirección y Planificación de la Economía,* p. 31.

46. There are talks among some sectors of the population, that if Cuba were not so heavily committed in Africa there would be fewer shortages. See James Nelson Goodsell, "What'll Castro do for an Encore?" *Christian Science Monitor,* 22 January 1979.

47. Fidel Castro, "Address Before the 34th Session of the U.N. General Assembly," *Granma Weekly Review,* 21 October 1979, p. 3.

Chapter 4

1. The available data in Cuba are the composition of GSP by economic sector, but this excludes the value of nonmaterial services hence distorting the distribution. The methodology to estimate and assign material services has changed several times; for instance, in agriculture those services were disaggregated in 1962–69 and increased abnormally in the last two years, while the value of those services has not been reported since 1970. The price structure also introduces distortions;

prices are not fixed by demand and supply but by the state which overestimates the value of industrial output (fixing high prices to capital, intermediate and manufactured goods) and underestimates the value of agriculture (fixing prices to food below the market price). Still another statistical deformation is created by double counting in the process of aggregating GSP, more significant in industry (where a product is transformed and its value counted several times) than in agriculture (where the value of a product is usually counted once). Finally since data are not available in constant prices, structural changes are confounded with price changes, for instance inflation apparently affects commerce and transportation more than other sectors.

2. The decline of nine percentage points in the industrial share would be even more severe if the distortions explained in footnote 1 were corrected, while the decrease of nine percentage points in agriculture would be lesser, and the increase of fifteen percentage points in commerce (particularly in the inflationary years of the 1970s) would be somewhat smaller also.

3. I decided not to reproduce in this book the percentage distribution of GSP by major economic sectors and, within these, by production lines, because the percentages are too small and methodological shifts make the connections inaccurate (see *Boletín 1966*, p. 22; *Anuario 1972*, p. 32; *Anuario 1973*, p. 36; *Anuario 1975*, p. 40; and *Anuario 1976*, p. 40). Instead I reproduced the distribution of both agricultural and industrial products in appendices 2A and 2B.

4. *Anuario 1973*, p. 36.

5. Discussion of the 1959–70 sugar policy in this section comes mostly from *Revolutionary Change in Cuba*, C. Mesa-Lago, ed. (Pittsburgh: University of Pittsburgh Press, 1971), pp. 283, 297–99, 301–8. The best analysis of the 1965–70 sugar plan is Heinrich Brunner, *Cuban Sugar Policy from 1963 to 1970* (Pittburgh: University of Pittsburgh Press, 1977). Discussion of the 1970s sugar policy in this section comes mostly from Carmelo Mesa-Lago, *Cuba in the 1970s: Pragmatism and Institutionalization*, 2nd ed. (Albuquerque: University of New Mexico Press, 1978), pp. 49–54.

6. In 1959 there were 161 sugar mills—mostly built before the end of the 1920s—but deterioration and lack of spare parts reduced their number to 152 in the late 1960s.

7. The most comprehensive and documented study of the subject is Sergio Roca, *Cuban Economic Policy and Ideology: The Ten Million Ton Sugar Harvest* (Beverly Hills: Sage Publications, 1976).

8. Manuel Moreno Fraginals (author of the classic *The Sugar Mill*) lecture at the University of Pittsburgh, 23 March 1979.

9. *Ibid.*

10. A Cuban economist has proven that the cost curve in the sugar industry declines as the number of harvest days increases to about 175 days; thereafter the curve rises due to both low productivity induced by rains and decrease in the sugar content of the cane. Juan Ferrán Oliva, "Economía de la duración de la zafra," *Economía y Desarrollo*, 35 (May–June 1976): 75–99.

11. Author estimates based on "Fidel's Interview with U.S. Journalists," *Granma Weekly Review* 26 June 1978, p. 3; and *Caribbean Monthly Bulletin*, 12:17 (July 1978): 40. The official figure of canecutters for 1979 was 130,000 (see *Granma*, 4 August 1979, p. 1).

12. "7,300,000 Tons of Sugar Already Produced," *Granma Weekly Review*, 2 July 1978, p. 1.

13. The U.S. Department of Agriculture has estimated the 1979 sugar harvest at 7 million tons, one million tons below the official figure. See *Sugar and Sweetener Report*, 5:5 (May 1980):5.

14. "Heavy Rain Brings Problems for Cuban Sugar Harvest," *Latin America Commodities Report,* 2 February 1979, p. 1; and Fidel Castro, "Speech Closing the 14th Congress of the CTC," *Granma Weekly Review,* 17 December 1978, p. 8; and *Granma,* 30 July 1979, p. 1.

15. Reported by Raul Castro, "Speech During the commemoration of the Disappearance of Camilo Cienfuegos," *Granma Weekly Review,* 11 November 1979, p. 3, and "Speech at the Main Event to Commemorate the 23rd Anniversary of the November 30 Uprising," *ibid.* 9 December 1979, p. 2.

16. Fidel Castro, "Speech at the Closing Session of the 3rd Congress of the FMC," *Granma Weekly Review,* 16 March 1980, p. 3; information provided by José Alonso, a technician from the Interamerican Development Bank who visited Cuba in January 1980; and Banco Nacional de Cuba, *Highlights of Cuban Economic Development 1976–80 and Main Targets for 1981-85* (Havana, January 1981), p. 8.

17. Comité Central del PCC, *Directivas para el desarrollo económico y social del País en el quinquenio 1976–1980: Tesis y resolución* (La Habana, 1976); *Caribbean Monthly Bulletin,* 12:4 (April-May 1978): 33; "Cuba Seeks Increase in its Free-Market Sugar Sales," *Latin America Commodities Report,* 15 December 1978, p. 194; and "Cuba: Political Consolidation and Economic Adjustment," *Bank of London and South America Review,* 13:2 (February 1979): 79–80.

18. Data combining the state plus the private sector, unavailable for 1962–67, show an increase from 36.5 percent in 1968 to 48.9 percent in 1970 and a decline to 34 percent in 1975 but probably the proportion in 1962 was substantially below that of 1968. Other Cuban statistical series show even higher shares for sugar cane in 1975; for example 39.6 percent (sugar cane as a percentage of all new sowings) and 67.7 percent (total sugar cane land as a percentage of total agricultural land). Author estimates based on *Boletín 1971,* pp. 56–58, 68; *Anuario 1972,* pp. 43, 46–47; *Anuario 1974,* pp. 48–49; *Anuario 1975,* pp. 53–55, 68–70; and *Compendio 1976,* p. 32.

19. United Nations, *Statistical Yearbook for Latin America 1976* (New York, 1977), pp. 220–21, Table 199.

20. F. Castro, "Speech at the Main Rally to Celebrate the 16th Anniversary of the CDRs," *Granma Weekly Review,* 10 October 1976, pp. 2–5.

21. For complete output series of the products discussed in this section see *Cuba in the World,* Cole Blasier and C. Mesa-Lago, eds. (Pittsburgh: University of Pittsburgh Press, 1979), Tables 9.2 and 9.3. A summary of output of these products is given in Table 3 of this book. Additional data on shares of state and private sectors come from the *Anuario.*

22. Roberto Veiga, "Informe Central al XIV Congreso de la CTC," *Granma,* 30 November 1978, p. 3; Raul Castro, "Speech at the Main Event . . .," p. 2; F. Castro, "Discurso en la Clausura del II Período de Sesiones de 1979 de la Asamblea Nacional del Poder Popular, Palacio de las Convenciones, 27 de diciembre de 1979, Departamento de Versiones Taquigráficas"; "Blue Mold and its Effect on the Cuban Economy," *Granma Weekly Review,* February 10, 1980, p. 4; F. Castro, "Speech at the Closing Session of the 3rd Congress of the FMC," p. 3; and "Tobacco Mold, Swine Fever, Sugar Rust Hit Cuba," *Los Angeles Times,* 19 May 1980, IV, pp. 1–2.

23. Discussion at the panel "Cuba: Twenty Years of Economics Under the Revolution," American Economic Association Meetings, Atlanta, 28 December 1979.

24. *Boletín 1966,* pp. 58–59; *Anuario 1972,* p. 201; *Anuario 1976,* pp. 141, 170.

25. Fidel Castro, "Main Report Presented to the 1st Congress of the Communist Party of Cuba," *Granma Weekly Review,* 28 December 1975, p. 6.

26. *Sobre las dificultades objetivas de la Revolución: Entrevista a Humberto Pérez por Marta Harnecker* (La Habana: Editora Política, 1979), p. 80. In 1979, the failure to deliver imports of poultry from the socialist camp, combined with an epidemic of porcine cholera, forced the slaughter of underweight cattle, and beef output declined by 13 percent in the first half of the year. See *La economía cubana, primer semestre 1979*, p. 8.

27. For sources and details see *Revolutionary Change in Cuba*, pp. 313–14. For a sympathetic, detailed analysis of livestock developments in the 1970s see J. R. Morton, "Agriculture and Rural Development," *Cuba: The Second Decade*, John and Peter Griffiths, eds. (London: Writers and Readers Publishing Coop, 1979), pp. 89–96.

28. Charles González Ferrer, "Modelo económico-matemático para la optimización del balance alimentario del ganado vacuno en la empresa," *Economía y Desarrollo*, 45 (January-February 1978): 9–36.

29. Veiga, "Informe Central," p. 3.

30. M. B. Willis, "Fertilidad de la vaca de carne," *Revista Popular de Divulgación Agropecuaria*, 1 (January-April 1971): 7–22.

31. Based on *Boletín 1971*, p. 86; *Anuario 1973*, pp. 87–88; *Anuario 1976*, pp. 76–77.

32. Estimate for 1979 based on Humberto Pérez, "Intervención en la Asamblea Nacional," *Granma*, 28 December 1979, p. 2; and *La economía cubana primer semestre 1979*, p. 5. See also chapter 3 footnote 37.

33. There are two long-range state fleets: Flota Cubana, the largest fleet, is equipped with 31 vessels carrying fish processing and fish-meal production on board, it operates in the Atlantic and the Pacific, fishing hake, cod, tuna, and scad; in 1976 this fleet caught more than half of the total catch. The second long-range state fleet is Flota Atunera, established in 1973 and equipped with 20 trawlers that operate in the Atlantic fishing tuna and gar. There are two state medium-range fleets: Flota Camaronera de Mariel, established in 1963, equipped with 155 shrimp trawlers which operate in the Gulf of Mexico and the Caribbean Sea; and Flota del Golfo established in 1968, equipped with 53 vessels, which operates in the Gulf of Mexico fishing red snapper and king fish.

34. See *Revolutionary Change in Cuba*, p. 316; *Boletín 1968*, pp. 99–100; *Boletín 1970*, pp. 103–34; *Anuario 1974*, pp. 105–20; *Anuario 1975*, pp. 91–92, 101; and *Banco Nacional de Cuba*, 1977, pp. 27–34.

35. Theodore H. Moran, "The International Political Economy of Cuban Nickel Development," *Cuba in the World*, pp. 257–72.

36. See *Ibid.*; Cole Blasier, "COMECON in Cuban Development," *Cuba in the World*, pp. 238–39; and K.S. Karol, *Guerrillas in Power: The Course of the Cuban Revolution* (New York: Hill & Wang, 1970), p. 50, n. 49.

37. See Mesa-Lago, *Cuba in the World*, p. 175; and Moran, pp. 262–263.

38. Banco Nacional de Cuba, 1977, p. 16; "Cuba Aims to Make Nickel Rank Equal with Sugar," *Latin America Commodities Report*, 12 January 1979; and *Proyecto de los lineamientos económicos y sociales para el quinquenio 1981–85* (La Habana, Comité Central del PCC, 1980), p. 14.

39. *Cuba en cifras*, p. 27. Felino Quesada has explained this decline in output as a result of the technological renovation which is taking place at the Moa plant. Havana, August 4–5, 1980.

40. Moran, p. 265.

41. F. Castro, "Discurso en la Clausura del II Período de Sesiones. . ."

42. Actually the twofold increase was achieved in 1963–68, there was a sharp decline in 1969–71, and a recuperation thereafter; but output in 1976 was still below the 1968 peak.

43. Castro, "Main Report Presented to the 1st Congress," p. 5.

44. Distribution of energy consumption from *Anuario 1976*, p. 93. For a 1957–75 series of electricity output see *Cuba in the World*, p. 177; data for 1976–78 come from *Anuario 1976*, and *La economía de Cuba 1977* and *1978*.

45. According to Jorge Pérez-López, overall energy consumption per capita grew at average annual rates of 7.6 percent in 1950–59, and 1.2 percent in 1959–78, while corresponding electricity rates were 7.6 and 3.3 percent. See "Energy Production, Imports and Consumption in Revolutionary Cuba," ACES Meetings, Atlanta, 28 December 1979, p. 37.

46. See Jorge Pérez-López, "The Cuban Nuclear Power Program," *Cuban Studies/ Estudios Cubanos*, 9:1 (January 1979): 1–42; Rafael Fermoselle, "Cuba's Energy Balances and Future Energy Picture," *ibid.*, 9:2 (July 1979): 45–58; and F. Castro, "Discurso en la Clausura del II Período de Sesiones. . ."

47. Distributed as follows: 40 percent Canadians; 18 percent from socialist countries; 15 percent from Western Europe; 15 percent from Latin America; and 12 percent from the United States.

48. Part of the information in this section comes from *Cuba in the World*, pp. 202–3. See also the interview with Jesús Jiménez, head of Cuba's tourist agency Cubatour in "Tourism in Cuba Growing by Leaps and Bounds," *Granma Weekly Review*, 10 December 1978, p. 6; and Banco Nacional de Cuba, 1977, p. 26.

49. "Cuban Silk Worms Head South," *Latin America Economic* Report, 2 February 1979; Helga Silva, "Cuba's Exile Tourist Boom," *Miami Herald*, 11 February 1979; and F. Castro, "Discurso en la Clausura del II Período de Sesiones. . ."

50. Fidel Castro, "Speech at the Closing of the 14th Congress of the CTC," *Granma Weekly Review* 17 December 1978, pp. 7–8.

51. "Cuba: Political Consolidation and Economic Adjustment," pp. 82–83.

52. See note 48.

53. Simon Malley, "20-Hour Interview with Fidel Castro," *Granma Weekly Review*, 22 May 1977, p. 3; and Castro, "Speech at the Closing of the 14th Congress of the CTC," p. 7.

Chapter 5

1. Fernando Henrique Cardoso and Enzo Faletto, *Dependency and Development in Latin America* (Berkeley: University of California Press, 1979), pp. xii, xxiii.

2. See among others, *ibid*, pp. xx–xxii; Theotonio dos Santos, "The Structure of Dependence," *American Economic Review*, 60:2 (May 1979): 231–36; James D. Cockcroft, André Gunder Frank and Dale J. Johnson, *Dependence and Development in Latin America* (New York: Doubleday & Co., 1972); and Ronald H. Chilcote and Joel C. Edelstein, *Latin America: The Struggle with Dependency and Beyond* (New York: John Wiley & Sons, 1974), pp. 26–46.

3. See David Ray, "The Dependency Model of Latin American Underdevelopment: Three Basic Fallacies," *Journal of Interamerican Studies and World Affairs,* 15:1 (February 1973): 8–10.

4. For previous analyses see Eric N. Baklanoff, "International Economic Relations," *Revolutionary Change in Cuba*, C. Mesa-Lago, ed. (Pittsburgh: University of Pittsburgh Press, 1971), pp. 251–76; Archibald Ritter, *The Economic Development of Revolutionary Cuba* (New York: Praeger, 1974), pp. 50–56, 87–90, 156–57, 334–41; Steven L. Reed, "External Economic Independence: Definitions and Measurements," University of Pittsburgh, 1976: Jorge I. Domínguez, *Cuba: Order and Revolution* (Cambridge: Harvard University Press, 1978), pp. 149–65; and my own "The Economy and International Economic Relations," *Cuba in the World*, Cole Blasier and C. Mesa-Lago, eds. (Pittsburgh: University of Pittsburgh Press,

1979), pp. 169–98. The most innovative, sophisticated and comprehensive study so far has been done by William M. LeoGrande, "Cuban Dependency: A Comparison of Pre-revolutionary and Post-revolutionary International Economic Relations," *Cuban Studies/Estudios Cubanos,* 9:2 (July 1979):1–28. I have benefitted greatly from the latter essay and borrow many of LeoGrande's ideas and approaches in this chapter.

5. Technological dependency is not discussed in this book due to scanty and difficult-to-evaluate data. There are some statistics on Cuban students sent abroad but none on the importation of foreign technicians. Data on purchase of patents and licenses are simply not available. Although there are figures on the acquisition of capital equipment, it does not support an evaluation of its degree of technological level.

6. Taiwan, South Korea, Singapore and Hong Kong have chosen an export-oriented strategy for development and achieved high rates of growth. But they did it by expanding the industrial sector so they have an assorted output mix and largely satisfy their own domestic needs for such goods. Foreign trade takes a high percentage of GNP in these countries and hence they are vulnerable to international market fluctuations. Nevertheless, the variety of both their output and trade partners makes these countries less vulnerable than monoexport economies (particularly those exporting nonstrategic raw materials) that also suffer from trade-partner concentration.

7. Based on data from Cuban Economic Research Project, *Study on Cuba* (Coral Gables: University of Miami Press, 1965). Subsequent references in this chapter on prerevolutionary trade, capital inflows, and foreign debt data come from this source.

8. High export figures in 1975 may have been caused by higher prices paid for Cuban sugar by the USSR and Eastern Europe, plus sugar sales to the West in 1975 signed by the end of 1974 at the record prices then prevailing in the international market.

9. SDPE, *Plenaria Nacional de Chequeo sobre el Sistema de Dirección y Planificación de la Economía* (La Habana: JUCEPLAN, 1979), p. 31: "Latin America Suffers from Sugar Price Fall," *Latin America Economic Report,* 24 September 1976, pp. 146–47; *ibid.,* 8 October 1976, p. 1; and "Cuban Economic Setback Threatens to Reduce Gains from any U.S. Opening," *Business Latin America,* 2 February 1977, pp. 33–34.

10. The first estimate of imports for 1978 was much higher (about 3,740 million pesos) than the one in Table 16 infra. See Comité Estatal de Estadística, *La economía de Cuba en 1978,* p. 18.

11. Fidel Castro, "Speech in Closing 14th Congress of CTC," *Granma Weekly Review,* 17 December 1978, p. 9.

12. A very high correlation was calculated in this period between the value of sugar exports and both GMP ($R=0.888$) and GSP ($R=0.886$).

13. For a summary of these studies and sources see Jorge Pérez-López, "Sugar and Petroleum in Cuban-Soviet Terms of Trade," *Cuba in the World,* p. 278, n. 10–14.

14. Quoted by Leon Gouré and Julian Weinkle, "Cuba's New Dependency," *Problems of Communism,* 21:2 (March-April 1972): 75. The authors do not give any specific source for their statement.

15. Cuba's trade with socialist countries is done through bilateral agreements mostly on barter evaluated in pesos (for example, exchange of sugar for machinery) and exceptionally in convertible currency. On the other hand, trade with market economies is mostly conducted in convertible currency, except with Spain, which is partly done in barter.

16. Central Intelligence Agency, *The Cuban Economy: A Statistical Review, 1968–76* (Washington, D.C.: December 1976), p. 13, Table 23.

17. Domínguez, pp. 155–56.

18. See Mesa-Lago, pp. 173–75; and "Cuba Seeks Increase in its Free-Market Sugar Sales," *Latin America Commodities Report,* 15 December 1978, p. 194.

19. *Anuario 1974,* p. 228; *Anuario 1975,* p. 228; and Fidel Castro, "Discurso en la Clausura del II Período de Sesiones de 1979 de la Asamblea Nacional del Poder Popular, Palacio de las Convenciones, 27 de diciembre de 1979, Departamento de Versiones Taquigráficas."

20. Information gathered by Cole Blasier in April 1979.

21. Pérez-López, pp. 286–91.

22. *Ibid.,* pp. 291–93.

23. CIA, pp. 14, Table 24.

24. Domínguez (p. 156) has offered some evidence that in 1960 and 1963–64 Cuba subsidized Soviet imports of machinery and industrial equipment at a higher rate than the subsidies paid by the USSR for Cuban sugar. But he believes that such a situation reversed in 1965–70 with Soviet subsidies to Cuban sugar exceeding Cuban subsidies to Soviet capital goods.

25. Rodríguez as quoted in *Le Monde,* 16 January 1975, pp. 1, 4.

26. Quoted by Benjamin C. Bradlee, "Conversation with Fidel Castro," *Miami Herald,* 6 March 1977. In the same sense James Nelson Goodsell, "Cuba Interested in U.S. Trade," *Christian Science Monitor,* 28 April 1977; and Kirby Jones, Statement at the International Conference "The Role of Cuba in World Affairs," University of Pittsburgh, 17 November 1976.

27. Robert Keatley, "U.S. Businessmen Return from Cuba," *Wall Street Journal,* 22 April 1977.

28. Humberto Pérez, "El Plan de la Economía Nacional para 1978," *Granma,* 27 December 1977, p. 2.

29. *Vneshniaia Torgovlia SSSR v 1977g.* (Moscow 1978), p. 275; and private correspondence with Jorge Pérez-López, 2 May 1979.

30. F. Castro, "Discurso en la Clausura del II Período. . ." Following the same comparisons of Table 19, the difference between the Soviet and world price was 23.13 cents per pound of sugar in favor of Cuba, and the difference for the barrel of oil was $23.70 per barrel of oil also in favor of Cuba. I appreciate Jorge Pérez-López' help in obtaining this information.

31. Banco Nacional de Cuba, 1977, p. 23.

32. "Letter from Havana I," p. 202; and "U.S. Business Trip to Havana Shows Keen Interest in Trade on Both Sides," *Business Latin America,* 4 May 1977, p. 137.

33. *Granma Weekly Review,* 25 April 1976, p. 9.

34. Pérez, "El Plan de la Economía Nacional para 1978."

35. Averages of Cuban sugar exports as well as other types of exports to socialist and market economies have been computed by the author based on *Anuario 1971,* pp. 240–44; *Anuario 1975,* pp. 176–81; and Banco Nacional de Cuba 1977, p. 21.

36. These are selected imports, however, which represented about two-thirds of the total value of Cuban imports, and there is no information on what the remaining one-third of imports was made of. (Notice that this is a proportion much larger than that of nonspecified imports in Table 18.) Another problem is that an average of 10 percent of the suppliers is not identified; but since most socialist suppliers are listed (even when their import shares are small), I assumed that "others" are market economics and added this category to the identified market economy suppliers (in rice imports, however, "others" meaning China, were added to socialist suppliers).

37. Jorge and René Pérez-López have compiled all Cuban bilateral agreements in 1959–76, showing that in 1974–75, the proportion of Cuban agreements signed with socialist economies reached the lowest point in the whole period (59.9 and 58.5 percent) while the proportion of agreements with developed market economies reached its highest (13.2 and 16.5 percent), and that with Third World developing economies it was also among the three highest years (26.9 and 25 percent). See "Cuban International Relations: A Bilateral Agreements Perspective," *Latin American Monograph Series* (Northwestern Pennsylvania Institute for Latin American Studies No. 8, 1979) p. 8, Table 2.

38. Same sources as Table 22 infra and *Anuario 1975*, pp. 132–97. In the 1970s the USSR also faced increasing difficulties in supplying some food items to Cuba resulting in the following decline in imports in 1967–75: wheat from 100 to 70 percent; corn from 100 to 27 percent; cheese from 82 to 55 percent; powdered milk from 56 to 15 percent; and fodder from 54 to 19 percent.

39. *Anuario 1975*, p. 114 and *Anuario 1976*, p. 93.

40. See Jorge Pérez-López, "Energy Production, Imports and Consumption in Revolutionary Cuba," ACES Meeting, Atlanta, 28 December 1979, p. 1.

41. Osvaldo Dorticós, "El combustible: Factor esencial para el mantenimiento de la actividad económica," *Economía y Desarrollo*, 12 (July-August 1972): 68–83.

42. Rafael Fermoselle, "Cuba's Energy Balances and Future Energy Picture," *Cuban Studies*, 9:2 (July 1979): 45–58.

43. "Russia's Oil, Gas Exports Set Record," *Oil and Gas Journal*, 75:33 (15 August 1977): p. 28.

44. Pérez-López, "Energy Production, Imports and Consumption in Revolutionary Cuba," p. 34.

45. See my "The Economics of U.S.-Cuban Rapprochement," *Cuba in the World*, pp. 205–6; "Mexican-Soviet Oil Deal Still On," *Latin American Economic Report*, 9 June 1978; "La operación cuadrangular entre España-Venezuela y Cuba-URSS," *El País*, (Madrid), 4 March 1978, p. 41; and *Newsweek*, 2 October 1978, p. 21.

46. Domínguez, pp. 162–65; Blasier, pp. 246–48.

47. Alfred Padula, "Oil and Revolution in Cuba," University of Maine, January 1979, p. 19. For a divergent viewpoint see Sergio Roca, "Economic Aspects of Cuban Involvement in Africa," *Cuban Studies*, 10:2 (July 1980): 63.

48. *Anuario 1975*, p. 131, and *Anuario 1976*, p. 109.

49. Lázaro Barrero Medina, "Development and Foreign Trade," *Direct from Cuba*, nos. 150–51 (1–15 August 1976), pp. 4–5. See also Business International Corporation, *Cuba at the Turning Point* (New York: BIC, 1977), pp. 117–18.

50. See CIA, p. 14; and Domínguez, pp. 150–54.

51. Cole Blasier, "COMECON in Cuban Development," *Cuba in the World*, pp. 225–29.

52. There are contradictions in the information on whether this loan has to be repaid in goods or in cash. Soviet scholars in Moscow assured Cole Blasier in the spring of 1979 that payment will not be in cash. But the National Bank of Cuba reported in 1977 (p. 22) that amortization will be in rubles.

53. See as examples my *Cuba in the 1970s: Pragmatism and Institutionalization*, 2nd ed. (Albuquerque: University of New Mexico Press, 1978); Edward González, *Cuba Under Castro: The Limits of Charisma* (Boston: Houghton Mifflin Co., 1974); and Domínguez, *Cuba: Order and Revolution*.

54. See Lawrence H. Theriot, "Communist Country Hard Currency Debt in Perspective," *Issues in East-West Commercial Relations*, Joint Economic Committee U.S. Congress (Washington, D.C.: Government Printing Office, 1979), pp. 179–85.

55. Bank of International Settlements, "Maturity Distribution of International Bank Lending, June 1979," Basel, Switzerland, January 1980.

56. F. Castro, "Discurso en la Clausura de II Período de Sesiones. . ."
57. Mesa-Lago, "The Economics of U.S.-Cuban Rapprochement," pp. 211–12. The reader should be aware that because of the different systems of national accounts these comparisons are not entirely accurate.
58. Theriot, p. 183.
59. Based on the 1963 budget *La Tarde,* 8 January 1963; and the 1979 budget, *Granma Weekly Review,* 21 January 1979 p. 3. In the 1960s there was a budget category of "payment of the foreign credits." In my calculations of the text I assumed that both categories were the same.

Chapter 6

1. For a thorough discussion of the subject see my "Unemployment in Socialist Countries: Soviet Union, East Europe, China and Cuba" (Ph.D. diss., Cornell University, 1968); and "Unemployment in a Socialist Economy: Yugoslavia," *Industrial Relations,* 10:1 (February 1971): 49–69.
2. The statistical yearbook has slightly increased the number of tables on the labor force and employment from one in 1966 to six in 1976 (out of about 250 tables), but the yearbook only reports on state civilian employment and the overall size of private employment hence leaving out military employment, unemployment, and the overall size of the labor force. The distribution of civilian employment by sex has only been published occasionally; its distribution by economic activity is reported more regularly (although replaced in some years by average employment in state agencies); recently the distribution by province has been published; and the distribution by age (except for 1970) and race is not provided. JUCEPLAN has conducted a few surveys and studies on the labor force but copies have not circulated outside of Cuba. In 1970, a population census was taken and it gathered information on employment and unemployment. Part of the census results have been published including valuable data on the distribution of the economically active population (EAP) into total employment and unemployment, by age, sex, province, urban and rural location, and economic activity. And yet census results on the composition of employment by state (civilian and military sectors) and private employee, self-employed, employer, small farmer and unpaid family worker have not circulated outside of Cuba. Furthermore, the information released in 1970 has not been published for other years hence we lack a historical series. Finally it is not possible to compare the EAP data for 1970 with the state civilian employment data regularly reported in the yearbooks.
3. Data on state civilian and private employment in the table come mostly from official sources while the overall labor force, military employment, and unemployment were estimated as follows. First the labor force was derived using a varying percentage of the total population; such a percentage was calculated based on historical prerevolutionary data as well as patterns of the total and working-age population under the Revolution. Then state civilian and private employment were subtracted from the labor force, and the residue became the combined figure for military employment and unemployment. Finally, the residue was roughly disaggregated into its two components using scattered information; these two components of the labor force, therefore, are probably the least accurate. Two consistency checks were done on the estimates using almost complete data (except for the military) available for 1962 and 1970. Earlier I had calculated the Cuban labor force for 1962–69 but lacked enough information and ended up overestimating it. See *The Labor Force, Employment, Unemployment and Underemployment in Cuba: 1899–1970* (Beverly Hills: Sage Publications, 1972), p. 40.

4. In 1958 the working-age population stood at 59.4 percent but due to the high birth rates in 1960–68 (an average of 3.3 percent with a peak of 3.5 percent in 1963), it declined to a trough of 47.8 percent in 1968. In 1969–72 the birth rate was almost stagnant (an average of 2.86 percent) and steadily declined thereafter (standing at 1.75 percent in 1977). But those born in the 1960s began to reach 17 years of age in 1977 hence the proportion of the working-age population, stagnant in 1969–76 (at 4.82 percent) started to rise in 1977 (4.89 percent). Author estimates based on Cuba's statistical yearbooks.

5. See Inter-American Development Bank (IADB), "Latin America: Labor Force and Employment," *Economic and Social Progress in Latin America 1977* (Washington, D.C., 1978), pp. 121–25.

6. In the five years prior to the Revolution, the 1953 census and the 1956–57 survey provided accurate data on the distribution of the labor force by economic activity. For the Revolution there were surveys conducted in 1960–61 and 1964, whose accuracy we ignore, as well as the 1970 census which provides the most reliable figures.

7. Prerevolutionary labor force data in this chapter comes from the 1943 and 1953 population census, and from a 1956–57 survey reproduced in Gustavo Gutiérrez, *El empleo, el subempleo y el desempleo en Cuba* (La Habana: Consejo Nacional de Economía, 1958).

8. Oscar Rodríguez Mazorra and Fernando Gómez Quiñones, "Fuerza de Trabajo," *La población de Cuba* (La Habana: Editorial de Ciencias Sociales, 1976), p. 191.

9. IADB, "Latin America: Labor Force," p. 128.

10. See Mesa-Lago, *The Labor Force,* pp. 16 and 22.

11. *Granma Weekly Review,* 31 August 1969, p. 4.

12. Vilma Espín, *Granma,* 30 November 1978, p. 5.

13. *La población de Cuba,* pp. 179–86. See also JUCEPLAN, *Aspectos demográficos de la fuerza laboral femenina en Cuba* (La Habana, September 1975); and Ramiro Pavón, "El empleo femenino en Cuba," *Santiago,* 20 (December 1975): 97–115.

14. About one-fifth of 5,186 interviewed in a national survey conducted in 1974 reported female discrimination which reduced opportunities for promotion. See Departamento de Orientación Revolucionaria del CC del PCC, *Sobre el pleno ejercicio de la igualdad de la mujer* (La Habana: Imprenta Federico Engels, 1976), pp. 32–33.

15. *Proyecto de los lineamientos económicos y sociales para el quinquenio 1981–1985* (La Habana, Comité Central del PCC, 1980), p. 10.

16. The questionnaire was reproduced in *Granma,* 4 September 1970, p. 4.

17. *La población de Cuba,* pp. 104–6.

18. Lourdes Casal, conversation in Pittsburgh, 8 April 1979.

19. See Marianne Masferrer and C. Mesa-Lago, "The Gradual Integration of the Black in Cuba," *Slavery and Race Relations in Latin America,* Robert B. Toplin, ed. (Westport: Greenwood Press, 1974), pp. 366–71.

20. See John Clytus, *Black Man in Red Cuba* (Coral Gables: University of Miami Press, 1970), pp. 23–24; and Elizabeth Sutherland, *The Youngest Revolution* (New York: The Dial Press, Inc., 1969), pp. 141–53.

21. Jorge Domínguez, *Cuba: Order and Revolution* (Cambridge: Harvard University Press, 1978), pp. 224–27.

22. Lourdes Casal, "Ethnic Composition of the Cuban Elected Popular Power Organs" (Paper delivered at The Woodrow Wilson International Center for Scholars, 1979.)

23. Mesa-Lago, *The Labor Force,* pp. 16, 22, 27.

24. *Ibid.,* pp. 35–43.

25. Banco Nacional de Cuba, *Desarrollo y perspectivas de la economía cubana* (La Habana, 1975), p. 19.

26. The 1959–70 policies have been summarized from Mesa-Lago, *The Labor Force,* pp. 47–61, while part of the 1970s policies come from *Cuba in the 1970s: Pragmatism and Institutionalization,* 2nd ed. (Albuquerque: University of New Mexico Press, 1978), pp. 38–40. See also Brian H. Pollitt, "Employment Plans, Performance and Future Prospects in Cuba," in *Third World Employment,* Richard Jolly, ed. (London: Penguin Books, 1973); and Archibald R. M. Ritter, *The Economic Development of Revolutionary Cuba* (New York: Praeger, 1974), chapter 7.

27. Raúl Curbelo, "Tenemos que aplicar la técnica," *Granma,* 28 August 1966, p. 6.

28. Fidel Castro, "Clausura de Curso del Instituto Tecnológico de la Caña de Matanzas," *El Mundo,* 15 November 1964, p. 12.

29. Pedro Ríos, "El por qué de las estadísticas," *Comercio Exterior,* 3 (January-March 1964): 38.

30. Ernesto Guevara, *El Mundo,* 5 May 1962 and transmission on CMQ Television, 20 December 1962.

31. "El desarrollo industrial de Cuba," *Cuba Socialista,* 6:57 (May 1966): 163.

32. CEPAL, "Apreciaciones sobre el estilo de desarrollo y sobre las principales políticas sociales en Cuba," MEX/77/22/Rev. 3, November 1978, p. 114.

33. F. Castro, "Resumen de la concentración de trabajadores por la batalla del sexto grado," *El Mundo,* 22 November 1964, p. 11; "Clausura de curso del Instituto," p. 12; and "En el IV aniversario de la creación de los CDRs," *Obra Revolucionaria* (September 1964), pp. 19–20.

34. F. Castro, *El Mundo,* 15 November 1964, p.4.

35. *Boletín* 1966, p. 16.

36. For a full discussion of work quotas in the first half of the 1960s see my book *The Labor Sector and Socialist Distribution in Cuba* (New York: Praeger, 1968), chapter 3.

37. Augusto Martínez Sánchez, "Información al pueblo sobre las normas de trabajo," *Hoy,* 28 December 1963, p. 4.

38. Osvaldo Dorticós, "Organización y normación del trabajo en 500 grandes centros industriales," *Granma,* 16 September 1970, p. 5.

39. See my article "Economic Significance of Unpaid Labor in Socialist Cuba," *Industrial and Labor Relations Review,* 22 (April 1969): 339–57.

40. Osvaldo Dorticós, "Análisis y perspectivas del desarrollo de la economía cubana," *Economía y Desarrollo,* 12 (1972): 52.

41. F. Castro, "Discurso en el acto de clausura del XIII Congreso de la CTC," *Juventud Rebelde,* 16 November 1973, p. 7.

42. Pavón, "El empleo femenino en Cuba," pp. 127–28; and Comité Estatal de Trabajo y Seguridad Social, *La seguridad social en Cuba* (La Habana, 1977), p. 42.

43. Susan Eckstein, "Cuba in the 1970s: The Changing Class Structure" (Paper, Boston University, 1979), p. 27.

44. *La población de Cuba,* p. 191.

45. R. Castro, "Speech at the Main Event to Commemorate the 23rd Anniversary of the November 30 Uprising," *Granma Weekly Review,* 9 December 1979, p. 2.

46. Roberto Veiga, "Informe Central al XXXIV Consejo Nacional de la CTC," *Granma,* 6 February 1975, p. 2.

47. R. Veiga, "Informe Central al XIV Congreso de la CTC," *Granma,* 30 November 1978, p. 4.

48. Francois Raiberger, "Cuba Puts Taxes on Self-Employed," *Christian Science Monitor,* 6 December 1976; Marcel Niedergang, "Cuba: le point de non-retour," *Le Monde,* 12 May 1978, p. 5; Fred Ward, *Inside Cuba Today* (New York: Crown

Publishers, 1978), p. 31; and Felino Quesada Pérez, remarks in a Seminar of the Institute of Cuban Studies in Washington, D.C., August 13–17, 1979.

49. Fidel Castro cited in "Resolución del VII Pleno," *Bohemia*, October 26, 1979, p. 45; and Humberto Pérez, "Intervención en la Asamblea Nacional," *Granma*, December 28, 1979, p. 3.

50. Fidel Castro, "Discurso en la Clausura del II Período de Sesiones de 1979 de la Asamblea Nacional del Poder Popular, Palacio de las Convenciones, 27 de diciembre de 1979, Departamento de Versiones Taquigráficas."

51. Fidel Castro, "Speech at the Closing Session of the 3rd Congress of the FMC," *Granma Weekly Review*, March 16, 1980, pp. 2–3.

52. Pérez, "Intervención en la Asamblea Nacional," p. 3.

53. CEPAL, "Apreciaciones sobre el estilo de desarrollo," pp. 113–114.

54. Ernesto Guevara, *Revolución*, 19 March 1962.

55. F. Castro, "Speech at the Closing Session of the National Plenary Meeting of Basic Industry," *Granma Weekly Review*, 20 December 1970, pp. 2–4.

56. Systematic data on labor productivity has been only published once, in the 1966 statistical yearbook, covering the period 1962–66 but without explaining the methodology used to compute it. Thereafter only occasional figures on overall labor productivity rates have been released. Neither do we have a clear Cuban definition of labor productivity but instead just occasional vague hints of how it is measured: at the micro level by the value of a product or service—limited to the material sector—turned out by a worker in a given time unit with a given quality and average intensity; at the macro level by contrasting the increases in GSP and employment (Banco Nacional de Cuba, *Desarrollo y perspectivas*, p. 23). From this scattered information I inferred that overall labor productivity could be estimated by dividing GSP by the sum of state civilian employment (minus employment in services and administration) plus private employment. Since GSP excludes nonproductive services, the armed forces and social services employment should not be used in the computation. To check if my approach was correct, I compared my estimates with the official data published in 1962–66 and got an almost perfect matching. (Unfortunately my estimates for the 1970s did not match the occasional figures released for a couple of years, suggesting that there may have been a change in methodology.) Labor productivity in each economic activity within GSP was estimated dividing the value of GSP in each activity by the state civilian employment of the corresponding activity. There is a problem with that technique, that is, since it excludes productive labor from the private sector, productivity is overestimated in some economic activities (mainly agriculture) and particularly in the early years when private employment was high.

57. Curbelo, p. 6. See also "Establishment of Work Norms," *Granma Weekly Review*, 19 October 1969, p. 4.

58. See *Cuba in the 1970s*, p. 39.

59. SDPE, *Plenaria Nacional de Chequeo sobre el SDPE* (La Habana: JUCEPLAN, 1979), p. 29.

60. Raúl Castro, "Palabras en la clausura del acto de constitución del Sindicato de Trabajadores Agropecuarios," *Granma*, 10 September 1973, pp. 2–3.

61. Banco Nacional de Cuba, *Desarrollo y perspectivas*, p. 23.

62. Veiga, "Informe Central at XIV Congreso de la CTC," pp. 3–4.

63. R. Castro, "Speech at the Main Event," p. 2.

64. Humberto Pérez, *Plan de la Economía Nacional para 1979* (La Habana: JUCEPLAN, 1979), p. 7; and "Intervención en la Asamblea Nacional," pp. 2–3.

65. "El desarrollo industrial de Cuba," pp. 107–11.

66. Veiga, "Informe Central al XIV Congreso de la CTC," p. 4.

67. *Ibid.*, p. 3.

68. F. Castro, *Granma Weekly Review*, 15 July 1979, p. 3.

69. F. Castro, "Speech at Río Verde Sheep Farm, Magallanes," *Granma Weekly Review*, 5 December 1971, p. 8.

70. F. Castro, "Franco debate obrero," *Granma*, 8 September 1970, p. 5. See Friedrich A. von Hayek's classic article, "The Use of Knowledge in Society," *The American Economic Review*, 35:4 (September 1945): 519–30.

Chapter 7

1. See as an example, Peter Wiles, *Distribution of Income: East and West* (Amsterdam: North-Holland, 1974).

2. Based in Banco National de Cuba, *Memorias* (1951–1959); and ILO, *Yearbook of Labor Statistics* (1948–1959).

3. Harry T. Oshima, "A New Estimate of the National Income and Product of Cuba in 1953," *Food Research Institute Series*, 2 (November 1961): 214; and Buró de Información y Propaganda de la Agrupación Católica Universitaria, ¿*Por qué reforma agraria?* (La Habana, 1958), pp. 1–6.

4. Gustavo Gutiérrez, *El empleo, el subempleo y el desempleo en Cuba* (La Habana: Consejo Nacional de Economía, 1958), Table 3.

5. See Felipe Pazos, "Comentario a dos artículos sobre la Revolución cubana," *El Trimestre Económico*, 29:113 (January-March 1962): 1–18; and Dudley Seers, et al., *Cuba: The Economic and Social Revolution* (Chapel Hill: University of North Carolina Press, 1964), pp. 32–34.

6. Arthur MacEwan, "The Distribution of Income in Cuba," an essay prepared for the ILO, September 1978; and Claes Brundenius, "Measuring Income Distribution in Pre- and Post-Revolutionary Cuba," *Cuban Studies*, 9:12 (July 1979): 29–44. MacEwan estimated family income distribution in 1958 using an average for the distribution of Argentina, Mexico, and Puerto Rico. His estimates for the 1962 distribution are even more conjectural since they are based on opinions of foreign scholars on the income gains of urban and rural workers and a good number of untested assumptions. Brundenius took a more sophisticated approach and estimated personal income distribution in 1953 based on labor force data from the census of that year and a survey of wages paid by ten leading companies (in manufacturing, public utilities, petroleum, and banking), mostly in Havana in 1955. He then assumed that such wage distribution was similar in other companies throughout the nation, and since the survey did not include agriculture he estimated the latter without explaining how. Brundenius' crude estimates for 1962 and 1973 are based on official wage averages per capita of various activities within the state civilian sector; to determine the distribution within each activity he assumed a differential ratio of 4 to 1 and that the income dispersion was normally distributed around the mean. The distribution, therefore, excluded military men and private farms (who may earn more than state civilian employees), as well as pensioneers and students (who have smaller incomes), and the unemployed and housewives (who do not have an income). Furthermore, data to be presented later indicate that in the mid-1960s the wage differential ratio was 10 to 1 rather than 4 to 1 and that there was a high concentration of the employed—both in agriculture and in industry—in the lowest income brackets. In summary the real income distributions in 1962 and 1973 had to be less egalitarian than in Brundenius' estimates. For other comments on Brundenius' estimates see Susan Eckstein, "Income Distribution and Consumption in Post revolutionary Cuba," *Cuban Studies*, 10:1 (January 1980): 91–99.

7. Tom Alberts and Claes Brundenius, "Growth versus Equity: The Brazilian Case in the Light of the Peruvian and Cuban Experiences," *Research Policy Studies—Lund University*, no. 126 (January 1979), pp. 20–21.

8. The survey was conducted, in April 1972, by JUCEPLAN, the National Bank and other official agencies, based on a sample of 6 percent of the total number of households. Full survey results have not circulated outside of Cuba. Figures in the text come from Chris Logan, "Economy and Planning," *Cuba: The Second Decade*, John and Peter Griffiths, eds. (London: Writers and Readers Publishing Coop, 1979), p. 58.

9. Income figures from F. Castro, "Speech on the 11th Anniversary of the Events of March 13, 1957," *Granma Weekly Review*, 24 March 1968, pp. 3–6; and population figures from *Boletín 1968*, p. 9.

10. The analysis of wage policies and differentials, until 1970, mostly comes from Roberto E. Hernández and Carmelo Mesa-Lago, "Labor Organization and Wages," *Revolutionary Change in Cuba*, C. Mesa-Lago, ed. (Pittsburgh: University of Pittsburgh Press, 1971), pp. 224–35, and Nelson Amaro and C. Mesa-Lago, "Inequality and Classes," in *ibid.*, pp. 342–46 and 360. See also my previous book *The Labor Sector and Socialist Distribution in Cuba* (New York: Praeger, 1968), pp. 74–115.

11. Author's calculations based on *Boletín 1971*, p. 49, and *Compendio 1976*, p. 59.

12. Ernesto Guevara in "Información al pueblo sobre las normas de trabajo," *Hoy*, 28 December 1963, p. 4. Although there is information available on the percentage distribution of state civilian employment by groups and hence scales, we do not know which is the distribution within each group—scale by grade—and, in the case of productive workers, which is the distribution between agriculture and nonagriculture. Other data on the distribution of state civilian employment by economic activities cannot be used for the disaggregation of productive workers, because within each activity there are not only productive workers but also administrative personnel, technicians and executives.

13. "El desarrollo industrial de Cuba," *Cuba Socialista*, 6:57 (May 1966): 109.

14. Hugo Chinea, "Organización del trabajo en la agricultura," *Teoría y Práctica*, no. 36 (May 1967), pp. 31–32.

15. Maurice Zeitlin, "Inside Cuba: Workers and Revolution," *Ramparts*, 8 (March 1970): 11, 14.

16. "El desarrollo industrial de Cuba," Table 9, p. 96.

17. Interview with Eugenio R. Balari, Havana, 13 July 1979.

18. See Adolfo Gilly, "Inside the Cuban Revolution," *Monthly Review*, 16 (October 1964): 42; Zeitlin, "Inside Cuba," p. 14; Rene Dumont, *Cuba est-il socialiste?* (Paris: Editions de Seuil, 1970), pp. 191–94; Castro, "Discurso en la plenaria provincial de la CTC," *Granma*, 10 September 1970, p. 2; Joseph Kahl, "Cuban Paradox: Stratified Equality," *Cuban Communism*, 2nd ed., Irving Louis Horowitz, ed. (New Brunswick: Transaction Books, 1972), pp. 283–306; and Jorge Domínguez, *Cuba: Order and Revolution* (Cambridge: Harvard University Press, 1978), pp. 229–33.

19. Most of these measures and ideals are expressed in Fidel Castro, "Discurso en commemoración del 15° aniversario del ataque al Cuartel Moncada," *Granma Resumen Semanal*, 28 July 1968, pp. 3–5.

20. The analysis of Cuba's wage and incentive policies of the 1970s is partly based on my *Cuba in the 1970s: Pragmatism and Institutionalization*, 2nd ed. (Albuquerque: University of New Mexico Press, 1978), pp. 38–49.

21. F. Castro, "Speech Closing the 14th Congress of the CTC," *Granma Weekly Review*, 17 December 1978, p. 8.

22. Personal conversations with authors in Havana, December 1978. Payment for articles and books by number of pages is a Soviet custom. See Cole Blasier, "The Soviet Latinamericanists," *Latin American Research Review,* 16:1 (1981):118.

23. Miguel Dotre, Asesor de JUCEPLAN, "Intervención sobre el Sistema de Dirección de la Economía en Cuba," V Seminario Latinoamericano de Periodistas, La Habana, 1980, pp. 2–3.

24. See footnote 21 and Roberto Veiga, "Informe Central al XIV Congreso de la CTC," *Granma,* 30 November 1978, p. 4. A General Wage Reform enacted early in 1980 and to be nationally enforced by the end of the year reportedly sets the maximum monthly wage at $450. Top executives are expected to lose their historical wages and receive the maximum wage without any additional supplements. On the other hand, technicians and other workers should keep the historical wage. Information given by Felino Quesada at a Seminar of the Institute of Cuban Studies held in Havana, August 4–5, 1980.

25. "El desarrollo industrial de Cuba," p. 100.

26. Although my computations are somewhat different, I gratefully acknowledge that the idea for this comparison came from Susan Eckstein, "Cuba in the 1970s: The Changing Class Structure" (paper, Boston University, 1979), pp. 4–5, 14–15, Table 2.

27. The 1962–66 series refers to average wages in economic activities (resulting from dividing the wage fund in each activity by the number of employees in it), and within each activity by specific branches with a fair degree of disaggregation. The 1971–76 series, shifted to average wages by government agencies, with less specificity, and clustered the agencies under apparently similar economic activities. There are no data for the period 1967–70.

28. For a statistical comparison of all the means in 1962–66 see Hernández and Mesa-Lago, "Labor Organization and Wages," pp. 232–34, and Table 3.

29. These changes are in part the result of the shift in methodology between 1962–66 and 1971–76, which inflated the average in agriculture and deflated the averages in all other economic activities. I was able to evaluate the shift in methodology since data for the wage fund in the two distributions was available for the year 1966: the old from *Boletín 1970,* pp.34–36 and the new from *Boletín 1971,* pp. 50–53. The comparison demonstrated the following differences by economic activities for the same year, resulting exclusively from the shift to the new methodology: agriculture (+5 percent), industry (−19 percent), construction (-7 percent), transportation and communication (-2 percent), commerce (-55 percent), and services (-5 percent).

30. "The Work-Week, Minimum Wage and Retirement Age," *Granma Weekly Review,* 9 July 1978, p. 10.

31. Reporting a ratio of 3.5 to 1.0 are Arthur MacEwan, "Incentives, Equality and Power in Revolutionary Cuba," *The New Cuba: Paradoxes and Potentials,* Ronald Radosh, ed. (New York: W. Morrow and Company, 1976), pp. 86–87; and Howard and Nancy Handelman, "Cuba Today: Impressions of the Revolution in its Twentieth Years," *American Universities Field Staff Reports,* no. 8 (1979), p. 6. Dumont (p. 91) gave a ratio of 10.6 to 1.0 in 1969, in the midst of the Mao-Guevarist stage; while Marcel Niedergang reported a ratio of 7 to 1 in 1978, see "Cuba: le point de non-retour," *Le Monde,* 12 May 1978, p. 5.

32. *Cuba in the 1970s,* pp. 76–79. According to Sergio Roca, military men stationed in Africa are paid 20 percent over national rates, can keep any monetary stipends offered by the host country, and receive an increase in pension benefits. See "Economic Aspects of Cuban Involvement in Africa," *Cuban Studies/Estudios Cubanos,* 10:2 (July 1980): 67.

33. Quoted by Carlos Rafael Rodríguez, "The Cuban Revolution and the Peasantry," *World Marxist Review,* 8 (October 1965): 14, 18.

34. Leo Huberman and Paul Sweezy, *Socialism in Cuba* (New York: Monthly Review Press, 1969), p. 118.

35. Jon Nordheimer, "20 Years with Fidel," *The New York Times Magazine,* 31 December 1978, p. 29; and Niedergang, "Cuba: le point de non-retour," p. 5.

36. F. Castro, "Speech at the Closing of the 5th Congress of ANAP," *Granma Weekly Review,* 29 May 1977, pp. 2–4. For an excellent analysis of government policies in relation to private farmers, see Domínguez, *Cuba: Order and Revolution,* pp. 450–63.

37. *Revista del Banco Nacional de Cuba,* 5: 5 (May 1959): 756–57.

38. A series for 1962–66 refers to national income per capita, while another for 1967 and the 1970s refers to "population monetary income."

39. Interview with JUCEPLAN officials Francisco Martínez Soler and Felino Quesada Pérez, Havana, 12 July 1979.

40. Eckstein, "Cuba in the 1970s: The Changing Class Structure," Table 3.

41. Eugenio R. Balari, "Cinco Años de trabajo del Instituto Cubano de Investigaciones y Orientación de la Demanda Interna," *Economía y Desarrollo,* 38 (November-December 1976): 118–31; and personal interview with Balari, Havana, 14 July 1979. The magazine *Opina,* published by the Instituto since mid-1979, inserts cartoons and stories critical of consumption deficiencies.

42. Seers, *Cuba: The Economic and Social Revolution,* pp. 35–36; Ricardo Leyva, "Health and Revolution in Cuba," in *Cuba in Revolution,* Rolando E. Bonachea and Nelson P. Valdés, eds. (New York: Anchor Books, 1972), pp. 462–64; and Felino Quesada Pérez, "La implantación del cálculo económico como sistema de dirección de la economía de la República de Cuba," Instituto de Estudios Cubanos, Washington, D.C., August 1979, p. 14.

43. Niedergang, "Cuba: le point de non-retour," p. 5; Seers, *Cuba: The Economic and Social Revolution,* p.36; and my own conversations in December 1978 and July 1979 with both supporters and opponents of government policies.

44. *Bohemia,* 16 February 1979, p. 22.

45. Sergio Roca has compared the per capita distribution of selected food and manufactures by provinces showing that Havana has the best allocation and Oriente the worst. See "Distributional Effects of the Cuban Revolution: Urban Versus Rural Allocation," American Economic Association Meetings, Dallas, 1975, pp. 73–76.

46. *Cuba in the 1970s,* p. 43.

47. *Ibid.,* p. 47; and Roberto Veiga, "Informe Central al XIV Congreso de la CTC," *Granma,* 2 December 1978, p. 3.

48. Humberto Pérez, *Sobre las dificultades objectivas de la Revolución* (La Habana: Editora Política, 1979), pp. 56–57.

49. See footnote 42.

50. This practice, as well as giving away state goods free to relatives and friends, has become notorious enough to force public acknowledgement and criticism. See Lesmes la Rosa, "Un caso de malversación, causa 1722," *Verde Olivo,* 50: 10 (December 1978): 24–25.

51. Neidergang, "Cuba: le point de non-retour," p. 5.

52. Pérez, *Sobre las dificultades objectivas de la Revolución,* pp. 85–87.

53. In August 1980, I visited a free peasant market in San Cristobal, one-and-one-half hours west of Havana. Some prices in pesos were: pork 2.50 per pound, black beans 1.25 per pound, coconuts 0.30 each, and avocados 0.20 each. Late in the day prices were reduced to clear the merchandise.

54. State budgets for 1962–65 and 1978–79 published in *Gaceta Oficial,* January 1962; *La Tarde,* 8 January 1963; *El Mundo,* 10 January 1964, p. 1; *Revolución,* 2 January 1965, p. 2; *Granma* 23 December 1977; and *Granma Weekly Review,* 21 January 1979, p. 3.

55. For a summary of the literature and systematic comparisons see Sergio Roca, "Methodological Approaches and Evaluation of Two Decades of Redistribution in Cuba," American Economic Association Meetings, Atlanta, December 28, 1979.

56. For detailed studies on Cuban education see Richard Jolly, "Education," *Cuba: The Economic and Social Revolution,* pp. 159–280; Rolland G. Paulston, "Education," *Revolutionary Change in Cuba,* p. 375–97; Nelson P. Valdés, "The Radical Transformation of Cuban Education," *Cuba in Revolution,* pp. 422–55; Michel Huteau and Jacques Lautrey, *L'éducation à Cuba* (Paris: Maspero, 1973); CEPAL, "Apreciaciones sobre el estilo de desarrollo y sobre las principales políticas sociales de Cuba," MEX/77/22/ Rev. 3, November 1978, pp. 119–44; Domínguez, *Cuba: Order and Revolution,* pp. 165–73; and Martin Carnoy and Jorge Wertheim, *Cuba Economic Change and Education Reform: 1955–1974* (Washington, D.C.: World Bank Staff Working Paper, No. 317, January 1979).

57. Jolly, "Education," p. 204.

58. JUCEPLAN, *Censo de población y viviendas 1970: Datos fundamentales de la población* (La Habana: Instituto Cubano del Libro, n.d.), pp. xii–xvii, 5. An analysis of illiteracy and education by race is done by the Center for Demographic Studies comparing all Cuban censuses from 1899 to 1953 but without releasing any data from the 1970 census. See *La población de Cuba* (La Habana: Editorial de Ciencias Sociales, 1976), pp. 108–116.

59. However, Roca has shown that by 1970 rural elementary schools still lagged far behind those in urban areas in student-teacher ratios, construction expenditures, and student promotion rates. See "Distributional Effects . . . " pp. 45–64.

60. *Boletín 1971,* pp. 266–69; and *Anuario 1975,* p. 209.

61. Pérez, *Sobre las dificultades objetivas de la Revolución,* p. 50.

62. For detailed studies on Cuban public health see Cuban Economic Research Project, *Social Security in Cuba* (University of Miami, 1964), pp. 155–70, 248–76; Leyva, "Health and Revolution in Cuba," pp. 471–95; Milton I. Roemer, *Cuban Health Services and Resources* (Washington, D.C.: Pan American Health Organization, 1976); Domínguez, *Cuba: Order and Revolution,* pp. 221–24; CEPAL, "Apreciaciones sobre el estilo de desarrollo," pp. 162–97; and Ross Danielson, *Cuban Medicine* (New Brunswick: Transaction Books, 1979).

63. *Social Security in Cuba,* pp. 163–65, 255–59; Leyva, "Health and Revolution in Cuba," pp. 480–84; CEPAL, "Apreciaciones sobre el estilo de desarrollo," p. 171; and Fidel Castro, "Speech at the Inauguration of the Cienfuegos Clinical and Surgical Hospital," *Granma Weekly Review,* 1 April 1979, p. 2.

64. *Social Security in Cuba,* pp. 160–61; *Boletín 1966,* p. 154; *Anuario 1974,* p. 232; *Anuario 1976,* p. 232.

65. Leyva, "Health and Revolution in Cuba," p. 486; and footnote 52.

66. Pérez, *Sobre las dificultades objetivas de la Revolución, p. 44; and Anuario 1976,* pp. 31–32, 233. For a detailed discussion of urban-rural differences in health care in 1959–70, see Roca, "Distributional Effects . . . ," pp. 16–18, 28–33, 64–71.

67. *Boletín 1966,* p. 154; *Boletín 1968,* p. 187; *Anuario 1974,* p. 261; *Anuario 1975,* p. 232; and *Anuario 1976,* pp. 233–35.

68. Kahl, "The Cuban Paradox," pp. 286–87.

69. Domínguez, *Cuba: Order and Revolution,* pp. 226–27 and Appendix C.

70. *Social Security in Cuba,* pp. 69–157.

71. *Ibid.*, pp. 173–282; Basilio Rodríguez, "La seguridad social en Cuba," *Cuba Socialista,* 6:64 (December 1966): 14–30; and Comité Estatal de Trabajo y Seguridad Social, *La Seguridad Social en Cuba* (La Habana, 1977), pp. 26–52.

72. *Anteproyecto de Ley de Seguridad Social* (La Habana: CTC, 1979); and "Aprobó la Asamblea Nacional del Poder Popular la Ley de Seguridad Social," *Granma,* 5 July 1979, pp. 1–2.

73. Fidel Castro, "Discurso en el sexto aniversario de la Revolución," *Obra Revolucionaria,* 1 (January 1965); CMQ Radio transmission of 5 January 1965 and Radio Progreso transmission of 6 January 1965.

74. Leyva, "Health and Revolution in Cuba," p. 470.

75. Veiga, "Informe Central del XXXIV Consejo Nacional de la CTC," p. 5.

76. *Desarrollo y perspectivas de la economía cubana,* p. 104.

77. See Rodney Mace, "Housing," *Cuba: The Second Decade* (London: Writers and Readers, 1979), pp. 122–29; Sergio Roca, "Housing in Socialist Cuba," International Conference on Housing Problems, Miami, 1979, p. 14; and *Anuario 1976,* p. 97.

78. See my "Availability and Reliability of Statistics in Socialist Cuba," *Latin American Research Review,* 4:2 (Summer 1969): 69–72; Maruja Acosta and Jorge Hardoy, *Urban Reform in Revolutionary Cuba* (New Haven: Yale University Antilles Research Program, 1973); and Domínguez, *Cuba: Order and Revolution,* p. 186.

79. Official figures for 1959–67 are contradictory and may be inflated; Castro, for instance, has reported annual average housing construction in that period as 10,000, one-third of the figure reproduced in Table 46 infra. F. Castro, "Speech at the Inauguration of a new community of 120 homes," *Granma Weekly Review,* 14 January 1968, p. 2.

80. F. Castro, "Discurso de Clausura del Congreso Nacional de Constructores," Radio Havana, 26 October 1964; and speech of 29 August 1966 quoted by Leyva, p. 468.

81. Author estimate based on the increase in population (3 million inhabitants which at the rate of 4.5 persons per home required 650,000 units), minus the homes built (310,000), minus the homes left by exiles (130,000), plus the houses destroyed by lack of repair (500,000). According to Castro in 1964, 200,000 homes were badly in need of repair; and the President of JUCEPLAN reported in 1979 that 25,000 homes were destroyed annually by lack of repairs (Pérez, *Sobre las dificultades objetivas de la Revolución,* p. 92). Other Cuban officials reported in 1968 and 1978 that over 50 percent of the houses needed extensive repairs (Roca, "Distributional Effects . . . ," pp. 7–8, 19). In 1978 and 1979 I was able to appraise directly the effects of housing deterioration in the cities of Havana, Pinar del Río, and Matanzas.

82. The 1976–80 plan set an annual goal of 30,000 homes, but it was reduced in 1978 to 24,000 and this was unfulfilled by 30 percent. For various goals see my "Availability and Reliability of Statistics," pp. 71–72; "La construcción de viviendas y centros comunales en Cuba," *Economía y Desarrollo,* 19 (September-October 1973): 172; and F. Castro, "Speech Closing the 14th Congress of the CTC," p. 8.

83. Veiga, "Informe Central al XIV Congreso de la CTC," p. 3.

84. See *Cuba in the 1970s,* p. 48; F. Castro, "Speech Closing the 14th Congress of the CTC," p. 8; and Pérez, *Sobre las dificultades objetivas de la Revolución,* pp. 94–96.

85. Census of 1953; and *Desarrollo y perspectivas de la economía de Cuba,* p. 104. Roca (pp. 9–10) has accumulated evidence that suggests that most housing construction even in the 1960s, took place in urban instead of rural areas.

86. *Censo de población y viviendas de 1970* reproduced in CEPAL, "Apreciaciones sobre el estilo de desarrollo," pp. 211–12.

87. *Anuario 1974,* p. 148.

Chapter 8

1. LeoGrande in his excellent comparison of Cuban dependency in the prerevolutionary period (centered in 1946–58) and the postrevolutionary period of 1959–75 concludes that out of twenty-eight indicators six failed to show any significant change in dependency while the other sixteen showed some improvement. However, of those sixteen indicators, ten were used to measure one variable (trade partner concentration in which a significant reduction in dependency was registered) while in another variable (that is, the foreign debt that showed a significant increase in dependency) only one indicator was used. There are other methodological problems (like the distorting effect of sugar in many of the indicators), some of which the author acknowledges. Furthermore, LeoGrande qualifies his findings by saying that even in those indicators that showed reduction of dependency vis-à-vis the prerevolutionary period the "absolute level of these indicators remains too high for us to conclude that Cuba has successfully escaped dependency." Finally, he found that in the first half of the 1970s all indicators except one "show a marginal rise in dependency." In the second half of the 1970s, I have shown in this book a worsening in dependency. See William M. LeoGrande, "Cuban Dependency: A Comparison of Pre-Revolutionary and Post-Revolutionary International Economic Relations," *Cuban Studies/Estudios Cubanos,* 9:2 (July 1979): 22–24.

2. See Susan Eckstein, "Capitalist Constraints on Cuban Socialist Development," Working Papers, No. 6, Latin American Program, The Wilson Center, Washington, D.C., March 1978.

3. Composite excerpts from F. Castro, "Closing Speech of the Second Session of the National Assembly of People's Power," *Granma Weekly Review,* 1 January 1978, pp. 2–4; and "Speech Closing the 14th Congress of the CTC," *Granma Weekly Review,* 17 December 1978, p. 9.

INDEX